Researching Language and Digital Communication

This student guide is an introduction to research on language and digital communication, providing an overview of relevant sociolinguistic concepts, analytical frameworks, and methodological approaches commonly used in the field. The book is a practical guide designed to help students develop independent research projects on language and digital communication. Topics covered include: the emergence of research on Computer Mediated Communication (CMC), interactional affordances and the design infrastructures of digital platforms, practical and ethical guidance in designing and implementing a research project on digital communication, contemporary approaches in the sociolinguistics of digital communication such as Computational Sociolinguistics (CS) and interactional analyses, and the impact of social and digital media on language change.

Chapters are organised thematically, each supplemented with examples from various platforms and sociolinguistic contexts, as well as further reading and activities to scaffold students' learning.

The interdisciplinary relevance of this topic makes it a key reading for students from A-level English language to undergraduate and postgraduate students in linguistics, English language, media studies, digital culture, and communications.

Additional online resources are available on the Routledge Language and Communication Portal.

Christian Ilbury is a Lecturer in Sociolinguistics at the University of Edinburgh. His research focusses on the interrelation of digital culture and language variation and change, with a concentration on the linguistic and digital practices of young people.

Researching Language and Digital Communication

A Student Guide

Christian Ilbury

Routledge
Taylor & Francis Group
LONDON AND NEW YORK

Designed cover image: Polinmr

First published 2025
by Routledge
4 Park Square, Milton Park, Abingdon, Oxon, OX14 4RN

and by Routledge
605 Third Avenue, New York, NY 10158

Routledge is an imprint of the Taylor & Francis Group, an informa business

British Library Cataloguing-in-Publication Data
A catalogue record for this book is available from the British Library

ISBN: 9781032490113 (hbk)
ISBN: 9781032457499 (pbk)
ISBN: 9781003391838 (ebk)

DOI: 10.4324/9781003391838

Typeset in Sabon
by Newgen Publishing UK

Access the Support Material: www.routledgetextbooks.com/textbooks/languageandcommunication

To my students, my mentors, and my family.

Contents

1 Introduction

1.1 About this Book

This book is about language and digital communication. The term **digital communication** refers to digital sites, platforms, and technologies that are used by people to share messages, post content, and interact with others. This includes:

- **Social media platforms**: such as Sina Weibo, Douyin/TikTok, Facebook, Instagram, and Snapchat
- **Instant messaging services**: such as WhatsApp and Telegram
- **Electronic mail (i.e., email) platforms**: such as Outlook and Gmail
- **Video chat and streaming software**: such as Zoom, Teams, Twitch, and Skype
- **Online blogs and forums**: such as Tumblr, Mumsnet, and Blogger

On a daily basis, individuals from across the globe will use a range of digital platforms, services, and apps for a variety of different personal and professional reasons. This includes interacting with friends, conducting business meetings, and sharing photographs of recent holidays.

The aim of this book is to provide an overview of research which explores the language used in digital communication. Although researchers from a variety of different disciplines are interested in digital communication such as those working in media, digital communications, marketing, and the digital humanities, this book focusses specifically on **sociolinguistic** approaches to analysing language and digital communication. The main aim of this book is to introduce and describe sociolinguistic research which explores the types of interactions and language varieties that people use in digital contexts. One of the main areas that this book will focus on is **language variation**. The types of research questions and projects that are discussed in this book include:

DOI: 10.4324/9781003391838-1

1. Are there differences in the distribution of laughter variants (e.g., <lol>, <haha>, <hehe>) between men, women, and non-binary users in WhatsApp conversations?
2. Why do people use alternating caps (e.g., WhY AM I LikE ThIS?) in Reddit posts?
3. What are the linguistic characteristics of doge memes?
4. Why do people describe features of African American (Vernacular) English (AAE/AAVE) as TikTok language?
5. Does digital communication and social media cause language change?

All these questions are *sociolinguistic* in nature because they concern the interrelation of social (e.g., identity) and linguistic (e.g., language variation) issues. Given that very many of our daily interactions take place in and through digital technologies, understanding how language is used in digital contexts remains a central goal for sociolinguists interested in contemporary patterns of social interaction.

As this book is intended to be a student guide to studying language and digital communication, my aim is to provide students of different levels with a solid understanding of sociolinguistic research on the topic so that they can design their own research projects. To do this, I provide a survey of both earlier and more contemporary research in sociolinguistics and digital communication. This includes discussing some key foundational studies, as well as summarising the major methodological and theoretical approaches in studying digital communication from a sociolinguistic perspective.

The book is aimed at students who are more advanced and who already have some training in sociolinguistics as well as those who are starting out studying this area. Given the interdisciplinary nature of this research area, we will introduce perspectives, approaches, and concepts from related fields, including digital culture and media, sociology, computational linguistics, communications and marketing, and very many others. Subsequently, although this book focusses mainly on sociolinguistic approaches to studying digital communication, I anticipate that the content will be relevant to a wide range of readers from different disciplines. It is hoped that this book will be useful not just for the student reader who may be developing a term project or dissertation on digital language but also for instructors and teachers who are designing courses that explore topics on language, social media, and digital communication.

The impetus for writing this book comes from teaching a course that I designed and now teach at the University of Edinburgh called *'The Sociolinguistics of Digital Communication'*. The content of this book is based heavily on the course syllabus and the activities that are suggested throughout are those that have been tried and tested in class. The reason that I decided to write this book is related to my experience of teaching this course. When it got to the final assignment – a project on a digital communication topic of the student's choice – I found that students often struggled to identify a single feasible research project. They were often overwhelmed by the sheer number of possible research projects and many found it difficult to approach these issues from a sociolinguistic perspective. As noted above, very many researchers are interested in studying digital communication; however, not all those topics or practices are relevant to sociolinguistics. Although a solution would have been to use a class textbook, I realised there wasn't really a single resource that provided both an overview of sociolinguistic research on digital communication and guidance on designing a student project on these topics. Although there are now numerous textbooks, edited volumes, and journal articles which use sociolinguistic approaches to explore a wide range of digital topics, I felt that the field was lacking a single resource that could be used by students on my course. The purpose of this guide is to be this resource: To offer students a broad overview of sociolinguistic research on digital communication as well as equip them with the sufficient research and analytical skills to be able to design and operationalise their own research projects.

Before I describe the outline of this book, I should briefly note why I use the terms 'digital communication' and 'Digitally Mediated Communication' (DMC) throughout this book rather than 'social media' or a term that some readers may be more familiar with, 'Computer Mediated Communication' (CMC). First, unlike Page and colleagues' (2022) book in this series, *'Researching Language and Social Media: A Student Guide'*, the current book refers to research on technologies and platforms that are not typically grouped under the umbrella label of 'social media'. This includes WhatsApp, blogs, SMS, and emails. Although lots of the research we discuss *does* focus on language in social media, I consider these platforms as subtypes of 'digital communication'. The tools, approaches, and methods we discuss in this book are not specific to social media but rather can be used to explore patterns of digital communication more generally. Second, the use of the term 'digital communication' is intended to signal a theoretical departure from earlier research CMC which focussed on the influence of computer mediated infrastructures on language practice. DMC is a label which more accurately describes the ways in which people use digital technologies as interactive and communication technologies in contemporary society (Androutsopoulos, 2021). We will discuss this issue in more detail in Chapter 2.

1.2 About the Chapters

The book is structured into nine chapters. Each chapter is organised thematically. The first four chapters focus on theoretical approaches, introducing some key concepts in studying digital communication. The methodological and ethical issues of working with digital data are introduced in Chapter 5. The next three chapters introduce 'big', 'small', and 'mixed' data approaches. The final chapter looks beyond digital technologies to ask how these practices are embedded within our everyday communicative practices. The chapters of this book are organised chronologically but they can be read as standalone texts. A more comprehensive description of the chapters is provided here.

Chapter 2 provides an overview of digital communication and sociolinguistics. I first introduce this field of study before turning to a discussion of how digital communication and online interaction has been analysed in the field. This chapter introduces earlier CMC research which attempted to isolate the language of the internet on a scale of written-spoken registers. We consider the emergence of terms such as 'netspeak', 'txtspeak', and 'netlish', before critically evaluating these approaches. Finally, it will introduce some more contemporary approaches in studying in digital communication to sketch out the agenda for the following chapters of the book.

Chapter 3 introduces some key concepts that have been employed to analyse patterns of language and communication in digital contexts. This chapter examines the interactional architectures of digital platforms, providing a detailed overview of 'affordances', 'audiences', and 'contexts'. The chapter first explores the ways in which the functions of an app or platform ('affordances') influence the content of what we post and how we post. It then goes on to consider how people design their posts with a particular viewer or audience in mind ('imagined audience'). Finally, the chapter concludes by discussing the potential for social media to flatten audience dynamics, creating a space where multiple audiences such as family, friends, and co-workers are bought together ('context collapse').

An overview of research on language, identity, and online communities will be introduced in Chapter 4. This chapter first introduces sociolinguistic approaches to language and identity before expanding this to the study of digital communication. From here, it provides a discussion of social and digital media as 'participatory culture', exploring internet memes as a case study. The focus in this chapter is on how individuals use digital technologies to develop and maintain (online) communities that establish their own norms, values, and language styles. We will ask whether the identities we perform online are similar to or different from those we perform in the offline.

Chapter 5 introduces some common methodological approaches and ethical challenges in researching digital communication. The aim of this chapter is to help students take a seed of an idea and develop that initial idea into a feasible research project. Most of this chapter focusses on the ethics of using digital data, interrogating the notion of 'public domain', asking students to critically reflect on the types of content they are analysing in their projects. The discussion is designed to provide guidance on making responsible and ethical decisions. After this, some of the main sociolinguistic approaches in analysing digital communication (e.g., variationist, corpus, ethnographic, blended) are briefly introduced and described. Finally, the chapter concludes with some practical advice and recommendations for tools and programmes that can be used to collect and analyse digital and social media data.

In Chapter 6, I introduce and describe research that takes a 'big data' approach to analysing patterns of language variation and change in digital communication. The focus here is on the emergence of a new field of study: 'Computational sociolinguistics'. Through this discussion, I explore work in 'Twitter dialectology', using a recent paper that uses geolocated tweets to examine the diffusion of a variety of English across the UK (Multicultural London English) as a case study.

The preceding discussion will be complemented by 'Small data' approaches which will be introduced and examined in Chapter 7. The focus in this chapter is on approaches which have explored discourse-level phenomena in digital communication. After a brief discussion of emoji and emoticons, I cover four interactional issues in more depth: Language alternation, stylisation, metadiscourse, and politeness. The chapter introduces relevant sociolinguistic concepts and frameworks in each of these topics before expanding this to DMC.

Chapter 8 brings 'small' and 'big' data approaches together by introducing work which has used a 'mixed methods' approach. This type of research uses tools and methods from computational linguistics in combination with analytical approaches developed in sociolinguistics. To do this, three case studies are examined in detail. The purpose of this chapter is to demonstrate how a mixed-methods approach can be used to explore a wide range of digital phenomena.

The final chapter (Chapter 9), critically examines a long-standing question in the field: Whether (social) media leads to language change. It first introduces two opposing perspectives, considering arguments for and against the claim that media influences language change. The chapter then goes on to introduce more contemporary perspectives on the relationship between media and language by exploring the concepts of 'mediatisation' and 'sociolinguistic change', reframing the debate away from 'influence' and 'effect'. The chapter will encourage students to critically reflect on the ways in which digital technologies are embedded in 'offline' structures of social interaction. It concludes by sketching out an agenda for future research by introducing the 'post-digital' turn.

1.3 Conventions

This book uses several stylistic and linguistic conventions which readers should take note of. Where necessary, I have transcribed elements of spoken language into the International Phonetic Alphabet (IPA). The IPA is the standardised phonetic notation system commonly used in linguistics. Transcriptions in IPA are provided either in 'broad' / / or [] 'narrow' form, e.g., [wɔːkɪŋ]. For those who have not studied phonetics or the IPA before, readers are directed to *'A Course in Phonetics'* by Ladefoged and Johnson (2014). Orthographic features (i.e., spellings) are transcribed using < >, e.g., <fink> vs. <think>. This is to distinguish the orthographic representation from the spoken realisation of that word. *Italics* are used to refer to specific words, e.g., *walking* vs. *talking*. **Bold** is used to emphasise words of specific interest. This includes key words and concepts. Unless otherwise stated, underlined words and phrases are part of a hyperlink. Where quotes and examples are used, the original grammar, spelling, and style is maintained. Thus, spelling errors and non-standard spellings are commonly found in the examples in this book. Finally, I briefly explain the use of the term 'Twitter'. In April 2023, Twitter was rebranded 'X'. Given that most of the research discussed in this book predates the rebrand of this platform, I continue to refer to this platform as 'Twitter', not 'X'.

1.4 References

Androutsopoulos, Jannis (2021). Polymedia in interaction. *Pragmatics and Society*, 12: 707–724.

Ladefoged, Peter & Keith Johnson (2014). *A Course in Phonetics*. Belmont: Wadsworth Publishing.

Page, Ruth, David Barton, Carmen Lee, Johann Wolfgang Unger, & Michele Zappavigna (2022). *Researching Language and Social Media: A Student Guide*. Abingdon: Routledge.

2 Digital Communication and Sociolinguistics

2.1 Introduction

In this chapter we cover the following topics:

- Defining digital communication
- Introducing sociolinguistics
- Sociolinguistics and Computer Mediated Communication
- 'Netspeak'
- Contemporary sociolinguistic approaches.

Very many researchers are interested in studying digital communication. The topics and aims of this research, however, vary from field to field. For instance, media scholars are often interested in the social impacts of digital communication technologies, considering how digital technologies are used in contexts such as politics, culture, and society. Researchers in the fields of marketing and business, on the other hand, are often interested in understanding how businesses use digital technologies to engage consumers and market new products.

As discussed in the introduction, this book is about *sociolinguistic* approaches to digital communication. A sociolinguistic approach focusses on examining the interrelation of society, digital technologies, and language and communication. A common aim in this type of work is on understanding why and how people use different varieties of language in digital interactions. A productive area of sociolinguistic research on DMC has been to analyse patterns of language variation in social and digital media texts. Consider, for instance, the following post, which is taken from the social media platform, Twitter (or 'X' as it is now known):

(1) User
Work dat pole gurl! @VENUE <link to photo>

The example in (1) is a tweet written by a user from the UK. The tweet was posted to their timeline and originally was accompanied by a photo of their friend dancing in a nightclub, represented here as

DOI: 10.4324/9781003391838-2

<link to photo>. The @VENUE is used to tag the nightclub where the photo was taken. Although this tweet is relatively short (five words), it contains some interesting features that we might want to explore in more detail. We might, for instance, start to wonder about the use of the non-standard spellings in the tweet. We could ask 'why did the user spell 'that' as <dat> and 'girl' as <gurl>?' To answer these questions, we'd need to think about the functions of these spellings: What is it that these non-standard spellings 'do' that their standard counterparts <that> and <girl> do not? Perhaps these spellings reference an internet meme or perhaps they're being used to emulate someone's voice. To understand why they are being used in this way, we'd first want to collect more tweets and see if the user consistently writes in this way. This would give us a sense of the distribution of these spellings. We could then go on to try to determine *why* the non-standard spellings are used. In other words, we could try to identify the *social meaning* of the variation.

To take another example, consider the following excerpt taken from a group chat on WhatsApp:

(2) Kate Guess what guys, I'M COMING HOME IN AUGUST!!!!!!
Becca SHUT UP! NOOOOOOOOO. Literally the best news ever ✨

Like the tweet above, we see quite a few features that are potentially interesting to sociolinguists. Notably, there are a few written features that appear here that are not common in other written genres. For instance, we don't tend to see things like all caps (I'M COMING) or emoji (✨) in other non-digital written genres, like letters. However, these features are common in DMC, like in the WhatsApp message above. A sociolinguist might want to know *why* and *how* people use these features. This could lead us to ask the following questions:

- What is/are the function(s) of all caps (e.g., SHUT UP!)?
- Why does Kate use multiple exclamation marks (I'M COMING HOME IN AUGUST!!!!!!)?
- Why is the vowel in <no> repeated in Becca's message (NOOOOOOOOO)?
- What is the function or purpose of the 'sparkle' emoji (i.e., ✨)?

All of these questions are *sociolinguistic* questions. This is because they consider the relationship between a linguistic feature (e.g., ✨) and the social identity of the user or the context of the conversation. To answer these questions, we will need to explore how that feature is used in conversation, what its function is, and whether it is used by a particular demographic of people. In some contexts, the variation could be explained by the authors' social identity or background. The tweet in (1), for instance, is actually drawn from my own research on Twitter where I argue that this is a linguistic style commonly used by gay men. The non-standard spellings here emulate spoken features of African American Vernacular English but they have also become associated with a 'gay style' more generally (Ilbury, 2019). Alternatively, it might be that the variation is explained by what is being said in the conversation. This could include things like the user trying to signal their emotional response to a message or trying to convey their politeness. McCulloch (2019), for instance, finds that all caps are often used to signal excitement or to represent shouting. This is a very plausible explanation for the use of all-caps in the WhatsApp conversation in (2).

The purpose of this chapter is to introduce the study of digital communication as a *sociolinguistic* area of inquiry. To do this, I will first provide a brief historical overview of earlier research – an approach which has often been referred to as 'internet linguistics'. I will then go onto sketch out the research agenda of more contemporary research on digital communication.

2.2 What is Digital Communication?

This morning, within moments of waking, I picked up my phone from my bedside table. Shortly after unlocking my phone, I replied to a WhatsApp message from my friend about my weekend plans, liked a meme I'd been DM'd (i.e., direct messaged) on Instagram, and answered an email from a colleague about a meeting. Whilst walking to work, I uploaded a picture of my morning coffee to my Snapchat story, and 'liked' a recent music video of a band I follow on YouTube. When I got to work, I logged onto my desktop computer and set myself up for the day. I then checked my schedule on my Outlook calendar. My first meeting was on Zoom. I met with a filmmaker about an upcoming documentary that I'm going to be interviewed in. I then unlocked my phone and replied to the group WhatsApp chat about my friend's wedding this coming weekend. At this point, I check my watch: The time is now 9.42 am.

Within the span of a couple of hours of waking, I have used a variety of digital platforms (e.g., email, Snapchat, WhatsApp), across a range of devices (mobile phone, desktop computer) to interact with people from various different social and professional groups (friends, colleagues, and unknown users). Many of these people are based elsewhere: Most of my friends live in London, my colleague works at a German university, and the filmmaker is based in Ireland. All these interactions have been enabled by digital technologies. The email conversations I send, the Snapchat stories I upload, and so on, are subtypes of what we can label **digital communication**. In this book, we define digital communication as any type of interaction which is made possible by digital technologies. The subtypes of digital communication that we explore in this book include:

- **Electronic mail** or **emails**: are messages that are sent via electronic means from one user to others. It is the digital counterpart to mail. Platforms which facilitate this type of interaction include Gmail, Microsoft Outlook, and Yahoo! Mail.
- **Social media**: are digital platforms which enable users to share messages, information, and other types of content with others. A more formal definition is offered by Carr and Hayes (2015: 50) who define social media as '[i]nternet-based channels that allow users to opportunistically interact and selectively self-present, either in real-time or asynchronously, with both broad and narrow audiences who derive value from user-generated content and the perception of interaction with others'. Typical examples of social media platforms include Facebook, TikTok (or 'Douyin'), Instagram, Snapchat, and 'micro-blogging sites' Twitter, Sina Weibo, and Tumblr.
- **Instant Messaging (IM) platforms**: are those that allow users to communicate in real-time via the internet. Typically, instant messages are text-based but more recently, platforms have expanded to include other multimodal content such as photos, videos, and voice notes. Examples of IM software include Telegram, WhatsApp Messenger, and WeChat.
- An abbreviation of 'weblogs', **blogs** are centred on informational content that comprise discrete, informal text entries. Examples of these platforms include Blogger, Wix, and Wordpress. A subcategory of 'micro-blogs' (short posts without titles) includes Twitter, Sina Weibo, and Tumblr which are cross-referenced in the social media section here.
- **Video sharing platforms**: are those which focus on the sharing and creation of videos. Users can often leave comments and responses on posts. Examples include Dailymotion and YouTube as well as the social media app, TikTok.
- Platforms which allow users to engage in video-based telecommunications are called **video communication platforms**. This includes services and platforms such as Zoom, Skype, and Microsoft Teams.
- **Virtual worlds**: are computer-simulated environments where users create avatars which they use to communicate with others and participate in activities. Examples of virtual worlds include Second Life, World of Warcraft, and RuneScape.

Other platforms and services such as websites and chatbots are often included in definitions of 'digital communication'. However, these will be explored to a lesser extent in this student guide. The main subtypes of digital communication that we focus on in this volume are social media, video platforms, and instant messaging platforms. This is largely due to the concentration of sociolinguistic research on these platforms. Nevertheless, the approaches, methods, and frameworks we discuss are relevant to most types of digital communication and can be applied to platforms and services beyond those explicitly discussed here.

Key Term: Digital Communication

Digital communication refers to those online platforms, tools, and services which enable users to share ideas, messages, and content with others. This includes social media (e.g., Facebook, Twitter), email (e.g., Outlook, Gmail), blogs (e.g., Blogger, Tumblr), interactive streaming services (e.g., TikTok Live, Twitch), and instant messaging platforms (e.g., Viber, Telegram, WhatsApp).

My morning routine I describe above and the subtypes of digital communication I have introduced are likely to be familiar to very many readers. For many people across the globe, the use of digital devices such as mobile phones, computers, and tablets, and digital platforms and services are now a common and relatively unremarkable fact of everyday life. Whilst we still spend a great deal of our time interacting with people in face-to-face conversation, more and more of our interactions are taking place in and through digital technologies. It is perhaps uncontroversial to suggest that digital technologies have had quite a significant impact on language and society.

One of the most significant developments in the use of digital communication technologies has been the introduction and now widespread use of smartphones and mobile data roaming. Before the introduction of mobile technologies, accessing the internet was done via a desktop computer. In the 1990s, when the internet became widespread, users would need to be physically present at a computer which they would use to 'log on' to the internet via a dial-up modem. Users would then spend hours 'surfing the net' before logging off and leaving the 'cyber-world' behind. Being 'online' was very much constrained to 'being on the computer'.

Today, however, most people will use smartphones and other mobile devices such as iPads and laptops to communicate via the internet without ever actually logging on and logging off. With the introduction of mobile technologies, users are no longer tethered to a single location: They can communicate wherever and whenever, often whilst they are engaged in other activities. People now frequently send emails, IMs, upload Snapchat Stories, and participate in other types of digital communication whilst doing other things like taking the dog for a walk or waiting at a bus stop. In my description of my own morning routine, I sent emails, organised meetings with colleagues, and interacted with family who are based in various locations all while I was engaged in other activities: getting ready for work, leaving the house, walking to work, and ordering a coffee.

The increasing availability of digital platforms and technologies – particularly mobile technologies – has meant that society is now 'hyper-connected'. Digital technologies have become so embedded in our everyday lives that it is very hard to really and truly be 'offline'. Even when you are asleep, it's likely that some device is still connected to the internet. If, like me, you sleep with your phone on your bedside table, plugged in and tethered to the internet you will probably continue to receive messages through the night. How many times have you woken up in the morning to a message from a friend or received a notification of someone liking your Instagram story? The fact that are always connected to the internet, never really switched off, is what the researcher, danah boyd has called the 'always on lifestyle' (boyd, 2012).

For many people across the globe, the 'always on lifestyle' is now the social norm. People spend more time now than ever using social and digital media platforms. According to a recent survey, an estimated 4.9 billion people use social media across the world with the average user spending around 145 minutes on social media per day. Nigeria tops the global list of social media usage with Nigerians estimated to spend on average four hours per day using social media platforms (Buchholz, 2022).

In recent years, global events such as the COVID-19 outbreak have accelerated our reliance on digital communications. In March 2020, when the first coronavirus lockdowns were imposed and directives to work from home and isolate were enforced, many of us had to move our lives online. Practically overnight, offices, universities, and schools became 'virtual spaces', with classes, meetings, and lectures hosted via digital communication technologies like Zoom and Microsoft Teams. Even doctors offered remote appointments via services like Google Meet, whilst estate agents offered virtual property tours via Zoom. There is now a lot of academic research which has argued that digital technologies were crucial in shielding labour and productivity during the COVID-19 pandemic.

Even today, in what is sometimes labelled the 'post-pandemic era', many companies continue to offer remote working opportunities and digital technologies now take a more central role in our working lives. For instance, many companies continue to conduct business meetings entirely on video-conferencing platforms like Zoom and Microsoft Teams. In some professions and businesses, physical offices may not even exist. Colleagues might be spread across different countries and time zones and work activities might be conducted entirely via digital technologies. Similarly, in a work revolution initiated by the pandemic, more and more people are becoming 'digital nomads', using digital technologies to work whilst travelling. Some countries such as Germany, Norway, and Taiwan, have even introduced 'digital nomad' work visas to encourage people to work remotely there.

All of these technological developments have dramatic consequences for society. As noted previously, very many researchers are interested in studying these consequences. From the impacts of digital cultures on personal connections to the potentials of digital communications in marketing and advertisement, researchers from a range of different disciplines have studied the effects of this digital revolution on society. As digital technologies become increasingly embedded in our social and professional lives, understanding how people use digital technologies to communicate has now become a central goal of contemporary sociolinguistic research. The main aim is to understand the consequences of these technological developments for language and social interaction.

Points for reflection

- Make a diary of your digital engagements by recording your use of digital communication platforms and technologies from the moment you wake up to two hours later. What platforms do you use? What types of posts do you upload to those platforms? If you upload similar posts to different platforms, are there any differences in how you write/create them across platforms? Who do you interact with and where are those individuals based?
- Compare your digital diary with your friends' or classmates'. Do you see any similarities or differences in the types of platforms you use? Why?

2.3 What is Sociolinguistics?

As discussed in the above section, the focus of this book is on *sociolinguistic* approaches to digital communication. For those who have never studied linguistics before, it's possible that you've never encountered the field of 'sociolinguistics'. This section briefly introduces the field of study that we call 'sociolinguistics', before extending this approach to DMC.

Broadly speaking, sociolinguistics is an academic field of research which studies the relationship between language and society. Sociolinguists are primarily interested in understanding how language is used in two main ways: (i) as a means of establishing and maintaining relationships with others, and (ii) as means of deducing social information about interlocutors.

Let's explain this using a real-world situation. Imagine you are at a bus stop on a sunny day. You take a seat and someone walks up, sits down next to you, and says 'nice weather!'. Now, on the face of it, the comment 'nice weather!' isn't really that interesting: It's a simple remark – an observation of the fact that the sun is shining. We could stop here and just assume the person is being friendly. But to a sociolinguist, what's interesting is that the person is speaking at all. There's no real need for the individual to speak to you – you are, after all, strangers. And observing that it is a nice day when the sun is shining is, well, stating the obvious. This type of interaction is what we call 'phatic communication'. In this situation, the comment 'nice weather!' doesn't just comment on the state of the weather (that it's sunny) but, more importantly, it fulfils a social function. The comment 'nice weather!' initiates conversation and establishes some type of *social* relationship between you and your interlocutor (i.e., the person speaking to you).

Now, imagine that the initial 'nice weather!' comment leads to a much longer conversation between you and your fellow passenger. They might ask you about your day, comment on the fact that the bus is late, and then ask about your plans for the evening. When you reply, you obviously give the person a response to their question, but you also start to reveal things about who you are as a person. This is because how we speak or sign is influenced heavily by our social background like where we're from, our sexuality, our age, and so on. Simply responding to the individual gives them a chance to infer what type of person you are from how you speak or sign. For instance, you might provide clues about how old you are if you start describing the weather as 'peng' (a British term for 'good/attractive' often associated with younger individuals) or, if you are older, 'A1' (an adjective meaning 'very good' that was popular in the late 1980s). In this way, language functions as a 'social cue'. These cues are used by your interlocutor to infer things about your social identity, in this case, your age. We do this type of social inferencing on a daily basis. When we communicate with others, we often try and deduce an individual's social background based on their accent, the words they use, or their communication style. This type of social inferencing often means that we don't have to explicitly ask people about their background. This is a useful social tool because, whilst it may be socially taboo to ask someone who you do not know very well their sexuality, for instance, we *might* be able to infer this information from how they speak.

One of the main goals of sociolinguistics is to understand how language varies across different groups. Lots of research explores how social identities (or 'factors') like age, gender, social class, and ethnicity, influence how people use different language varieties. In the UK, although most people speak a common language (English), there is a great deal of variation in how different people and groups use that language. In the previous example, I used the example of variation in lexis (i.e., words). In the British context, whether you refer to the weather as 'A1' or 'peng' might tell us something about how old you are. Younger people will tend to use the word 'peng' whilst older people may use the phrase 'A1'.

Language can also tell us about where someone is from. In England, a good example of this is what has been called the 'TRAP–BATH split'. Speakers in the South of England generally say the word *bath* as [bɑːθ] whilst those in the North of England will often say [baθ]. The pronunciation of this vowel often depends on your regional background, i.e., whether you are from the North or South of England. Similarly, if you say the word *down* /daʊn/ more like [dʌʉn] 'doon', that might mean that you are from Scotland.

Decades of sociolinguistic research has identified consistent patterns between social factors like socio-economic class, ethnicity, sexuality, and gender with particular linguistic features. For instance, there is now quite a lot of work on 'TH-fronting'. In the UK, in particular, it is common to hear people pronounce /θ/ as [f] in words like *think* – hence [fɪŋk]. Research has shown this pronunciation to be influenced by social factors like age, social class, and gender (see Ramsammy & Schleef, 2013).

The above examples focus on two types of language variation: lexis or 'words' (e.g., *A1* vs. *peng*) and phonology (e.g., [fɪŋk] vs. [θɪŋk]). In addition to phonology and lexis, we see variation across all levels of language. This includes:

- **Grammar**, e.g., *she* ***were/was*** *home*
- **Discourse**, e.g., *he was running to me and* ***he said*** *'yes'/* ***he was like*** *'yes'/* ***he goes*** *'yes'*
- **Spelling**, e.g., *I love* ***u/you***

Given that lots of digital communication is text-based (e.g., WhatsApp, IM, Twitter), in this book we will focus heavily on spelling or 'orthographic' variation. Orthographic variation refers to spellings which are not typical, conventional, or standardised. In other words, these spellings aren't typically those that you'd find in the dictionary. For instance, in the above example we can see that the word 'you' can be represented in two ways: The standardised spelling <you>, and the non-standard spelling <u>. We could say that <you> is the 'standardised' spelling because it's the one that has been 'codified' and put into a dictionary. <u>, on the other hand, is the 'non-standard' spelling because it deviates from the expected spelling. These spellings have often explicitly been taught to learners, and the rules of the spelling system are enforced by gatekeepers. Most editors and teachers would correct <u> for <you> in written texts.

Whilst orthographic variation like the use of <u> for <you> is generally rare in formal written registers like books, letters, and public notices, these types of spellings are very common in DMC because this is a 'deregulated space'. In other words, on platforms like Twitter and WhatsApp, the 'formal rules' of written communication which we associate with letters and published work, are not always followed. There is no expectation that people will write in the same way that they do in a formal letter. In fact, people often use non-standard spellings for creative and stylistic purposes. Similar types of non-standard spellings are found in other 'deregulated spaces' like graffiti, magazines, dialect literature, shop signs, and so on.

Orthographic variation and non-standard spellings are not just a quirk found in English language DMC. We can find lots of examples of non-standard spellings and inventive written practices in other languages too. For instance, although Greek speakers generally write in the Greek alphabet, in social media, emails and other types of DMC many users will write in 'Greeklish'. Greeklish is a spelling system or orthographic style in which authors use the Latin alphabet to represent Greek. An example is found in Georgakopoulou's corpus of Greek emails (1997: 151):

(3) Katarxin se epishma keimena parakalo to onoma mou na anagrafetai ws XXXXX kai se epishma documents efoson etsi me kseroun oli tous edo. 2. I tipissa lei oti mas voleyei na katevoume san Ellhniko prama …
'First of all, I request that my name is written as XXXXX in formal documents since this is how I am known here. 2. The chick says it's better if we go on the pitch as a Greek team ...'

As we will see throughout this book, this type of variation is especially common in DMC. It is perhaps unsurprising that many researchers have therefore applied tools, concepts, and theories developed in sociolinguistics to understand *why* and *how* people use non-standard spellings, creative punctuation marks, and other strategies across a variety of different platforms and contexts.

Although the variation in these messages may appear, at first, to look random or unprincipled, a great deal of sociolinguistic research has demonstrated that language variation is systematic and rule-governed.

People don't just write (or speak or sign) in whatever way they want. The variation is influenced by particular social and linguistic rules or constraints.

The systematic nature of language variation was first described in two seminal studies that are often thought of as the foundations of the field of sociolinguistics: Fischer (1958) and Labov (1963). These were the first studies to demonstrate that language variation was systematic and could be explained by a series of linguistic and social factors. In Fischer's (1958) work in New England, he found that the variable pronunciation of the suffix <-ing> (i.e., [ɪn] vs. [ɪŋ]) in words like *running* and *fishing* was predicted by the speakers' sex and class. Similarly, in his work on rhoticity in New York City, Labov (1966) demonstrated that the pronunciation of post-vocalic /ɹ/ in words like *forth* and *floor* was influenced by the social class identity of the speaker and whether the word was produced in a 'careful' or 'casual' manner.

Because linguistic differences map onto social differences (e.g., young vs. old, working-class vs. upper-class), we go through life learning to recognise these differences, associating forms of language with different types of people. In other words, we learn the *social meaning* of variation. If we return to the example of the pronunciation of *bath* above, it's very unlikely that anyone in the UK is ever explicitly told that one pronunciation is typical in the North and the other in the South of England. But over the course of our lives, we come to recognise these differences and we learn their social associations. The ability for language to refer to social information like where the individual is from is what sociolinguists call **indexicality**. Simply put, social indexicality refers to the fact that language can point to non-linguistic (i.e., 'social') meanings. This includes social information like where the person is from, how old they are, their sexuality, and so on. To use our earlier example, we could say that 'peng' and 'A1' might *index* different types of people or qualities associated with those people, like being 'young', 'cool', or 'old'.

Key term: (Social) Indexicality

Indexicality refers to the property of linguistic signs to point to or signal non- linguistic attributes. This includes social categories like 'woman', 'working class', or 'gay', or more fine-grained meanings like 'coolness, 'dominance', or 'masculinity'.

Given that the field of sociolinguistics emerged in the 1960s, it is perhaps unsurprising that most sociolinguistic research has focussed on variation in speech and face-to-face conversation. For most of its history, the most common approach in the field has been to record and analyse variation in spoken interactions. However, other researchers have demonstrated that the concepts and approaches developed in this field can be usefully applied to other modalities, including signed languages, written registers, and – most relevant to the focus of this guide – digital communication. In the 1990s, as the internet became widespread, very many sociolinguists started to turn their attention to the language used online – to the study of 'Computer Mediated Communication' (CMC).

2.4 Computer Mediated Communication

The earliest sociolinguistic research on digital communication can be traced back to the early 1990s. Following the emergence of the World Wide Web (WWW) in 1991, many researchers started to become interested in understanding the types of language that were used in this new domain of interaction. The focus here was on documenting and describing linguistic patterns found in 'Computer Mediated Communication' (CMC). In this work, CMC was defined as 'any human communication achieved through, or with the help of, computer technology' (Thurlow, Lengel, & Tomic, 2004: 15). Work which followed this trend started to examine the language used in CMC subtypes, including emails, blogs, and Instant Messaging (IM).

Given that CMC interactions of the time were largely text-based on platforms and services such as IMs, emails, and weblogs, most of this work focussed on describing patterns of orthographic or spelling variation. A common approach was to develop taxonomies of CMC features which were said to be typical of the language used on the internet. Many of these accounts included features such as abbreviations (e.g., <u ok?>, <hun>), non-standard spellings (e.g., <fink>, <wot>), and alphabetisms (e.g., <gr8>, <2> for *to*).

Observing these trends, a consensus started to emerge regarding the nature of CMC. Many researchers claimed that the language used in CMC was a 'new variety' that was a hybrid of spoken and written registers. This perspective is evident in Davis and Brewer's account, where they claim that CMC is writing that 'very often reads as if it were being spoken – that is, as if the sender were writing talking' (1997: 2). Subsequently, many researchers set about attempting to determine where CMC could be placed on the spoken-written continuum (e.g., Ferrara, Brunner & Whittemore, 1991; Collot & Belmore, 1996). This agenda influenced the output of CMC research for some time, with investigations directed specifically at answering what David Crystal referred to as the fundamental goal of CMC research: To identify which features the variety takes from speech and which features it takes from writing (2006: 20).

Research which addressed this question concluded that CMC had features of both spoken and written registers such that it could be said to exist 'on a continuum between the context-dependent interaction of oral conversation and the contextually abstracted composition of written text' (Foertsch, 1995: 301). **Synchronous** genres of CMC – where the message is sent and received in real time – were said to resemble spoken discourse more closely, whilst **asynchronous** genres of CMC – where there is a delay between the sending and response of a message – were claimed to be more like written discourse.

Key Term: (A-)synchronous

Synchronous CMC occurs in real-time. The message is sent, received immediately, and then (typically) responded to by the interlocutor. All parties involved in the conversation are simultaneously engaged at the same time. Examples of contemporary forms of synchronous CMC include Skype conversations, FaceTime, and Zoom meetings.

In **asynchronous** CMC, there is a time lapse between the message being sent and the message being received. In these conversations, there is unlikely to be an immediate response from the receiver of the message. Examples of asynchronous CMC include emails, forums, and SMS messages.

This type of perspective is found in David Crystal's highly influential book, *Language and the Internet,* where he categorises the different types of CMC (e.g., web, emails, IMs) based on which features they take from written and spoken language. Table 2.1 is adapted from Crystal's (2006) book. The first three elements (time bound, spontaneous, and face-to-face) are features of spoken language. The last three qualities (space-bound, contrived, and visually decontextualised) are typically associated with written discourse. According to Crystal's taxonomy (Table 2.1), Instant Messaging – a synchronous type of CMC interaction – exhibits more features associated with spoken discourse (time bound, spontaneous) than blogging, an asynchronous type of CMC, which is more comparable to written discourse (contrived, visually decontextualised).

Having concluded that the language used on the internet was an 'emergent register' (Ferrara et al., 1991), researchers developed a set of terms and labels which referenced the written-spoken hybrid of CMC. This included terms such as 'netspeak', 'netlish' (Crystal, 2006), 'electronic language' (Collot & Belmore, 1996), 'electronic discourse' (Davis & Brewer, 1997), 'chatspeak' (Vandekerckhove & Nobels, 2010) and 'interactive written discourse' (Ferrara et al.,

Table 2.1 Spoken and written discourse features of 'netspeak' (adapted from Crystal, 2006)

	Web	**Blogging**	**e-mail**	**Virtual worlds**	**Instant messaging**
1. time bound	no	no	yes, but in different ways	yes, but in different ways	yes
2. spontaneous	no	yes, but with restrictions	variable	yes, but with restrictions	yes
3. face-to-face	no	no	no	no	no, unless camera used
4. space-bound	yes, with extra options	yes	yes, but routinely deleted	yes, but with restrictions	yes, but moves off-screen rapidly
5. contrived	yes	variable	variable	no, but with some adaptation	no
6. visually decontextualised	yes, but with considerable adaptation	yes	yes	yes, but with some adaptation	yes, unless camera used

1991). Features which were often considered characteristic of this variety included:

- Smileys and emoticons: :-) :-(;-(:-]
- Paralinguistic glosses: <laughs>, *coughs*, ~eye roll~
- Letter homophones: lol, cya, lmao, IMHO, tldr
- Non-standard spellings: wot, u, gr8, fankz, luv, dese
- Non-standard punctuation: !!!!!!!!, ?!?!
- Non-standard grammar: how pronounce, very disagreement

Points for reflection

- Do you use 'netspeak' features (e.g., abbreviations, non-standard spellings) on social media?
- If you do use 'netspeak' features, why do you use them? If you do not use features of netspeak, consider why you avoid using them.

As is evident in Crystal's taxonomy (Table 2.1), a common assumption in this type of work was that the medium (e.g., written vs. spoken language, instant messaging vs. email) was the main influence on the language used on the internet. Variation in text – like turn length, non-standard spellings, and other novel linguistic features – were understood not in reference to the context of the interaction or the users' identities, but were rather assumed to be determined directly by the medium. This assumption led to an outpouring of work which attempted to define specific features of CMC subtypes. This included publications which described 'the language of emails' and the 'linguistic features of IM'. A tendency in this work was to compare the language used in different CMC genres, leading to generalised claims like 'the language of text messaging is more 'conversational' than the language of emails'.

Points for reflection

- Is it possible to identify a distinct language variety used on the internet?
- Do you agree with the claim that the language of text messaging (e.g., SMS, WhatsApp) is more 'conversational' than emails?

The approach I have outlined so far which argued that language variation in CMC was determined by the medium subscribes to a determinist view of the relationship between technology and society. **Technological Determinism** (TD) is the idea that technology independently influences society. Within CMC, a TD perspective can be seen in the extent to which scholars argued that users' linguistic choices were determined by the medium (e.g., spoken vs. written) or the CMC genre (e.g., IM, email, blogs), as opposed to contextual or conversational factors like topic, identity, or interlocutor.

Key Term: Technological Determinism (TD)

The idea that technology autonomously influences society. Technology is the primary cause of major social, cultural, and historical change. In earlier work on CMC, scholars often subscribed to a TD perspective by arguing that the medium (e.g., written vs. spoken) and the genre (e.g., email, IM, blogs) of interaction determined the linguistic style (e.g., turn length, non-standard spellings) used online.

As the field became more established, researchers started to consider not just the effects of the medium on language, but also whether social and contextual factors influenced different styles of interaction. Some of this research asked whether variation in CMC could be explained by users' identities. This included work which attempted to identify differences between CMC styles used by men and women. For instance, in Herring's (2000) research on gender in CMC, she finds significant differences between the types and content of messages that men and women post. She observes that, in discussion lists and newsgroups, men were more likely to post longer messages, start and end discussions in mixed-sex groups, and use taboo and crude language such as insults and swearwords. Women, on the other hand, were more likely to post short messages, qualify and justify their assertions, apologise, and express support of others.

Nevertheless, whilst work by Herring (2000) and others signalled a departure from medium-focussed analyses of CMC, these approaches still seemed to neglect the relevance of context. To take Herring's (2000) study of gender in CMC as an example, the content and style of the message is assumed to be predicted solely by the gender identity of the author. What the users were writing about or who they were communicating with is not considered here. We know little to nothing about the context of the message. This seems like an oversight. Evidently, both men and women can be crude and use 'taboo' language. But crucially, it often depends on who we're talking to (i.e., friends vs. family) and what we're talking about (i.e., a positive vs. a negative topic). It's possible, then, that while gender might be a relevant factor in patterns of CMC, it might not be the *only* factor that influences how people use language online.

The type of work I have been describing so far has often been called the 'first wave' of CMC research. In Georgakopoulou's (2006) overview of the field, she argues that, whilst this line of work was important in establishing CMC as an independent area of linguistic inquiry, the first wave approach has various methodological and theoretical shortcomings. One of the main issues with this type of work was that many of the claims made in first-wave studies were generalisations based on anecdotal observations or small datasets. The relatively modest sized datasets used in the first-wave is likely indicative of the fact that accessing digital data at this time was still relatively difficult to do. Ideally, to make claims about the nature of 'the language of CMC' (as scholars were attempting to do) we would need lots of examples to argue that our examples are *representative* of broader patterns. This wasn't always feasible and so researchers often had to rely on anecdotal or fabricated examples. For instance, in his book, *Language and the Internet,* Crystal (2006) acknowledges the 'difficulty of obtaining large samples of [CMC] data', which he attributes to concerns about the public or private nature of CMC. As a workaround, Crystal uses 'constructed examples' (i.e., hypothetical examples he created himself) throughout his book to demonstrate CMC phenomena (2006: x). Whilst fabricated examples might help illustrate certain features or processes, we have next to no idea of knowing how widely they were used.

Another shortcoming of the first-wave of CMC research is this work seldom considered how the context may have influenced how a feature or language style was used. As we discussed above in relation to Herring (2000), it seems that context and topic are likely to be relevant to how crude or long a message is – not just the authors' gender identity. The omission of contextual issues was likely indicative of the agenda of first-wave CMC research: To develop an account of CMC/internet language as a distinctive and unique variety – as opposed to considering how context might shape different types of digital interactions.

A final shortcoming of first-wave CMC research was its apparent lack of engagement with other fields of study. Problematically, early CMC research seldom engaged with theories, concepts, and frameworks that had been developed in related fields like sociolinguistics, media studies, and digital sociology. Although concepts developed in these fields were clearly relevant to studying digital communication, first-wave approaches rarely engaged with work in related fields. Subsequently, researchers inevitably dealt with issues that had already been resolved or discussed elsewhere. The outcome of this was that CMC scholars continued to focus on answering a very restricted set of research questions mainly concentrating on the effects of the medium on language use or explaining language in terms of broad social categories like 'men' and 'women', rather than responding to contemporary developments in sociolinguistics and other fields.

2.4.1 A New Variety?

As we have discussed above, a core argument of the first-wave of CMC research was that the linguistic variety used online was fundamentally different to that used elsewhere. Whether scholars referred to this variety as 'netspeak', 'chatspeak', 'txtspeak', 'netlish', or 'internet slang', it was generally agreed that the language used on the internet was a fundamentally new variety that was specific to the medium of the internet. This type of perspective is evident in Crystal's definition of 'netspeak' which he calls 'a type of language displaying features that are *unique* to the Internet' (emphasis added 2006: 20).

However, though 'netspeak' features like <bbz> *babes,* <2> *to,* <!!!!!> were perceived to be new features that had emerged on the internet, in reality, the novelty of these features was overstated. Many of the supposedly 'unique' features of the 'internet variety' were found to actually predate the internet. Similar kinds of abbreviations and respellings to those found in CMC were observed to be common in older written genres including notetaking, telegrams, and magazines (see Janda, 1985; Baron, 2008; Androutsopoulos, 2000).

Points for reflection

- Have you ever seen 'netspeak' features in other contexts than DMC? If so, why do you think these features are used in these contexts? (Hint: Think about graffiti.)
- Do you associate the use of 'netspeak' with any types of people or users?

We see similar types of spellings and written conventions across written genres because they share similarities in their structure, form, and design. In the case of SMS and telegram messages, both are technologies constrained by character limits. Similar to SMS messages, which are charged based on the number of characters, telegrams were charged by the number of words. Abbreviations and other non-standard spellings were often used to minimise the costs of sending a message. This style of writing became known as 'telegram style'. Unsurprisingly, the types of abbreviations and the style of telegram messages look very similar to those used in SMS. Consider, for instance, the following example (4) from a textbook on telegraphs in the early 1900s (Dodge, 1901):

(4)

Q. Hw sun wi 1st 74 b rdy
'How soon will 1st No. 74 be ready?'
A. Sun as ty gt C & W
'Soon as they get coal and water'
Q. Wr r ty gg r 9
Where are they going for No. 9?'
A. SX
'Wanatah, office call'
Q. Cld ty mk K A if I gv em 10 mins on 9
'Could they make Hanna if I gave them 10 minutes time on No. 9?'

The above example contains many abbreviations which look very similar to those we defined as 'netspeak' in earlier sections – just some 90 or so years before the internet was introduced! Importantly, like those used in CMC and SMS, the abbreviations and spellings people used in telegrams weren't random or illogical. They are linguistically principled: Vowels tend to be omitted (e.g., <Hw> *how*, <rdy> *ready*, <Cld> *could*) or reduced (e.g., <Sun> *soon*), whilst other spellings appear to represent processes commonly found in speech (e.g., <em> *them* → [ɛm]).

Similar spellings and abbreviations are found in SMS. For instance, consider the following data from Thurlow and Brown's (2003) paper on SMS messages sent by young people in the UK (Extracts (5) and (6)):

(5) AS IF,wot ugly unsespectin minga has got u?only jokn fatsy,I new ud laf,dats i sent it-erd ur doin levis proj,did u 12 borrow mine?
'as if, what ugly unsuspecting minger has got you? Only joking, fatsy. I knew you'd laugh. That's [why] I sent it- heard you're doing Levi's project. Did you 12 borrow mine?

(6) R WE DOIN LUNCH THIS WK?CHE
'are we doing lunch this week? Che'

We see very many similar spellings and abbreviations in these messages to the telegram in (4). This includes the deletion of vowels (e.g., <R> *are,* <WK> *week,* <u> *you*) and representations of spoken language phenomena (e.g., <erd> *heard* [ɜːd], <dats> *that's* [dats]). These spellings, like the telegram style, are not random or incoherent, but are principled and systematic.

Based on this evidence, it seems that the language used in CMC was unlikely to have ever been truly *unique* to the internet (cf. Crystal, 2006). Rather, it seems that features and strategies common in other genres of written communication (e.g., telegrams) were recycled and extended in CMC. On the internet, these features were used in similar ways and, perhaps, for similar reasons. A more accurate definition of CMC language, then, is not that it is 'a variety unique to the internet' but rather: 'A linguistic style that is characterised by standard and non-standard spellings, abbreviations, emoticons, and other features that are found in other written genres, but are often associated with the internet'.

So far, we have focussed on one main critique of internet language: The novelty of netspeak forms was overstated. A second and related issue, however, focussed not on the supposed novelty of 'netspeak' forms per se, but more the extent to which these features were actually used in CMC. Although features like <bbz>, <gr8>, and emoticons were claimed to be typical or iconic of CMC, there was little evidence on the extent to which these features were used in practice. As noted previously, many of the arguments made in earlier work about the nature of the language of CMC were often based on limited datasets and/or anecdotal observations (e.g., Crystal, 2006). It was unclear to what extent these arguments could be generalised.

In fact, when researchers examined the quantitative distribution of 'characteristic' CMC features in naturalistic conversations, they found these to be much less common than initially claimed. For instance, in Tagliamonte and Denis' (2008) analysis of 'netspeak' forms in a corpus of over 1.5 million words of Instant Messages (IM) sent by 72 Canadian teenagers, the authors find that features previously described as characteristic of IM were used very infrequently. Notably, they find that, in the corpus of 1.5 million words, the abbreviations <ttyl> 'talk to you later' and <btw> 'by the way' were used very infrequently: <ttyl> was used 298 times, whilst <btw> was used only 249 times. Although perhaps the most surprising finding is that the abbreviation <lol>, which is often claimed to be an iconic CMC feature, was used just 4506 times. Instead, the variant <haha>, was used more frequently than <lol>, occurring 16183 times in the corpus. Overall, the authors conclude that the use of so-called 'characteristic IM forms' were actually very infrequent in the corpus, with all forms combined representing only 2.4% of the word count of the dataset. Together, these findings suggest that whilst 'netspeak' features may be relatively interesting features of digital communication, their novelty and frequency were heavily overstated in earlier research on the topic.

2.4.2 Beyond 'Internet Language'

Acknowledging the limitations of the first-wave, researchers started to advocate for a move away from analysing features of CMC in relation to spoken-written registers or examining how a particular medium shapes language use or how macro-identities, such as gender, correlated with language choices. Scholars like Georgakopoulou (2006) and Androutsopoulos (2006) argued instead for a greater focus on the contextual aspects of digital communication. The call was made for research to examine how broader contextual, social, and cultural dynamics shape digital communication.

CMC research which followed this call started to focus less on the medium specificities of email, IM and other genres (cf. Crystal, 2006) but rather emphasised individual agency in digital communication. These types of studies demonstrated that users actively engaged in creative and sometimes unpredictable linguistic practices, appropriating and styling linguistic resources to do conversational and interactional work, as opposed to reproducing a set of expected and conventionalised practices determined by the medium of interaction.

The focus in this new line of inquiry was not on defining the 'language of the internet' or the 'linguistic characteristics of netspeak' per se, but rather on how linguistic variability was used in social interaction and its role in the construction of sociolinguistic identities. Androutsopoulos (2006: 419) summarises this development as a shift from studies which analyse the 'language of CMC' to those which focus on 'socially situated computer-mediated discourse'. Research which followed showed that CMC was not a single homogenous variety but rather that there was a great deal of linguistic diversity in users' digital interactions. These analyses did not attempt to explain the linguistic diversity solely in terms of the medium (i.e., email or IM), but rather emphasised the relevance of social, interactional, and contextual factors in shaping the content and style of digital communication.

The refocussing of research priorities away from medium-related to user-related language practices gave rise to what some scholars have termed the 'second wave' of CMC studies (Georgakopoulou, 2006; Androutsopoulos, 2006). Along with this development came a more sustained effort to engage with insights and arguments in related fields, such as sociolinguistics, sociology, and media studies.

An illustration of this development is found in Siebenhaar's (2006) analysis of code choice and code-switching in Swiss-German Internet Relay Chat (IRC) rooms. In that study, Siebenhaar finds that the variation in the use of Swiss-German dialects and Standard German in Swiss-German depends on both individuals' preferences and also the predominant variety used within a particular thread. Thus, in that analysis, it is not the medium (IRC) that is perceived to determine which style or type of language is used. Rather, it is social and contextual factors (individual preferences, the predominant dialect in a thread) that are argued to influence the code choice.

2.5 Current Approaches in Sociolinguistics

Since the publication of the special issue on 'Sociolinguistics and computer-mediated communication' in the *Journal of Sociolinguistics* (Androutsopoulos, 2006), sociolinguistic research on digital communication has gone from a relatively specialised and fringe research area to a productive and vibrant field of inquiry. Digital data and methods are no longer unusual or noteworthy. Rather, analyses of DMC take centre stage in contemporary sociolinguistic research.

This development reflects the changing technological landscape over the past 20 or so years. Over this period of time, digital technologies have become increasingly embedded in our lives to the point that, for most people today, social media and digital communication have become fairly unremarkable facts of social life. The types of digital media we engage with and the ways in which we engage with them have dramatically changed too. As noted in the introduction, mobile devices such as smartphones and tablets have replaced computers as the primary way that most people get online and users now access platforms primarily through apps rather than web-based browsers. As mobile technologies have become more sophisticated, the digital media content that we upload and interact with has shifted from primarily text-based to multimodal. That is to say that, along with text, we now upload content that combines images, music, and videos.

Sociolinguistic research on digital communication has responded to these developments. As discussed in Section 2.4, the earliest CMC research focussed mainly on 'text-based' CMC platforms and services, like IM and SMS. I suspect that most readers of this book, however, will be more familiar with multimodal platforms like Snapchat, TikTok, and Instagram. All these platforms place an emphasis on audio-visual content. As new platforms and practices emerge, sociolinguistic approaches of digital communication have shifted from focussing solely on textual patterns and orthographic variation towards approaches that analyse the interplay of visual, textual, and aesthetic features of platforms and messages.

2.5.1 Offline-Online

Arguably, one of the most dramatic developments that has complicated how we approach the study of digital communication is the increasing convergence of 'offline' and 'online' space. As described in the introduction, we don't really ever 'log off'. Instead, we move seamlessly between interactions in face-to-face and digital contexts. This reality is considerably different to the one that researchers were describing in the 90s. As I have already discussed, in the earliest CMC research, users' digital practices were assumed to be specific to the context of the internet (e.g., Crystal, 2006). Individuals were argued to use features of a distinct variety that was bounded to this domain, i.e., 'netspeak' or 'internet language'. This conceptualisation is heavily influenced by the framing of the online as some separate 'cyber world' or dimension.

Today, given that digital technologies are so embedded in our everyday lives, it no longer seems feasible to try to define a distinct 'digital world'. It seems unlikely that individuals will use a discrete linguistic variety that is restricted to the internet when people often continually move between offline and online contexts of communication.

To illustrate how difficult it is to separate offline-online contexts of social interaction, I'll introduce a hypothetical situation, partially illustrated in Figure 2.1. Imagine you are messaging a friend (Jack) on Snapchat about your day at school or uni. The conversation is initially text-based. You ask Jack how he is, he responds, and then he asks you what you're up to. Instead of sending a text message back, you decide you will send a picture of what you're doing at that time. Perhaps you're working on your coursework. Along with an image of your coursework, you add a Snapchat sticker of the time (22.19), along with two emojis that suggest you're not entirely happy to be working on your coursework.

After 20 minutes or so, you make little progress. You decide to send Jack a video selfie of you with the 'dog lens', and the comment '#bored'. By the time your friend has responded, you've finished your homework and you're relaxing by watching a film before bed. You send Jack a quick video of the film you're watching followed by a voice note saying you'll snap (i.e., message) him tomorrow. This very mundane – and

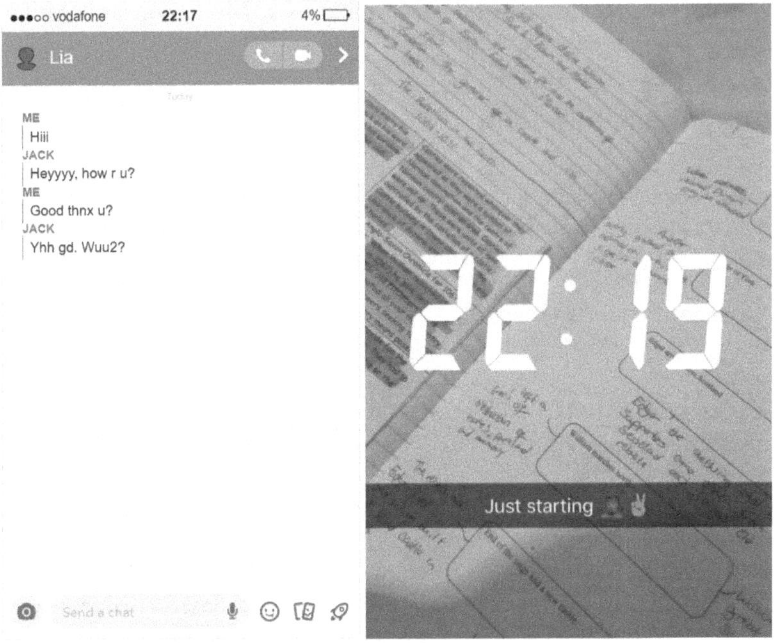

Figure 2.1 An example of a multimodal snapchat conversation

hopefully relatable – example which many of us engage in on a daily basis demonstrates the slippery offline-online divide. When you send an image of your homework, a context which we typically think of as 'offline' – your desk, your writing – becomes transformed into a digital message (a Snapchat). And when you see Jack in class tomorrow, your Snapchat discussion – the film, the coursework – becomes available as a potential topic to be discussed in face-to-face conversation. In this way, the boundaries between offline-online contexts of communication become blurred, if not indistinguishable.

Another issue which complicates any attempt to distinguish between offline-online contexts of interaction is the fact that many of us communicate *across* platforms. Although earlier research was focussed on defining the language used in specific platforms – 'IM', 'email', 'SMS' – today, people regularly engage in interactions that move across different networks, platforms, and devices. Returning to the Snapchat conversation above, it is possible to imagine a scenario in which the interaction takes place across multiple platforms. For instance, when 'coursework' becomes a topic of conversation, your friend Jack might send you a work-related meme on Instagram. It is then possible that the rest of the conversation will continue on a different platform even though it was initiated on Snapchat. This tendency is part of a phenomenon that the digital anthropologists, Madianou and Miller (2012) have called **polymedia.**

Key Term: Polymedia

A concept introduced by Madianou and Miller (2012), polymedia describes the tendency for mediated communication to take place not on a single platform, but across services and apps. People choose from this range of media platforms not based entirely on what that platform allows the user to do but rather on the social relationships that can be formed there.

As we will see, all these developments are extremely relevant to sociolinguistic approaches to digital communication. Today, the reality that we are faced with is really very different to that discussed in earlier work on 'CMC'. The computer has largely been replaced by a variety of different digital and mobile devices that we use. As platforms become more sophisticated, the new multimodal styles of social and digital media now look very different to the text-based conversations that were discussed in earlier work on CMC. Given that our relationship with technology and our digital practices have very clearly changed over the past 20 or so years, the label 'CMC' now seems a little outdated. It seems odd to refer to conversations on 'Snapchat' or 'Instagram' as types of CMC because these are very different platforms to those analysed in the first-wave of CMC research. At a very obvious level, they are accessed via a mobile device and whilst mobiles are *technically* computer-based devices, people don't really *think* of mobiles in this way. For these reasons, and to distinguish the approaches and research I discuss in the remainder of this book from earlier CMC research, I use the terms 'digital communication' and 'DMC' (see Androutsopoulos, 2021).

2.5.2 'TikTok Voice'?

The above discussion on the offline-online separation of social life brings me to an issue that I often get asked to provide some media commentary on. Over the past few years, I have been inundated with journalist requests asking me to comment on and describe the new variety of 'TikTok language' (or whatever platform was popular at the time!). There are now a good few newspaper articles which have been written on an apparently new TikTok voice or accent whilst others have claimed that Twitter has led to more informal or casual styles of interaction (presumably due to the character limit).

Before we progress, it is worth critically assessing some of these claims. I often argue that many of these claims are reflective of a tendency for people to overestimate the influence of (new) technologies and social media platforms on language and social interaction. As discussed above, in earlier research on CMC, researchers concluded that the internet had led to the emergence of a new variety of language. Many of the claims I see about 'TikTok voice' (or whatever platform voice) are reminiscent of those made in earlier CMC research. Most researchers who work on this topic, however, are less convinced that new platforms will lead to new varieties of language.

So why then do these narratives exist? In my work on this topic, I have argued that it is often to do with visibility. TikTok, especially, puts a lot of the language practices that we probably do in everyday face-to-face interaction under the microscope. You may not have recognised that people use words like 'rizz' or 'slay' or that when people speak, they use lots of hesitation markers (e.g., *erm, err, hmm*), or you may have never even heard a speaker from Shetland. But, on TikTok, those words, dialects, and other types of language practices are put on display and are intensely scrutinised. Those practices have likely existed for some time but platforms like TikTok and YouTube increase the *visibility* of those practices as they become viewed by new audiences. We now attend to something we've never thought of or heard about before, and so it's possible that we jump to the conclusion that those practices *emerged on the app/platform* simply because that's where we first heard or saw them. In a recent article, I was asked to comment on a new 'influencer voice' used on TikTok. However, what the journalist had heard on TikTok, predates the app. Before TikTok, it was Instagram. Before that, it was YouTube. We often have a tendency to assume that things are much newer than they are!

In fact, lots of the practices described as 'influencer voice' or 'TikTok language' are actually things people already do offline and have done for some time. Very recently, lots of journalists have asked me to comment on the emergence of a 'TikTok accent'. When I've analysed the content of the videos sent to me, many of the people in the videos use features of language we hear and see elsewhere. For instance, many influencers use 'uptalk' or 'High Rising Terminals' (HRTs), that is, the use of a rising intonation on a declarative statement (e.g., *I went to this party?*) – and creaky voice or 'vocal fry' – where speakers use a deep, creaky, breathy sound when they speak. Of course, whilst some influencers might use these features in an interesting way, it would be inaccurate to say that these features are distinct to TikTok or even part of a platform specific 'accent'.

To me, as a sociolinguist, a more compelling question is *why* do some influencers use these features? In my work, I have argued that these features are often used in TikTok (and other platforms) because they potentially make the content more engaging. For instance, sociolinguistic research on HRTs in speech has shown that these are often used to engage the audience in what the speaker is saying. It's highly likely that influencers and other creators who are fighting for space and attention on TikTok, use linguistic strategies in an attempt to engage their audience and keep them on their page. On many platforms, engagement means money. If you're a highly engaging creator, people will stay on your page and you will make more money!

In other work, journalists have been more interested in the appearance of so-called 'new words' or 'internet slang'. Much of this discussion neglects the fact that lots of what people think of as 'TikTok slang' – e.g., 'slay', 'ate it up', 'left no crumbs', and so on, have a much longer history than most people recognise. Many of these words and phrases originated in a variety of English called 'African American English' and/or are words which have been historically associated with queer communities. Most people are unaware of the etymologies of these words and so when they see words like 'slay' and 'yaas' being used on TikTok, they often assume that those words and phrases originated on that platform. In reality, they were used a long time before TikTok and by communities who have a long history of using the language. In this way, social media appears to raise the visibility of language varieties and their use, and so potentially increases the uptake of these words and phrases. We will continually to critically evaluate these issues throughout this book, but it's worth keeping in the back of your mind that language varieties and practices that we think of as being 'TikTok' or 'Twitter' language, for instance, often have a much longer history than we think.

2.6 Summary

This chapter has provided an overview of research on digital communication in sociolinguistics. In the chapter, we defined digital communication as any type of interaction that takes places via digital technologies. This includes services such as email, social media, video conferencing platforms, and weblogs. Earlier sociolinguistic research on digital communication focussed on describing patterns of 'CMC'. Much of this work tried to identify the distinctive features that were thought to be characteristic of the 'new variety' used on the internet (often labelled 'netspeak'). More recent approaches instead analyse the ways in which users creatively appropriate linguistic resources to perform their identities and to do conversational work, such as signal sarcasm or irony.

The chapter concludes by briefly summarising current approaches in the field. Research in sociolinguistics and digital communication has moved in lockstep with more recent technological developments such as the emergence of 'image-first' platforms like Instagram and TikTok. In contemporary sociolinguistics, researchers have turned their attention to multimodal social and digital media interactions, exploring the interplay of text, images, video, and emoji. Along with these developments, researchers have also questioned the traditional dichotomy of the offline-online. As we will see in later chapters, this has led researchers to explore how digital interactions are embedded in broader systems of sociolinguistic differentiation and use.

2.7 Activities

1. Make a list of linguistic features you consider to be typical of DMC. Now compare that list with that in Crystal (2006, Chapter 2). What similarities and differences do you observe?
2. Keep a diary of your 'polymedia' practices throughout the day. Are there particular platforms that you use to interact with specific people? Are there particular types of messages you send on one platform that you don't on another?
3. Navigate to a conversation on a text-based app or platform (e.g., a WhatsApp chat). Now search for the following features: <lol>, <haha>, <hehe>, <lmao>. First, write down how many times each of these are used. Do you use one form more than another? Are there any forms that you don't use at all? If you use more than one form, try to think about how that is used in your text messages. For instance, do you use <lol> in a different way to <hehe>?
4. After completing the task above, attempt to define the function of <lol>. Some scholars (e.g., Tagliamonte & Denis, 2008) consider <lol> along with <haha>, <hehe> and <lmao> to be 'laughter variants'. Do these features *always* function as signifiers of laughter in your texts?
5. Do you think there is a 'TikTok voice'? If yes, what are some features of this voice? Do you see these features being used elsewhere in face-to-face interaction or other contexts?

2.8 Further Reading

Sociolinguistics

Holmes, Janet & Nick Wilson (2022). *An Introduction to Sociolinguistics*, 6th edition. London: Longman.

Jones, Rodney & Christiana Themistocleous (2022). *Introducing Language and Society*. Cambridge Introductions to Language and Linguistics. Cambridge: Cambridge University Press.

Van Herk, Gerard (2018). *What is Sociolinguistics?*, 2nd edition. Oxford: Wiley-Blackwell.

CMC

Crystal, David (2006). *Language and the Internet.* Cambridge: Cambridge University Press.

Georgakopoulou, Alexandra & Tereza Spilioti (2016). *The Routledge Handbook of Language and Digital Communication.* Oxford: Routledge.

Herring, Susan (1996). *Computer-Mediated Communication: Linguistic, Social, and Cross-Cultural Perspectives.* Amsterdam: John Benjamins.

2.9 References

Androutsopoulos, Jannis (2000). Non-standard spellings in media texts: The case of German fanzines. *Journal of Sociolinguistics*, 4: 514–533.

Androutsopoulos, Jannis (2006). Introduction: Sociolinguistics and computer-mediated communication. *Journal of Sociolinguistics*, 10(4): 419–438.

Androutsopoulos, Jannis (2021). Polymedia in interaction. *Pragmatics and Society*, 12: 707–724.

Baron, Naomi S. (2008). *Always On: Language in an Online and Mobile World.* Oxford: Oxford University Press.

boyd, danah (2012). Participating in the always on lifestyle. In Michael Mandiberg (ed.), *The Social Media Reader*, pp. 71–76. New York: New York University Press.

Buchholz, Katharina (2022). Which countries spend the most time on social media? *World Economic Forum.* www.weforum.org/agenda/2022/04/social-media-internet-connectivity/ (accessed 21 April 2024).

Carr, Caleb T. & Rebcca A. Hayes (2015). Social media: Defining, developing, and divining. *Atlantic Journal of Communication*, 23(1): 46–65.

Collot, Milena & Nancy Belmore (1996). Electronic language: A new variety of English. In Susan Herring (ed.), *Computer-Mediated Communication: Linguistics, Social and Cross-Cultural Perspectives*, pp. 13–28. Amsterdam: John Benjamins Publishing Company.

Crystal, David (2006). *Language and the Internet*, 2nd edition. Cambridge: Cambridge University Press.

Davis, Boyd H. & Jeutonne Brewer (1997). *Electronic Discourse: Linguistic Individuals in Virtual Space.* New York: State University of New York Press.

Dodge, George M. (1901). *The Telegraph Instructor.* Indiana: Institute of Telegraphy.

Ferrara, Kathleen, Hans Brunner & Greg Whittemore (1991). Interactive written discourse as an emergent register. *Written Communication*, 8: 8–34.

Fischer, John L. (1958). Social influences on the choice of a linguistic variant. *WORD*, 14(1): 47–56.

Foertsch, Julie (1995). The impact of electronic networks on scholarly communication: Avenues for research. *Discourse Processes*, 19: 301–328.

Georgakopoulou, Alexandra (2006). Postscript: Computer-mediated communication in sociolinguistics. *Journal of Sociolinguistics*, 10: 548–557.

Herring, Susan C. (2000). Gender differences in CMC: Findings and implications. *The CPSR Newsletter,* 18(1).

Janda, Richard (1985). Note-taking English as a simplified register. *Discourse Processes*, 8: 437–454.

Labov, William (1966). *The Social Stratification of English in New York City*. Washington, DC: Centre for Applied Linguistics.
McCulloch, Gretchen. (2019). *Because Internet: Understanding the New Rules of Language*. London: Penguin Random House.
Schleef, Erik & Michael Ramsammy (2013). Labiodental fronting of /θ/ in London and Edinburgh: A cross-dialectal study. *English Language and Linguistics*, 17(1): 25–54.
Siebenhaar, Beat (2006). Code choice and code-switching in Swiss-German internet relay chat rooms. *Journal of Sociolinguistics*, 10(4): 481–506.
Tagliamonte, Sali & Derek Denis (2008). Linguistic ruin? Lol! Instant messaging and teen language. *American Speech*, 83(1): 3–34.
Thurlow, Crispin & Alex Brown (2003). Generation Txt? The sociolinguistics of young people's text-messaging. *Discourse Analysis Online*, 1(1).
Thurlow, Crispin, Laura Lengel & Alice Tomic (2004). *Computer Mediated Communication*, 1st edition. London: Sage Publications.
Vandekerckhove, Reinhild & Judith Nobels (2010). Code eclecticism: Linguistic variation and code alternation in the chat language of Flemish teenagers. *Journal of Sociolinguistics*, 14: 657–677.

3 Affordances, Audiences, and Contexts

3.1 Introduction

In this chapter we cover the following topics:

- Platform affordances
- Audience design and the imagined audience
- Contexts and context collapse.

Imagine you're on an exotic holiday in some far-flung destination. You're spending a day on a beautiful white sand beach surrounded by palm trees with a nice cold drink in hand. As the palm trees sway and the sun starts to set you think to yourself: 'I can't wait to upload this moment to social media so all my friends can see what an amazing time I'm having'. Now, here comes a dilemma: Which app do you use the document this moment? You've got accounts on all the main platforms (Twitter, Instagram, TikTok, Facebook, and Snapchat). Do you post the same video across all your accounts? Or perhaps you upload a photo to Snapchat and a video to your Instagram story.

What we post and where we post, is often a carefully made decision. We tend to create content and upload posts with an awareness of what the platform allows you to do (**affordances**) and who we expect to see that post (**audiences**). Take, for instance, the example above of uploading a post whilst you are on your summer holiday. On an app like Instagram, you could upload a single post with multiple images that documents various aspects of your trip to the beach: Relaxing on a sunbed with an ice-cold drink in hand, snorkelling in crystal clear waters, and an aesthetic shot of the sun setting over the beach (see Figure 3.1 for example). For the purposes of this discussion, let's say that your Instagram profile is public. You then carefully curate this post by adding some related hashtags (e.g., #holiday, #summer2024, #sunset). You might even tag the location of the beach. By tagging the post in this way, you have now linked the post to others which have also used the same hashtags and location. It's possible that people looking for their next summer holiday

DOI: 10.4324/9781003391838-3

Figure 3.1 An Instagram post of a day at the beach

may come across your post and interact with it, possibly leaving a comment or a like. Your followers may also interact with the post. All of these possibilities are enabled because of the **affordances** of Instagram.

Now, let us imagine that you want to post about your day at the beach on a different platform. Let's use BeReal as a counterexample. BeReal is a French social media app launched in 2020 where posts are uploaded as part of a daily randomly selected 2-minute window. When users receive a daily notification, they are encouraged to upload a post of what they are doing within that given moment. What that post will look like will depend entirely on what you're doing in that 2-minute window: You may be relaxing on a sunbed; you may be watching the sunset go down; or you may miss this window entirely because you've gone for a swim. But unlike Instagram where you've uploaded a post with multiple different images of your day, the BeReal post will capture only a small part of your day. And unlike the post on Instagram which becomes a permanent fixture of your profile (unless you delete it), the BeReal content will disappear once opened by those you sent it to. And, unlike on Instagram where users who do not know or follow you might interact with the post, on BeReal, posts are shared only with friends. This example reveals that different platforms have different affordances which leads us to design our posts in different ways.

For sociolinguistic analyses of DMC, audiences are important because concerns about who might see a post are likely to have an influence on the content and style of a post. Because posts might be seen by different audiences, users will often design posts with an intended audience in mind. For instance, in reference to the example above, on Instagram, where profiles are very often set to public, an awareness that the post may be seen by people who are not close friends might lead you to design a relatively inoffensive post that can't be misinterpreted by people who don't know you. Whereas on apps and platforms that are 'closed' (i.e., your post can only be seen by your friends, such as BeReal), it's possible that you might design this post in a different way. It may be more casual or include 'in jokes' that only you and your friends know.

What we've acknowledged here is that people don't just upload the same post to different platforms. Rather, they *design* their posts and messages based on the affordances of the platform and the perceived audience of that post. As sociolinguists and researchers interested in language online, when we analyse DMC, we want to ask whether audience effects or platform affordances influence or constrain the style and content of a post. We might be interested in the following questions:

- Do users create different styles of posts across different platforms?
- Are users language choices influenced by the design of the app or platform?
- What types of linguistic strategies and resources do users employ to negotiate different audiences (e.g., friends vs. family) on different apps and platforms?

In this chapter, we explore these questions in more detail. We start out by introducing some important concepts that have been employed to understand the language of DMC. Our focus here is on three main issues: Affordances, audiences, and contexts. We consider how these issues might influence how we design our posts and the implications of these issues for sociolinguistic analyses of DMC.

3.2 Affordances

Any person who has spent more than five minutes on Facebook or Instagram or on any other social media will quickly be aware that different digital platforms allow users to do different things. For instance, on Facebook – a platform typically associated with the affordance of the 'status update' – we can respond to the prompt 'what's on your mind?' by creating a post about what we've been up to or how we're feeling. If we wanted to, we could write quite a detailed post. Facebook currently permits status updates of up to 63,206 characters. If we compare the status update with the 'tweet', we'll quickly realise that the style, length, and type of update is going to be quite different on Twitter. This is because Twitter, as a platform which has long emphasised brevity, generally limits tweets to a maximum of 280 characters. What we have identified here is one main difference between Twitter and Facebook: Character limit.

There are very many other differences beyond the length and size of posts on the two platforms. For instance, on Facebook, we can share posts with our friends and family to our own profile. These posts will only be seen by those who we have accepted a request from. Whereas, on Twitter, we can retweet the post so it's seen by people from a much larger audience, many of whom we do not follow. Similarly, on Facebook, we can now respond to a post by 'liking' it or using an appropriate emoji reaction to convey 'anger', 'care', 'sadness', 'love', 'laughter', or 'surprise'. Whereas on Twitter, the button responses are more restricted – we can only 'like' a tweet (by pressing the 'love' button). An example is found in the tweet below (Figure 3.2), taken from my public profile. The affordances of comment, retweet, like (or 'love'), bookmark, and share are below the tweet. As the owner of the tweet, I can also post a comment, see the 'post engagements', and see the number of views the tweet generated.

What a platform or digital technology allows you to do and what activities are enabled by those functions are called **affordances**. We can think of affordances as properties of social and digital media. Often these affordances are shared across social and digital media platforms. For instance, Instagram and Snapchat both afford users the ability to upload posts to their stories. On both apps, users can upload a 24-hour 'story' that is accessible by followers (and potentially others if their account is public). In this way, the story function is an affordance that both Instagram and Snapchat (and some other platforms, e.g., WhatsApp) share.

Figure 3.2 Example tweet showing Twitter's various 'like', 'retweet' and 'share' affordances

Not all platforms will have the same affordances. For instance, although Instagram and Snapchat have similarities (e.g., the story function), there are also several differences in their design. The main difference is the way content and user profiles are organised on the two apps. On Instagram, user profiles comprise a grid of historic image uploads which users can scroll back through. Whereas on Snapchat, user profiles are only likely to contain the users' most recent content, such as uploads from the last 24 hours.

An often-made distinction in the literature is the difference between so-called 'high' and 'low' level affordances. **Low level affordances** are things that are dependent on the specific medium or platform or interaction, such as particular features, buttons, and styles of post. This includes those already discussed such as the like button on Facebook and stories on Snapchat and Instagram.

High level affordances are those dynamics enabled by social and digital media technologies that operate above specific platforms. In other words, these are affordances that are typical of social and digital media platforms more generally. danah boyd (2014) argues that social media are principally defined by four high level affordances. These are (1) persistence, (2) visibility, (3) spreadability, and (4) searchability.

Persistence refers to the fact that social and digital media services exist beyond the specific moment that the user is online or active. Unlike in face-to-face interaction which occurs within a specific time and space and ceases to exist beyond that moment (unless recorded!), conversations on social media are often 'on record'. In other words, messages, conversations, posts, and other online content persist beyond the moment in which they are sent. Users do not need to be online or using the service to receive the content. This means that platforms like Snapchat which enable users to send disappearing content are still considered persistent platforms because those services are continuously accessible, even if particular messages are not.

The persistent nature of content means users can often retrieve and review historic posts. A good example is the 'memories' affordance on Facebook (see Figure 3.3). This function allows users to review past moments shared with friends, including posts and photos, new friendship connections, and major life events. It is precisely because content persists that we can view and access this historic content. Some institutions have even capitalised on the persistent nature of social and digital media data by creating archives of social media data. For instance, the British Library added Twitter to its UK Web Archive whilst in the US, the Library of Congress kept a Twitter Archive.

The persistent nature of social media is relevant to sociolinguistic analyses of DMC because the fact that posts stick around might lead to new engagements and interactions. For instance, imagine you are rifling through an old friend's Instagram posts from 2016 and 'like' a

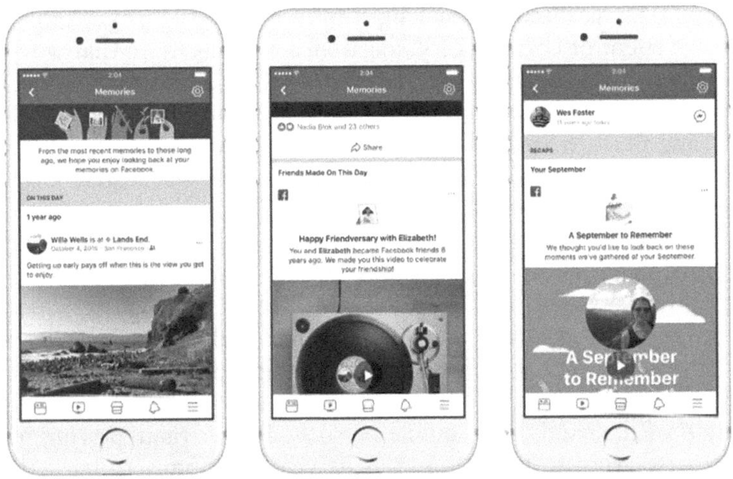

Figure 3.3 Facebook Memories (Meta, 2018)

post before commenting something like 'old memories!'. Liking and commenting on this historic post could lead to a new conversation between you and the user about the memories you made back in 2016.

Another, albeit dramatic, example of the interactional potentials of 'persistence' is the common request for evidence or so-called 'receipts'. Because social media posts are on record in a way that face-to-face interactions usually are not, users can often provide screenshots of conversations to support their claims. In this way, persistence has implications for sociolinguistic analyses of social and digital media.

The next affordance of social media that boyd discusses is **visibility**. This refers to the fact that posts on social media are highly visible. Although we often design posts with a specific audience in mind, they are often seen by users beyond those who we intend to engage with. For instance, when we post a tweet, we might write that tweet as if that tweet is only going to be seen by other users who follow us. But Twitter also has built in affordances that maximise the visibility of the tweet meaning that it is likely to be seen by a larger audience of users than just our followers. This includes the 'retweet' function which enables users to re-post tweets, which in turn shares that tweet with their own followers. The hashtag also functions in a similar way. If we upload a tweet with a hashtag, that tweet is directed into a larger conversational stream of tweets each containing the same hashtag. Say, for instance, we were watching a television programme, we could use the hashtag for that programme to filter our tweet into a 'channel' of other tweets about that programme.

The heightened visibility of social media posts can lead to situations where posts are viewed by people who are not part of our expected audience. This is discussed at length by boyd (2014) in her ethnographic account of US teenagers' social media practices. In that work, boyd recounts that she had been contacted by an admissions tutor at an Ivy League institution who was concerned about the application of a young Black student. The student had submitted an outstanding application which detailed his aspirations of getting a degree, enabling him to leave behind his crime-ridden neighbourhood where he'd grown up. However, after Googling the candidate, the admissions committee came across his MySpace profile which was filled with gang symbols, explicit language, and references to criminal activities. The committee concluded that the candidate had fabricated a back story in order to increase his chances of being accepted at the prestigious institution. boyd, however, argued that was this was a misinterpretation of the candidates' online persona. Rather than viewing his online persona as an indication that he was attempting to trick the admissions panel, boyd proposed that the student was using his profile as a 'survival technique' to get by in his neighbourhood. The difference in understanding here is indicative of the heightened visibility of the students' MySpace profile and the fact that it was seen by someone outside of his intended audience. The user evidently wasn't posting for the university admissions officer – he was posting for his classmates and peers.

Another high-level affordance is **spreadability.** This refers to the fact that digital and social media technologies enable us to circulate content far and wide. In face-to-face interaction we often communicate with a ratified (i.e., known) and restricted set of individuals. That information tends to stay with those individuals unless they discuss it with other people. The transmission of information from one person to the next is likely to be relatively slow. On social and digital media, however, information can be spread from user to user very easily and very quickly.

In fact, we've already discussed one example of the spreadability of social media in the above. The 'retweet' function on Twitter is a great example of the potential for social media content to become spreadable. As discussed above, we often write tweets intended to be read by our followers, but they're often seen by people beyond these contexts. This is because the retweet function is especially useful in spreading the content of that message beyond the limited number of followers that a user might have.

Spreadability is also enabled through 'screenshots'. For instance, on WhatsApp, a closed platform where users communicate with ratified users in a private conversation, users could share screenshots of messages with individuals who are not part of the group. Similarly, if users follow a private Instagram account that their friends do not, they might take screenshots of content to share with their friends. In this way, content can be spread easily and quickly beyond the immediate audience in which the original message was conveyed.

The final high-level affordance that boyd discusses is **searchability.** This refers to the fact that social media content can be found and uncovered via search functions. On Instagram, for instance, we can search for specific hashtags to follow, on TikTok we can find our friends by searching for their username, and on Facebook Marketplace we might use filters to narrow our search to find the perfect second-hand item we've been looking for.

Key Term: Affordances

Affordances refer to what a platform allows you to do. We can make a distinction between 'high' level affordances which are properties of social/digital media technologies more generally (e.g., the fact that digital conversations generally persist beyond the moment), and 'low' level affordances which refer to the specific functions of a platform or service (e.g., On Twitter: The 'like' button, the retweet function).

Points for reflection

- Think about some of the main (low-level) affordances of a social media platform (e.g., Twitter).
- Consider how these affordances influence the types of interactions that people engage in on that platform.
- Reflect on whether other platforms share these affordances. Are these affordances designed to be used in similar ways across different platforms?

Although affordances like *persistence* and *searchability* have been suggested as general properties of social media technologies, we should be mindful that users may engage with platforms in ways that subvert or question these affordances. In Costa's (2018) ethnographic work in Mardin, Turkey, she argues that *persistence* is only partially found in the users' practices, given that they would regularly open and close accounts. Similarly, users would intentionally subvert *searchability* by using fake names or accounts. She argues instead for affordances-in-practice emphasising the situated nature of affordances and the relevance of user engagements in exploiting those affordances.

3.2.1 Imagined Affordances

Some scholars have proposed an additional type of affordance that are not specific to the app or service – so-called **imagined affordances.**

Nagy and Neff (2015: 1) define imagined affordances as those that exist between 'users' perceptions, attitudes, and expectations; between the materiality and functionality of technologies; and between the intentions and perceptions of designers'. In other words, imagined affordances are those perceptions and expectations about how a platform or technology works which ultimately impact how a user engages with those platforms/technologies. This includes expectations about how the algorithm of a platform works. A good example of an imagined affordance is the Facebook News Feed. Often, people perceive this to be an objective and chronologically organised stream of their friends' and families' posts. In other words, people presume that their News Feed just presents them with a stream of users' latest updates. However, in reality, this is an algorithmically tailored selection of posts arranged in a non-chronological order according to the user's interests and past interactions.

3.3 Audiences

So far, we've discussed a few properties of social media that influence the style and content of how people post. Many of these relate in some way to the perception or response of the viewer – or the **audience**.

Lots of research has examined the role and effect of audience on DMC. This is because there are often considerable differences in the types of audiences in face-to-face and digital communication and how we manage them. In face-to-face conversation we generally interact with a known and ratified person or group of individuals. The style of interaction that we use (e.g., the words, the formality, etc.) is likely to be influenced by who we are speaking to. We often change the way we speak or communicate depending on the interactional context. This includes things like the age, gender, or social status of our interlocutor(s), as well as the context of the interaction. We can say then that we *design* our language based on the norms and expectations of the speaking context and the audience(s) we are communicating with. We're usually quite good at doing this because we have developed an awareness of the typical expectations of the context over time.

3.3.1 Audience Design

What we have started to describe above is called **stylistic** variation. Also called intra-speaker/signer variation, this refers to linguistic variation within the language of a single individual. For instance, you may use the word 'peng' with your friends, but 'nice' when speaking to your parents. This is called **style-shifting**. We all style-shift to some degree. Very clearly – and for good reason! – young people do not speak the same way to their friends as they do to their grandparents.

Rather, they will style shift: They will use words, pronunciations, and phrases associated with 'young people' (sometimes labelled 'youth language' or 'slang') with their peers and then shift to a more formal style of interaction when speaking with their grandparents.

Key Term: Stylistic Variation

Stylistic or intra-speaker/signer variation refers to variation within the language of a single individual. Style-shifting occurs when we move between different styles of interacting. For instance, you may speak or communicate one way with your friends and then style-shift to another way of speaking/communicating when interacting with your colleagues or family.

Decades of sociolinguistic research has showed that people are very adept at doing this type of stylistic variation. Several models of stylistic variation have been proposed to explain why people shift. In the earliest research on the topic, it was the formality of the speech context that was argued to be the central motivation for style-shifting. Sociolinguists such as William Labov (1966) and Peter Trudgill (1974) found that, as the formality of the interaction context increased, speakers used more of the standard or prestige speech style. For instance, research on the variable pronunciation of (ING) (i.e., the alternation of the pronunciation of *–ing* as either [ɪŋ] or [ɪn]) found that speakers were more likely to say words like *walking* as [wɔːkɪn] in more casual speaking contexts such as an informal interview or conversation. In more formal speaking tasks such as when reading a word passage or a list of words, however, they were more likely to use the standard, [wɔːkɪŋ]. To explain this pattern, scholars concluded that stylistic variation could be measured in relation to the degree of 'attention paid to speech'. That is to say that as the formality of the speech context increased, it was expected that individuals would pay more attention to their speech, and so would use more of the standard or prestige variant.

However, whilst individuals clearly adapt their linguistic behaviour in response to the perceived formality of the interactional context, there are some contexts where style-shifting cannot be understood in relation to the formality of the speech context. Research which followed demonstrated that other extralinguistic factors, like the interlocutor or audience, were also factors that influenced style-shifting.

In the 1980s, sociolinguist Allan Bell proposed a radical model of stylistic variation which he called 'Audience Design'. The framework was heavily influenced by trends in social psychology at the time, specifically Giles' (1973) framework of Communication Accommodation Theory (CAT). This framework argued that people make changes to their own behaviour either to align or to disalign from those they are interacting with. Extending this to linguistic behaviour, Bell argued that individuals "*design* their style primarily for and in response to their audience" (Bell, 1984: 143).

Bell's arguments were primarily based on an analysis of the pronunciation of different radio newsreaders in New Zealand. In that work, he found stylistic variation in the speech of two newscasters across the different radio stations they presented on. Bell argued that this pattern could not be interpreted in relation to attention paid to speech because the speaking task and formality were consistent: Both were formal news reports. He instead argued that the newscasters were style-shifting in response to the audiences of each show. In other words, Bell argued that the speakers *designed* their linguistic behaviour to match the norms and expectations of the two different audiences who tuned into the shows.

A radical element of Bell's model was the introduction of 'referee design'. Unlike audience design which is responsive in nature – i.e., individuals adopt a linguistic style in *response* to the expectations and norms of the audience – referee design was conceptualised as 'initiative'. In these contexts, Bell argued that individuals diverge from the typical expectations of the interactional context, instead using a language style associated with an absent third-party.

Key Term: Audience Design

Audience Design is a concept developed by Allan Bell (1984) which argues that stylistic variation occurs because people change how they speak or interact in relation to who they are interacting with (i.e., their audience). People design their speech in response to the expectations and norms of the audience.

3.3.2 The Imagined Audience

Though the concept of Audience Design was developed to account for patterns in spoken language, it is clearly relevant to our discussion of digital communication. As we discussed above, people often *design* the content of their posts in relation to their audience. Across different platforms, we might upload different posts in anticipation of who might see that post. The language choices we make, therefore, are potentially influenced by concerns of the audience.

However, and arguably, the notion of audience is a little more complex in digital communication. In most DMC contexts, we have no clear understanding of who our audience actually is or who might see the post. Take, for instance, Twitter. Though you might initially write a tweet in the hope that it will be seen by your followers, if the post is retweeted or hashtags are used, it's very likely going to be seen by people beyond the original audience.

Of course, this dilemma is not specific to digital communication – it is comparable to other types of asynchronous, one-to-many types of communication, such as radio and television. Bell's (1984) radio presenters had some idea about the type of audience who would listen to their shows but they had no real way of knowing who was really listening. This is also an issue that writers contend with. In fact, it's something I'm thinking about as I write this book. Although I have some predictions about who will read this book, and whilst it's true that I am writing this book in a particular style for the intended audience, in reality, I have no real way of knowing who will read this book and whether the style that I've adopted is truly that successful. Like the radio presenters in Bell's study, I am making linguistic choices based on my assumptions or expectations about who the audience might be and what they might use this book for. To use Bell's terminology, we could say that I am *designing* my writing for the student and/or teacher who I expect will use this book.

In social media and digital communication, these issues are arguably heightened. This is because high level affordances like *spreadability* and *searchability* mean that our messages, posts, and other content might be seen by people way beyond those we had ever thought would see it. If we go back to our earlier example of posting an image of our beach holiday on Instagram, when uploading this image, I would very likely assume that the audience of my post will be my friends and family. Many of my friends and family follow me, so it is logical to assume that this post will appear in their newsfeed. So, I will make several design choices with this audience in mind. But, as I discussed earlier, if I tag this post with hashtags, add a location tag, and make my profile public, it's possible – if not inevitable – that people beyond my immediate social circle will see this post. So, who are we posting for?

The answer is the **imagined audience.** In these contexts, and "in the absence of certain knowledge about audience, participants take cues from the social media environment to imagine the community" (boyd, 2007: 131). In this way, when we write a tweet or put together an Instagram post, we construct it in a way that we think is going to be familiar and interpretable by those who we expect to see that post – people who we *imagine* to be our audience (Litt & Hargittai, 2016).

Points for reflection

- Who do you post for? Who is your imagined audience?
- Do you post for different audiences on different platforms? How do you design your messages?
- Have you ever experienced a situation where someone (e.g., family) saw a post that you had not intended for them to see?

The type of audience that we imagine is based on a number of different factors including, the social network of the user, the platform which they post on, the affordances of that platform, and our past interactions. In a now seminal study of audience design on Twitter, Marwick and boyd (2011) asked participants a series of questions about their imagined audience. In response to the questions 'Who do you imagine reading your tweets?' and 'Who do you tweet to?', users generally responded that they designed their tweets for their friends, followers, or themselves. Some users also noted that the audience that they imagined was dependent on the content of the tweet. Others viewed the audience as the 'ideal' person – an imaginary interested party that shares their interests and preferences. The concept of the imagined audience is extremely relevant to studying digital communication. We'll discuss later the relevance of the imagined audience and ethics in Chapter 5 but, for now, we'll focus on the influence of the imagined audience in shaping how we communicate online.

Key Term: Imagined Audience

On social and digital media, unable to ascertain who might see a post, users design their messages and content for an expected or assumed audience. This audience is imagined to be a particular type of person, such as friends, family, and people who are similar to the poster.

Since we design our messages for an imagined audience, the choice of language we write in, the types of emoji we use, the spellings that we employ, or even the words we decide to use are all likely to be a design choice based on who we expect to see the post. Research has shown that multilingual posters will often decide which language to use on the basis of an imagined audience. For instance, in Androutosopoulos' (2014) analysis of language alternation on Facebook, he demonstrates that, in multilingual conversations, the code choice is influenced by the expectations and linguistic proficiency of the expected audience. The choice of language, he argues, is fundamentally motivated by the need to make the post as maximally interpretable and accessible to as many users as possible. By analysing four individuals' Facebook posts, he shows that the users adopt three strategies for maximising the audience. They either: (i) use a lingua franca; (ii) replicate the content of a message in multiple languages; and (iii) avoid using linguistic resources altogether. In this way, the users adapt the content of their message to respond to the expectations of the imagined audience.

Similar practices are observed by Liu (2021). In that study, Liu shows that Chinese multilingual users of the social media platform WeChat use highly complex design strategies to target different audiences. For instance, one individual, Amy, was seen to switch between English and Chinese in different posts that she uploaded. As an international student in Melbourne, her choice of language was highly variable. Some posts were in English, others in Chinese. However, when she took a summer vacation, her posts were almost entirely in Chinese. In interviews when Liu asked about these posts, Amy revealed that the posts she uploaded during her vacation were designed solely for her schoolmates and teachers in China. She commented that her choice to use Chinese was directly motivated by recommendations of her teachers back in China. They had suggested that she uploaded posts for those who did not have the opportunity to study abroad or for those considering applying for foreign universities. Here we see that the language that Amy posted in was directly influenced by the expectation of *who* might see the post, i.e., the imagined audience.

3.4 Contexts

Some of the tensions we've discussed so far in terms of audience design are related to the fact that social media brings people from different contexts together. In offline face-to-face situations, these contexts are quite easy to disentangle. From home to school to work to the cinema, we participate in different social circles depending on the context in which we find ourselves. At school, we might spend time with our friends and occasionally interact with our teachers, whilst at work, we spend time interacting with our colleagues and, potentially, customers or clients. The ways that we speak, dress, and interact are all dependent on the norms and expectations of a given context. How we interact with our peers and co-workers at school or at university is likely to be very different to how we communicate with our family or superiors (e.g., bosses, teachers, lecturers).

The above point describes a basic fact about social life: We present different versions of ourselves in different contexts. This observation was first theorised by sociologist Erving Goffman (1967) in his discussion of 'face'. Here, **face** refers to the individual's public self-image; it is how we present ourselves to the world. Because there are different norms and expectations in different contexts, we often change our public self-image. This is what Goffman refers to as **face-work**. We can think of face as a type of mask that we put on (or take off) depending on the audience and the context of social interaction. Goffman argues that a person can be seen to be in face when the image they claim for themselves is one that is "internally consistent, that is supported by judgments and evidence conveyed by other participants, and that is confirmed by evidence conveyed through impersonal agencies in the situation" (1967: 6).

In life, we often participate in this type of face-work as we move between contexts like work or home. There are often types of interactions or topics of conversation that are deemed appropriate for some social contexts and inappropriate for others. For instance, at work, where we are often expected to act 'professionally', we spend most of our time conversing with colleagues and, potentially, customers or clients. At work, sharing intimate details about your love life, for instance, is unlikely to be a socially appropriate topic for this context. Discussions about the current tax year or the budget for stationery may be more appropriate (depending on your job, of course). Evidently, topics deemed suitable for work are not the same as those you might engage in with your friends. Here, we see that in different contexts, we engage in different types of interactions depending on the norms and expectations of different communicative contexts. Generally, people have a good awareness of what is expected for a given social context. We know when to do our 'work-self' or 'friend-self' and when to switch that side of us off. It would be weird to go home and speak and act the same as we do when we're at work or at school!

3.4.1 Context Collapse

Generally speaking, the contexts that we find ourselves in are relatively distinct in space and time. Work, school, and home are domains that we can often separate from the rest of our lives. For instance, the 'work' domain is often specified by your contractual obligations of attending work at a designated time and place. Many people in white collar (i.e., office) jobs commute to a workplace and will work 'office hours', such as from nine to five. 'Professional life' and the roles that we engage in as a 'receptionist', 'banker', or any other such job are only roles that we fulfil when we're in the office during work hours. We can manage the boundaries of this context relatively easily. We might discuss the end of the tax year in a 9.30 am meeting with our colleagues but when we get home at 7 pm, outside office hours, we switch to the domain of 'home' and discuss social topics with family members. The two contexts seldom overlap: They are distinct and bounded.

However, sometimes the boundaries between different contexts (e.g., 'work', 'family', 'friends') may not be as easy to separate as the example above. In some situations, they may be blurred or in others, they may disappear entirely – they can be said to *collapse*. **Context collapse** occurs when there is a flattening of distinct contexts. This happens when the boundaries between the different domains that the individual participates in become blurred or even indistinguishable such that the individual's private, personal, or familiar networks might converge.

As we will see, context collapse in social media is a phenomenon that has been discussed at length. However, it is important to recognise that context collapse isn't specific to social media – it happens elsewhere. A classic case is the example of a family wedding where it is very typical for guests to be invited from various different social and professional circles: Family, friends, colleagues, and so on. Until the day of the wedding, those circles are likely to have been relatively separate – colleagues at work, family at home, friends in social settings. However, when all of those guests are bought together at the wedding, the boundaries that used to separate those groups of people disappear. Contexts collapse as colleagues talk to family, family talk to friends, and so on.

Key Term: Context Collapse

Context collapse refers to the flattening of distinct communicative contexts. In social media, context collapse occurs when users from various different social networks (e.g., work, family, school) are bought together. Users must contend with context collapse when designing the content of their posts.

Context collapse is relevant to the notion of 'face' because it can lead to individuals being in the 'wrong face' or 'losing face' in the situation that they find themselves in. For instance, in the example of a family wedding in the UK, it is common for the wedding celebration to feature a speech by the 'best man'. Typically, this will include humorous stories about the groom. Some of these stories include personal or embarrassing narratives. It is possible that the groom has not disclosed these details to colleagues or acquaintances. In these contexts, the public self-image that the groom has constructed (i.e., his face) may be contradicted or undermined due to the collapse of these different contexts. This is what researchers describe as 'losing face'.

The wedding example above shows us that context collapse isn't specific to social media. However, arguably, context collapse is heightened in digital and social media. This is because people often use social media to make connections with people from a variety of different social and professional circles. Social media brings these people together in much the same way as a family wedding.

A good example of context collapse on social media is the organisation of Facebook friends. Whilst writing this chapter, I navigated to my Facebook friends and checked who I'd accepted friend requests. I seem to have connections with people from just about every social and professional circle I've ever participated in. I have connections with users I went to primary school with, family from Australia and the UK, colleagues from a former workplace, current colleagues, old secondary school teachers, and others. Given that these individuals are all associated with specific social or professional contexts ('school', 'work', etc.), these connections have been kept separate. But on Facebook, they are now bought together. Now, if I were to think about uploading a post, I'd have to consider that this post is likely to be seen by all these different users from different social and professional circles. The design of this post is therefore very likely to be influenced by an awareness of the imagined audience and a concern for the context collapse that Facebook enables. In this way, context collapse influences not just the types of posts we share but also how we share them.

Points for reflection

- Have you ever experienced context collapse in social media?
- Do you use any strategies (e.g., privacy and security settings) to manage context collapse?

We can think of context collapse in social media as occurring in two distinct ways. The first, **context collusion** occurs when users "intentionally collapse, blur, and flatten contexts," while **context collision** occurs when "different social environments unintentionally and unexpectedly come crashing into each other" (Davis & Jurgenson, 2014: 480). Ultimately, the difference between collusion and collision is in the level of intentionality. For instance, updating a relationship status on Facebook is likely to lead to context collusion, with this information intentionally shared among members of different social networks (work, family, friends). Context collision, on the other hand, often occurs "without any effort on the part of the actor, and sometimes, unbeknownst to the actor with potentially chaotic results" (Davis and Jurgenson, 2014: 481). For instance, a user may be tagged in photos of a night out which then may be viewed by users from different social networks.

3.4.2 Managing Contexts

Given the potential for social media to collapse contexts, users will often employ strategies to manage the potential for content to be seen by multiple audiences. According to Marwick and boyd (2011), an awareness of context collapse and the imagined audience often leads users to develop an online presence that is maximally inoffensive to all possible imagined audiences. This type of 'self-censorship' often leads to a style of self-presentation that can be viewed as a "lowest-common denominator effect" (2011: 9). In other words, users may intentionally avoid posting about sensitive topics or uploading content that may be misinterpreted by different users.

An additional strategy that Marwick and boyd observe is that users often tend to balance authentic and public styles of self-presentation. They suggest that this allows users to "maintain equilibrium between a contextual social norm of personal authenticity that encourages information-sharing and phatic communication [...] with the need to keep information private, or at least concealed from certain audiences" (2011: 11). This may be done within a single post or across different combinations of posts.

Users might also change the privacy and security affordances of platforms to manage context collapse. For instance, lots of research has shown that users exploit the privacy settings of a platform to make posts more or less visible to their different social networks (e.g., boyd, 2014). Other work has shown that users use the 'block' and 'hide' affordances to prevent users from accessing their content (e.g., Stutzman & Hartzog, 2013; Vitak & Kim, 2014). More recently, the introduction of the 'close friends' function on platforms like Instagram has given users more control over who sees and can respond to the post.

A more radical type of social media boundary management is seen in the use of different accounts or platforms for different audiences. Simply put, some people might not use certain platforms because they do not want certain people to see what they upload to that platform. In my ethnography of young people's digital practices in East London (Ilbury, 2022), I found that young people did not actively post on Facebook because they were conscious that family members had accounts on the platform. If they uploaded something to Facebook, they were worried that their parents or extended family would see it and, possibly, misinterpret it. Instead, many of the young people resorted to using just one platform: Snapchat – an app which none of their parents used. By shifting entirely to Snapchat, they avoided the potential for context collapse to occur by using an app that was almost exclusively used by their peers and people their age.

Finally, users might create additional profiles to manage context collapse. For instance, many users have a 'work' profile that is shared with colleagues and a 'personal' profile shared with friends and family. Multiple or alternative ('alt') accounts have been documented on various different platforms, including Instagram (Kang & Wei, 2020) and Reddit (Triggs et al., 2021). There are several reasons why users might create 'alt' accounts. This includes the finding that users often create multiple accounts to manage professional and personal personas that are oriented to different audiences (Stutzman & Hartzog, 2013). In other contexts, using multiple accounts may be considered standard practice. For instance, in Costa's (2018) ethnographic account of digital practices in Mardin, Turkey, she finds that it is common for users to have multiple Facebook profiles. Often, these accounts are used with different networks of users and are generally listed under fake names and pseudonyms. The content and style of posts uploaded to a platform are likely to vary substantially across the different accounts.

Multiple accounts might also be used to avoid the disclosure of sensitive personal information, such as an individual's sexual or gender identity. For instance, in a study of queer communities on Reddit, Triggs and colleagues (2021) observe that these users avoid context collapse through a number of differentiation strategies, including maintaining a 'main' and 'alt' account. Across the two accounts, LGBTQ+ users report uploading and engaging with different types of content in line with the expectations of their imagined audience. On the 'alt' account, users were able to obscure their offline identities, therefore removing the possibility that their engagements could be linked back to their main account. This is especially necessary for users who may not be 'out' to friends and/or family.

3.4.3 Do Contexts Collapse?

Though context collapse has been useful in theorising the 'networked public' (boyd, 2010), recent work has questioned the universality of this concept. Costa (2018), for instance, argues that context collapse only really describes the ways in which people engage with social media in the West. She argues that context collapse is not an inherent property of social media, nor the effect of 'social media logic'. Rather, she argues for a greater focus on how specific communities of users adapt their practices to mitigate the potential for context collapse to occur.

Other critiques have focussed on the stability of contexts. Tagg and Seargeant (2021), for instance, argue that context collapse infers that contexts are fixed, predetermined sets of situational factors when, in fact, contexts are co-created discursively in and through interaction. Similarly, Szabla and Blommaert (2018) argue that users rarely address audiences but rather specific addressees, and so design their messages not for *audiences* but rather for *individuals*.

In response, Tagg and Seargeant propose a move away from context collapse to context *design*. Drawing inspiration from Bell's (1984) audience design framework, context design suggests that, in creating a message, users actively contribute to the construction of the context, rather than simply responding to some pre-existing norm. In other words, users actively *design* the content and style of their messages in response to a set of contextual variables.

3.5 Summary

This chapter has introduced and discussed some key media theories and concepts in studying language and digital communication. We have argued that digital content is often shaped by the affordances of a given platform. What users post and how they post it is influenced by what a platform allows them to do. We have also seen that users often have to contend with the fact that they can never be sure who will see their post. Subsequently users will often design posts, content, and other messages in anticipation of an imagined audience. Finally, we have discussed the potential for context collapse to occur in social media. As users from various different social networks are bought together, users may develop strategies to negotiate which communities and friends can access content.

3.6 Activities

1. Compare your user profiles (or that of a celebrity) across at least two social media sites that you use for different purposes and/or different audiences (e.g., LinkedIn, Facebook, Instagram). What differences in the style and content of your posts can you identify? Are any of these linked to the expectations of the imagined audience or context collapse?
2. Choose a social media platform. Now write down the platform affordances which could be used to manage the imagined audience and context collapse (e.g., security and privacy settings). In what ways would these affordances affect the style, content, and audience of the post?

3.7 Further Reading

Brandtzaeg, Petter Bae & Marika Lüders (2018). Time collapse in social media: Extending the context collapse. *Social Media + Society*, 4(1): 1–10.

Bucher, Taina & Anne Helmond (2018). The affordances of social media platforms. In Jean Burgess, Alice E. Marwick & Thomas Poell (eds.), *The SAGE Handbook of Social Media*, pp. 233–253. London: Sage Publications.

Burgess, Jean, Alice Marwick & Thomas Poell (eds.) (2018). *The Sage Handbook of Social Media*. London: Sage Publications.

Fuchs, Christian (2021). *Social Media: A Critical Introduction*, 3rd edition. London: Sage Publications.

Humphreys, Ashlee (2016). *Social Media: Enduring Principles*. Oxford: Oxford University Press.

Van Dijck, José (2013). *The Culture of Connectivity: A Critical History of Social Media*. Oxford: Oxford University Press.

3.8 References

Androutsopoulos, Jannis (2014). Networked multilingualism: Some language practices on Facebook and their implications. *International Journal of Bilingualism*, 19(2): 185–205.

Bell, Allan (1984). Language style as audience design. *Language in Society*, 13(1): 145–204.

boyd, danah (2014). *It's Complicated: The Social Lives of Networked Teens*. New Haven: Yale University Press.

boyd, danah & Nicole Ellison (2007). Social network sites: Definition, history, and scholarship. *Journal of Computer-Mediated Communication*, 13(1): 210–230.

Costa, Elisabetta (2018). Affordances-in-practice: An ethnographic critique of social media logic and context collapse. *New Media & Society*, 20(10): 3641–3656.

Davis, Jenny L. & Nathan Jurgenson (2014). Context collapse: Theorizing context collusions and collisions. *Information, Communication & Society*, 17(4): 476–485.

boyd, danah (2010). Social network sites as networked publics: Affordances, dynamics, and implications. In Zizi Papacharissi (ed.), *Networked Self: Identity, Community, and Culture on Social Network Sites*, pp. 39–58. New York: Routledge.

Giles, Howard (1973). Accent mobility. *Anthropological Linguistics*, 15(2): 87–105.

Goffman, Erving (1967). *Interaction Ritual: Essays on Face-to-Face Interaction*. London: Aldine.

Hartzog, Woodrow & Frederic Stutzman (2013). The case for online obscurity. *California Law Review*, 101(1): 1–50.

Ilbury, Christian (2022). Discourses of social media amongst youth: An ethnographic perspective. *Discourse, Context, and Media*, 48: 1–9.

Kang, Jin & Lewen Wei (2020). Let me be at my funniest: Instagram users' motivations for using Finsta (a.k.a., fake Instagram). *The Social Science Journal*, 57(1): 58–71.

Labov, William (1966). *The Social Stratification of English in New York City*. Washington, DC: Centre for Applied Linguistics.

Litt, Eden & Eszther Hargittai (2016). The imagined audience on social network sites, *Social Media + Society*, 2(1): 1–12.

Liu, Kaiwen (2021). Language choices as audience design strategies in Chinese multilingual speakers' Wechat posts. *Global Media and China*, 6(4): 391–415.

Marwick, Alice E. & danah boyd (2011). I tweet honestly, I tweet passionately: Twitter users, context collapse, and the imagined audience. *New Media & Society*, 13(1): 114–133.

Meta (2018). All of your Facebook memories are now in one place. https://about.fb.com/news/2018/06/all-of-your-facebook-memories-are-now-in-one-place/ (accessed 24 April 2024).

Nagy, Peter & Gina Neff. 2015. Imagined affordance: Reconstructing a keyword for communication theory. *Social Media + Society*, 1(2): 1–9.

Szabla, Malgorzata & Jan Blommaert (2018). Does context really collapse in social media interaction? *Applied Linguistics Review*, 11(2): 1–29.
Tagg, Caroline & Philip Seargeant (2021). Context design and critical language/media awareness: Implications for a social digital literacies education. *Linguistics and Education*, 62: 100776.
Triggs, Anthony Henry, Kristian Kristian Møller & Christina Neumayer (2021). Context collapse and anonymity among queer Reddit users. *New Media & Society*, 23(1): 5–21.
Trudgill, Peter (1974). *The Social Differentiation of English in Norwich*. Cambridge: Cambridge University Press.
Vitak, Jessica & Jinyoung Kim (2014). 'You can't block people offline': Examining how Facebook's affordances shape the disclosure process. In *CSCW '14: Proceedings of the 17th ACM conference on Computer Supported Cooperative Work & Social Computing*, pp. 461–474.

4 Identity and Online Communities

4.1 Introduction

In this chapter we cover the following topics:

- Sociolinguistic approaches to identity
- Theories of online identity
- Online communities
- Participatory culture
- Internet memes.

If you have a social media account on a platform like Facebook, Twitter, Instagram, or LinkedIn, take five minutes of your time and navigate to your profile page. Once there, take a few moments to think about the content of that page. It's highly probable that your profile will contain various bits of information about you. This is likely to include things like your name, where you work or study, your interests, and where you live. You may have even uploaded a profile photo of yourself. What you see in front of you is a digital representation of your life: It is your digital identity.

Very many of us use social media platforms to create and maintain digital representations of ourselves. Often, users will spend quite a lot of time designing an online presence that is interpretable by an imagined audience of their peers. This is because most people use social media to interact with people they know and have met in other contexts like work or school. For many people, the profile they create will need to be interpretable to their friends and family. For public figures, on the other hand, their profiles need to be recognised by the public. For instance, let's consider the Twitter profile for the current President of the Republic of South Africa, Cyril Ramaphosa. His profile includes various bits of information which tell us things about his identity (see Figure 4.1). This includes his:

- Name and username: *Cyril Ramaphosa, @CyrilRamaphosa*
- Nationality: 🇿🇦 *(A South African flag emoji)*
- Verified status

DOI: 10.4324/9781003391838-4

Figure 4.1 Cyril Ramaphosa's Twitter profile page (screenshot from August 2024)

- Professional roles and duties: *President of the African National Congress, President of the Republic of South Africa, and Chair of the African Union 2020*
- Location: *South Africa*
- Birthday: *November 17, 1952*
- Image: *A profile image which comprises a professional headshot and a banner which includes the oath of office.*

The above example shows us that user profiles are central to our online identities. By using the affordances of different platforms (e.g., bios, photos, emoji, and so on), we can create a digital representation of our professional and social identities.

As was discussed in Chapter 2, sociolinguistic research has long been interested in the relationship between language and identity in digital communication. This is because the style, content, and character of digital interactions are potentially influenced by authors' social backgrounds and the identities they wish to claim for themselves. For instance, it is possible that people use non-standard spellings (e.g., <wot>, <4>, <u>, for *what, for, you*) and other features (e.g., emoji, memes, and acronyms) to index some identity. When an individual uses a particular spelling, emoji, acronym or meme, they may be attempting to signal to others what type of person they want to be interpreted as. Lots of research, for instance, has examined how particular words, spellings, or phrases become associated with specific types of users or online communities. This includes the language used by members of social categories like 'women' and 'men', but also smaller groups like friendship networks and internet communities, such as fandom and meme cultures. The 2023 word of the year *rizz* ('charm, charisma'), for instance, was originally associated with a particular type of internet community – Twitch – where it appeared to be associated with the streamer, Kai Cenat. It then went on to become popular outside of this community, particularly amongst 'Gen Z'. If someone were to use this word, it may be an attempt to signal their engagement with Twitch or 'young person identity'.

Sociolinguistic analyses of language and identity in digital communication ask questions like: Do younger texters use more non-standard spellings than older texters? Are there differences between men, women, and non-binary people in emoji use? Do British and American teens use <lol> in different ways? All of these questions focus on the relationship between social identities (e.g., age, gender, region) and language use.

This chapter introduces some main theories of identity in sociolinguistics. It then goes onto discuss some popular theories of 'digital identity'. The chapter then considers a range of different identity-related practices in the context of a 'participatory culture'. Our focus here is on how users participate in the formation, negotiation and maintenance of digital communities, influencer cultures, and internet meme cultures.

4.2 Identity in Sociolinguistics

Identity is notoriously a difficult concept to define. The most straightforward definition of identity is simply *who you are*. Your identity is what makes you an individual. If someone asks, 'who are you?', it's highly likely that you will initially reply with your name. Your name is clearly one aspect of your identity but it's very likely that the person asking the question will want to know other things about your identity. This might include your age, ethnicity, gender identity, or social class.

As noted in the introduction, we rarely ask these questions outright, particularly if they are socially taboo. However, we can often infer information about someone's social identity from how they speak or interact. A case in point is that we can often determine where a speaker is from on the basis of their accent or dialect. Here we see how language and identity are closely related.

Points for reflection

- If someone asked you to describe your identity, what would you say?
- What elements of your identity are important to you (e.g., social class, gender identity, race)? Do you think these elements influence how you speak or interact?

A common approach to studying language and identity in sociolinguistics has been to identify and define the linguistic varieties that are used by different social groups. A great deal of work in the field has described varieties used by members of different ethnic groups. Examples include 'African American English' (AAE) and 'Chicano English'. The two varieties, AAE and Chicano English, are generally spoken by members of two ethnic groups: African Americans and Mexican Americans. If a speaker uses one of these varieties, they are able to index their membership of the ethnic group that the variety is associated with. In this way, language can become a marker of in-group identity. Use (or non-use) of a variety can signal membership of the community (or possibly lack of membership in the case of non-use).

To explore the relationship between social identities and language varieties, sociolinguists have typically attempted to identify correlations between linguistic features (e.g., the pronunciation of *my* as [mä:]) and social categories (e.g., African Americans). If the researcher observes significant differences in the use or rate of a feature from one group to the next, they can conclude that there is some social differentiation in the use of that feature. This difference is likely to be influenced by a social factor, like age, ethnicity, gender, and social-class.

To illustrate this approach, we will use a hypothetical example. Let's say we are interested in the variation in the use of the word *flat* vs. *apartment*. Both of these words essentially mean the same thing – something like 'a self-contained housing unit that occupies part of a building'. However, imagine that you have, anecdotally, heard younger family members and friends using the term *apartment* more often than your older family members/friends. This leads you to suspect that the use of this feature might be related to age. To test this hypothesis, we could go out, record some older and younger people speaking in casual conversation. For the sake of this example, let's say we recorded exactly the same number of tokens and speakers and we can easily separate them into the two age-groups (younger – 18–30 vs. older – 50–70). Once we had finished our recordings, we would go back to the lab and calculate the number of times the speakers said *flat* and *apartment*. We would then see if the use of *flat* or *apartment* correlates with a particular age group. Imagine you find that younger speakers use the word *flat* 30 times and the word *apartment* 70 times, whereas older people used the word *flat* 90 times and *apartment* 10 times. Here, we have identified a basic correlation between a lexical feature and a social group: Younger speakers use the word *apartment* more frequently than older speakers. This correlation would allow us to conclude that the choice of the lexical variant (i.e., *flat* vs. *apartment*) is influenced by the speakers' age.

What I have been describing so far is a common approach to analysing language and identity in a branch of sociolinguistics that has become known as 'first-wave variationist sociolinguistics'. In this work, the goal has often been to identify significant correlations between linguistic features and social groups. This approach suggests that an individual's identity is determined by their membership of a social group. Identity is therefore considered to be an almost static property of the individual: It is something that they have – 'they are female', 'they are working class', 'they are younger' – and this identity determines their linguistic practice – 'they use *apartment* more often than *flat* because they are younger/working-class/female'. The argument is that people speak or communicate the way they do because of the prevailing linguistic norms of the social groups that they belong to. We acquire these norms and go through life producing the norms of our community.

More contemporary research, however, has explored how people use language to *construct* and *perform* their identities, rather than simply deterministically producing the patterns of the social groups they belong to. From this perspective, identity is not a fixed or pre-given state. Rather, identities are constructed in and through language and interaction. In this way, we do not have one single identity that is fixed from childhood. Rather each of us can be seen to perform a repertoire of identities dependent on the context and type of interaction and the social goals of that conversation.

For instance, on paper, I am a queer male academic. This identity, however, is not a given. Rather, over the course of interaction, I may use language to either highlight or subvert this identity. And across different contexts – like home and work – I perform different identities. I am one type of person at work – a lecturer, a colleague, a mentor – and I am a different type of person outside of work – a friend, a family member, a stranger. In these contexts, I might perform different 'versions' of myself. I use language to construct my identity as a lecturer or as a friend. The versions of myself that I present will depend on who I am speaking to, the context in which I find myself in, and the kind of identity I wish to claim for myself. In some contexts, I will reveal or perform more of my queer identity, whereas in others I may construct a more reserved persona. Crucially, there is nothing inauthentic or unusual about this. We do this type of shifting all the time.

The shift towards more performative understandings of language and identity suggests that people have more control or **agency** in how they communicate. We make linguistic choices – whether they be conscious choices or otherwise – to signal what type of person we want to be perceived as. To take a very current example, concluding that a film was the 'ultimate slay' has different connotations to evaluating it as 'very good!'. The former is an evaluative phrase often associated with Gen Z (and the queer community) and so may tell us that the speaker is signalling their 'young person' (or queer) identity. Whereas if we were to evaluate the film as 'an artistic masterpiece' we may be trying to signal a more 'formal' or 'adult' identity.

In Section 3.3.1 we defined this type of variation as **style** or **intraspeaker variation.** In that section, we suggested that people change their ways of speaking and interacting depending on various factors, such as the formality of the context and who we are interacting with. In contemporary sociolinguistic research, style is considered central to language and identity. The idea is that we stylistically use linguistic features to construct our identities as we interact.

However, language is just one part of our identity. We will very likely use linguistic styles in combination with other resources and choices – things like clothing, hairstyles, and personalities – to communicate to others the type of person we want to be perceived as. We can think of this as a type of **bricolage** where people combine different resources to perform a recognisable type of identity. For instance, if I wanted to be a hippie (a countercultural movement that originated in the US in the 1960s and 1970s), I might start to adopt the fashions (e.g., grown my hair, wear tie-dye), beliefs (e.g., emphasise love and peace, adopt a liberal attitude towards drugs), and language (e.g., phrases like 'far out', 'out of sight', and the evaluation 'groovy') associated with the hippie movement. By combining different stylistic resources – fashion, beliefs, and language – I articulate to the world my identity as a hippie.

4.3 Online Identity

Our above discussion is relevant to digital communication because people will often spend great amounts of time and effort cultivating an online persona or digital identity. It is therefore perhaps unsurprising that, like in sociolinguistics, online identity has long been a topic of interest in media studies and digital sociology. As technologies and digital practices have changed, however, so too have theories and approaches to digital identity.

In the earliest work on internet practices, researchers tended to make a distinction between users' identities in digital and non-digital contexts. In this work, the 'offline' and the 'online' were viewed as separate 'worlds' or realities. Online spaces were defined as those services and platforms which were connected to the internet (e.g., instant messaging, social media) while the offline was defined as those spaces which were disconnected from the internet (e.g., the supermarket, the park). At this point, given that access to the internet was confined to the desktop computer, it was relatively straightforward to distinguish between the online and offline dimensions of social life. To get online, the user would simply log on to the internet. When they were finished, they would log off and so would be completely disconnected from the network. What they did online was very much separate from what they did offline.

Observing these practices, many researchers viewed the online as a distinct world – a 'cyberspace' – that was conceptually separate from the offline or 'reality'. In this space, users were seen to participate in various types of CMC. Researchers suggested that users created new identities and built relationships with others who were not part of their offline social networks. This led some scholars to argue that there was a theoretical binary between first (physical world) and second (digital or virtual) selves. Users' online identities were often considered to be more contrived, constructed, or performed whilst users' offline identities were thought to be more authentic and permanent.

The perspective towards online identity in earlier research was largely influenced by the observation that the internet appeared to expand the range of anonymous styles of self-presentation and communication. In digital communication, messages could be sent and received by individuals without either party revealing their 'true' identity. They could, it was argued, be whoever they wanted to be. Research on early internet adopters, for instance, found that users often experimented with new and unpredictable identities that were not necessarily related to their offline selves. In her book on digital identity and *'Life on the Screen'*, psychologist and digital scholar Sherry Turkle studied the practices of young people engaged in the computer cultures of MUDs (Multi-User Domains) or multiple-player virtual game worlds. She argued that "MUDs provide worlds for anonymous social interactions in which one can play a role as close to or as far away from one's 'real self' as one chooses" (1995: 12). Internet technologies, Turkle argued, led to a new sense of identity – one which was decentred and multiple where "you are who you pretend to be" (1995: 26). The widespread belief that the internet offered new anonymous and alternative styles of identity was famously depicted in a cartoon and internet meme, 'on the Internet, nobody knows you're a dog', published in the New Yorker in 1993.

At the time, the potential for the internet to offer new forms of anonymous interaction was hailed as transformational. Some researchers predicted that the internet would become a utopian space where people were liberated from prejudices experienced in the 'real world' (e.g., sexism, racism, homophobia, and so on). The internet was claimed to have initiated a new era of social interaction which was more democratic, equal, and decentralised.

In sociolinguistics, this perspective was adopted in work on identity and CMC. For instance, in her research on gender and language online, Danet (1998) argued that, in the emancipatory and anonymous spaces of the internet, users adopted textual resources that contradicted or obscured their offline identities – what she describes as 'text as mask'. Danet argued that users employed textual resources to subvert their expected offline gender identities. She observed that "[m]ales [were] masquerading as females, and females [were] masquerading as males" (1998: 129). Thus, users were seen to textually appropriate gender identities that had "no necessary physical reality behind them" (1998: 130).

Points for reflection

- Thinking about your own digital identity, do you think it is still accurate to claim that users appropriate online identities that are different from their offline selves?
- What consequences (if any) do you think the introduction of multimodal and 'image-first' apps like TikTok/Douyin and Instagram have had on digital identities?

The perspective that the offline-online are discrete spheres of interaction has since been heavily critiqued and has been viewed as a type of **digital dualism** (Jurgenson, 2012). For many readers of this book, this perspective may seem outdated when we think about how we now use social and digital media. A cursory glance at more recent research shows that even terms like 'cyberspace' and 'cyborgs' common in earlier internet research have fallen out of use. Today, it is far more common to see researchers talk about how users move *between* different offline-online environments, rather than attempt to separate what users do online and what they do offline.

However, it is important to recognise that the types of digital communication technologies that we are discussing now are quite different to those when Turkle, Danet, and their contemporaries were writing. In earlier digital research, the internet was still a relatively novel technology. The aim, as in earlier types of CMC research, was to understand how new technologies were being integrated into society and whether they were changing our relationships with each other and the social world. It is therefore perhaps unsurprising that people initially hailed the internet as transformational. Now, some years on and with digital technologies now deeply embedded in society, we can appreciate just how different the world is today.

Nevertheless, earlier research on digital identities still had its limitations. Notably because the earliest research predated the widespread use of the internet, researchers would often focus on the practices of early adopters. Unsurprisingly, many of these people were part of specialist communities or niche internet cultures. For instance, in the 1990s, much of the research on digital identities was based on the practices of people who engaged in role-playing or MUD games. In these games, users enter virtual worlds where they are encouraged to create avatars and alternate forms of self-presentation. These online identities were interpreted by some to be representative of different personalities of the user. For example, in Turkle's (1995) work on the use of MUDs by college students in the US, she argued that these different forms of presentation are experienced as different lives. According to Turkle, for these students MUDs allowed them to escape the real world and become part of another reality that was detached from everyday life.

However, the extent to which these practices could be generalised to those of society at large was unclear. Critics argued that the focus on MUDs and other role-playing games was problematic for several reasons. Notably, as virtual worlds, these types of platforms *encourage* users to adopt alternate identities that are distinct and completely separate to who they are offline. And although lots of research focussed on these contexts, these forms of online interaction comprised only a small proportion of internet based digital communication. In fact, many of these practices appeared to be typical of only a limited group of internet users: Teenagers. As Castells (2002: 118) acknowledges, this life stage often involves a great deal of self-discovery and experimentation with different forms of self-presentation. That we see teenagers adopting alternate identities in MUDs and other role-playing games is, perhaps, unsurprising given that we see similar practices elsewhere (e.g., at school).

4.3.1 Digital Identity and Social Networking Sites

One of the most important developments in developing a digital identity was the emergence of 'Social Networking Sites' (SNS). Early forms of social interaction on the internet were mainly facilitated through chat rooms and other types of instant messaging platforms. Some of these platforms enabled users to create webpages where they could share personal information and ideas. In the late 1990s, user profiles became a central feature of a group of new platforms which have been called 'Social Networking Sites' (SNS). The primary purpose of SNS were to facilitate the creation of social networks and relationships between users. Platforms like Six Degrees, Friendster, and Myspace were organised around profile pages which contained information about the user, such as their name, their location, and personal photographs. Users could make connections with others by compiling a friends list and searching for others with similar interests. In their overview of these platforms, boyd and Ellison (2007: 211) characterise SNS as internet-based services which permit users to '(1) construct a public or semi-public profile within a bounded system, (2) articulate a list of other users with whom they share a connection, and (3) view and traverse their list of connections and those made by others within the system'.

Key Term: Social Networking Sites (SNS)

An online social media platform which is organised around a profile page. SNS allow users to connect and communicate with others who share similar interests.

Importantly, given the central role of social networking, user profiles were (and continue to be!) designed to be maximally intelligible to an imagined audience. The information that users upload to their profiles tends to reference things about who they are in the offline, such as their current location, their profession, and their full name. Generally, individuals use these sites to connect with people they already know from 'offline' contexts like school or work (e.g., Ellison, Steinfield, and Lampe, 2007). In this way, most people do not create radically different identities to those they have offline. Rather, they use these platforms as an extension of their everyday or offline identities and networks.

Of course, whilst it is true that people use a variety of platforms to create different versions of themselves, it is important to recognise that these are not distinct identities. Rather, research has argued that users design their profiles according to the norms, expectations, and affordances of the platform. For instance, in her ethnographic work on US teens digital practices, boyd argues that:

> when a teen chooses to identify as "Jessica Smith" on Facebook and "littlemonster" on Twitter, she's not creating multiple identities in the psychological sense. She's choosing to represent herself in different ways on different sites with the expectation of different audiences and different norms.
>
> (boyd 2014: 38)

Because we present ourselves in different ways on different platforms, we often see that there are differences in how someone presents from one platform to the next. Consider, for instance, the differences between Instagram and LinkedIn. LinkedIn is a social media platform that is designed for business and employment purposes. The platform enables users to upload CVs, apply for advertised jobs, and network with recruiters and businesses. Instagram, on the other hand, is used mainly by people as a photo and video sharing app. If we compare the same user's LinkedIn and Instagram profiles, it is very likely that these will use different styles of self-presentation. All of these choices are linked to the expectation of the imagined audience as well as the norms and conventions of the platforms, in this case LinkedIn and Instagram.

This type of identity construction has been humorously depicted in a viral internet meme by the country music icon, Dolly Parton. The meme is a comical take on the various functions of four platforms and the different styles of self-presentation we engage in on four different platforms: LinkedIn, Facebook, Instagram, and Tinder. The LinkedIn image depicts Dolly dressed in formal attire in front of a chalkboard; the Facebook photo references the festive period with Dolly dressed in a 'Holly Dolly Christmas' sweater; the Instagram snap is a black and white vintage shot of Dolly leaning against a doorframe with a guitar, and the Tinder image is Dolly dressed in a bunny costume that references the men's lifestyle and entertainment magazine, Playboy (see Figure 4.2).

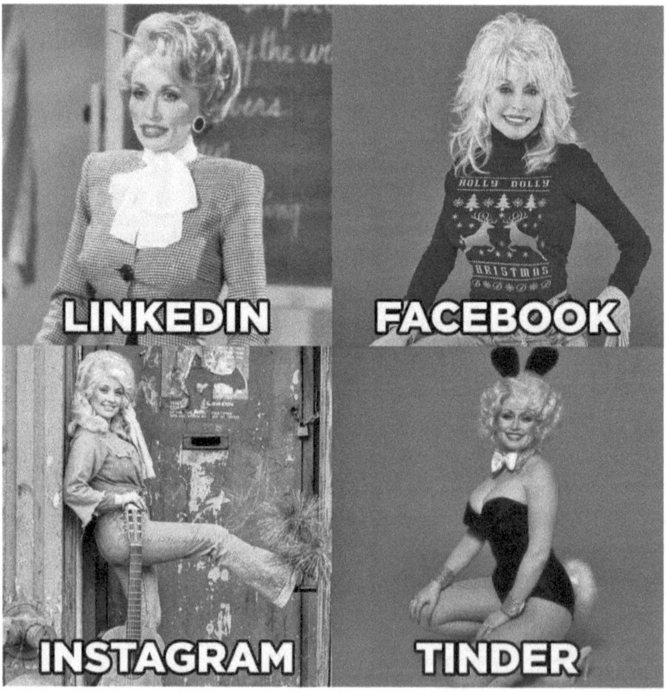

Figure 4.2 Dolly Parton and the 'LinkedIn, Facebook, Instagram, Tinder' meme

Acknowledging that platforms extend the possibilities for 'offline' identities and social networks, means we need to consider how these dynamics inform and constrain digital communication. Contemporary research has responded to this shift in perspective by analysing digital cultures and communities based on 'offline' social dynamics and identities like race, social-class, and nationality. This includes work on 'Black Twitter' – an internet community that mainly comprises members of the Black diaspora on Twitter. The fact that DMC operates across geographical borders means that users from different places can form online communities based on a common identity. In his seminal work on '*Distributed Blackness'*, Brock (2020) argues that digital media have enabled an aggregation of Black users from across the globe, leading to new forms and expressions of Black identity. A similar argument is made by Sobande (2020: 102) in her work on the '*Digital Lives of Black Women in Britain*', where she argues that, amongst other things, Black users across the globe employ digital technologies to connect with other members of the Black diaspora to share 'cues, references, and in-jokes that relate to the intricacies of their racial, ethnic, and cultural identities'. Evidently then, digital identities are not only shaped by social dynamics typically thought as 'offline' (e.g., race, sexuality), but they also shape those dynamics too. In later sections, we will see how users' social identities influence the content and style of their digital interactions.

Points for reflection

- Think about the social media platform you use most. Is your self-presentation (i.e., identity) on that app/platform similar to or different from your 'offline' self?
- Think about who you interact with on social media. Are these people you know from offline contexts (e.g., school, university, work)? Or are they people you met online?
- Is your online identity (e.g., user profile) consistent across the different platforms you use? If there are differences, why?

4.3.2 Anonymity and Identity

Although most users will maintain online profiles that are consistent with how they present offline, there are some situations where users will instead adopt deceptive or anonymous digital identities. Some of these motivations are positive. For instance, for minoritised and at-risk communities, the anonymity afforded by digital communication is potentially transformational. In countries where being LGBTQ+ is illegal or socially taboo, anonymity can afford users a way of engaging with other members of the community without the risk of being 'outed'

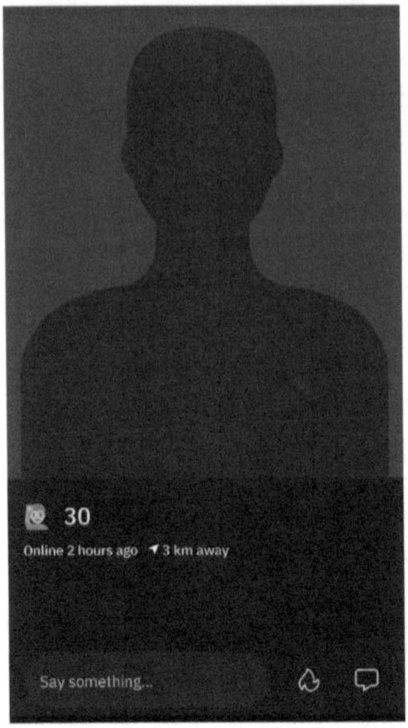

Figure 4.3 An example of an anonymous Grindr profile

or prosecuted. Users may adopt anonymous styles of presentation to obscure or hide their name, profession, or location (Triggs et al., 2020). This is a very common practice on the gay dating app, Grindr. In countries where being open about your sexuality is socially taboo or illegal, Grindr is either outright banned (e.g., United Arab Emirates) or is accessible, but users will often take steps to obscure their true identities (e.g., Morocco). Even in countries which are more LGBTQ+ friendly, individuals may use anonymous identities if they are not out. Figure 4.3 is an example of an anonymous profile on Grindr from the UK. The only indication of the person's identity is their age (which may or may not be accurate) and the emoji, which is presumably linked to the individual in some way. There is no personal bio nor any photos. The profile can in no way be linked to the individual's offline identity (unless, of course, we speak to that person and get that information directly and even then, we'd need to verify its accuracy).

Although the above examples discuss some benevolent potentials of anonymity, evidently these are not the only reasons why people use anonymous profiles. In recent years, research has focussed on the adoption of anonymous or bogus digital identities for deviant or malicious purposes. This includes **flaming** and **internet trolling**. These terms refer to the now (unfortunately) common social media trend for users to deliberately make aggressive, degrading, and/or derogatory comments in an attempt to cause offense. In some instances, these types of comments may constitute libel and trolls have been prosecuted for sending racist, homophobic, and other distressing messages. Given the potential repercussions for sending these types of messages (e.g., some people have lost their jobs), people will often use anonymous accounts in an attempt to hide their real name or profession.

Key Term: Trolling

The use of social and digital media for deviant and malicious purposes. Trolls often use anonymous accounts to send discriminatory and/or hurtful messages intended to cause offense and upset.

It should be noted, however, that although the internet has facilitated new types of anonymity and deception, this is not something new nor is it specific to digital communication. Authors have long concealed their identities to express unpopular opinions or dissent. This includes 'confession' sections in newspapers and articles penned by anonymous authors. Nevertheless, trolling is arguably more prevalent in social media because people can easily and directly send messages to individual(s) they would otherwise not have access to.

4.4 Online Communities

As discussed briefly above in relation to 'Black Twitter', one of the most important and transformative features of digital and social media is that it enables users to connect with others from across the globe. Users do not have to be in the same geographical location – they can send and receive messages with others who share similar interests, purposes, or identities. When multiple users come together around some shared goal or activity, **online communities** emerge.

Key Term: Online Communities

Groups of people who use digital technologies to connect with others who share similar interests and goals. Often, online communities will develop their own in-group norms and conventions. This includes things like: language, memes, and post topics.

In earlier work, online communities were considered types of 'virtual communities'. Rheingold (1993: xx) suggested that "virtual communities are social aggregations that emerge from the Net when enough people carry on those public discussions long enough, with sufficient human feeling, to form webs of personal relationships in cyberspace". However, as this definition suggests, much of the work on virtual communities has framed these aggregations of people and identities as some way specific to online sites and platforms.

More recent work, however, has emphasised the interaction between different contexts of use, concentrating on how social and digital media might extend the possibilities for mutual engagement and community formation. In her overview of this term, Herring (2004: 355) defines six main criteria for defining the online community:

1. Active, self-sustained participation; a core of regular participants
2. Shared history, purpose, culture, norms, and values
3. Solidarity, support, reciprocity
4. Criticism, conflict, means of conflict resolution
5. Self-awareness of group as an entity distinct from other groups
6. Emergence of roles, hierarchy, governance, rituals.

A good example of this criteria in action is the platform Twitch: A video-based live streaming service that is best known for its video game streaming services and esports competitions. Through the affordances of live content and group chat, the platform facilitates the creation and building of communities organised around titles of games or streams. Communities are created as users engage with one another. Twitch allows users to participate in streams that take place simultaneously across multiple locations. In a way comparable to watching television shows with friends, users of Twitch come together to watch their favourite streamer play video games, play music, cook, or other activities that they find interesting. In essence, the digital platform Twitch becomes a social forum in which users can 'hang out' and engage with others from various different locations who share similar interests (see Figure 4.4).

Figure 4.4 An example of a Twitch stream (from https://help.twitch.tv/s/article/stream-display-ads?language=en_US)

4.4.1 Communities of Practice

As social and digital media enable users from across the world to connect with others who share similar interests, when these users come together, they will often form a community of people who develop a shared in-group identity. This group will often create a set of norms and practices which become markers of the in-group identity. This includes language. Certain words, for instance, might become associated with particular types of internet communities, such as 'gamers' or 'streamers'. This has been discussed in the context of Twitch (see Figure 4.4).

In many ways, the communities and subcultures that emerge in digital contexts and platforms are similar to those elsewhere. To be a part of an internet community, we need to acquire and effectively use the in-group norms and conventions. This is similar to what people do when they participate in subcultures that we typically associate with 'offline' contexts, such as certain musical and political groups. If you wanted to be a 'hippie', 'punk', 'goth', 'skinhead', 'jock', or 'gopnik', for instance, you'd need to acquire the style and the norms of that culture. This would likely include mastering the language, the clothing, and the social practices associated with the in-group.

In sociolinguistics, collective groups of people who develop in-group norms have been called **Communities of Practice** (CoP). Initially developed by Lave and Wenger (1991), a CoP refers to a group of people who regularly come together and participate in a shared activity. This includes groups of people who are part of a football team, those who play an instrument as part of a band, people who participate in a musical subculture such as goths, or those who attend after school clubs (i.e., 'youth groups'). The idea that is within these CoP's, members develop a set of shared in-group practices such as distinctive ways of talking, beliefs, and social values.

There is now a lot of sociolinguistic research which has analysed how language is used within different CoPs. One particularly productive area of research has been to study the formation of CoPs in schools. This is because schools are often very rich sites where people organise themselves into different groups, each with their own distinctive identity. When I was at school, it was common for people to distinguish between CoPs like the 'geeks' who were considered studious and conscientious and the 'popular kids' who were fashionable and anti-establishment. Each of these CoPs had certain beliefs, values, and ways of speaking that were considered characteristic of the broader in-group identity that just about everyone in the school knew and recognised. Someone could signal their alignment with the 'popular kids' by dressing in the right way or using the language of the in-group.

Points for reflection

- Are you part of any CoPs? If so, what norms, values, beliefs, or language styles are associated with this CoP?
- Does this CoP have an online presence? If so, is it similar to or different from how those people interact or present in an offline setting?

We can see similar types of CoPs emerge in digital settings. Sometimes, offline CoPs like a football team will have an online presence too. It is common, for instance, for football teams to maintain an Instagram account where they upload photos of their latest fixtures and update fans with important announcements. Although some digital CoPs might not be directly related to any offline social network or group. When a CoP exists only in a digital environment it can be described as a '**Virtual Community of Practice**' (VCoP) (Dubé, Bourhis & Jacob 2005). These types of CoPs are found in digital forums like Reddit, Tumblr, and Mumsnet. Often users who participate in these forums probably do not know each other outside of this context. Nevertheless, they can be considered a CoP insofar that they establish community norms, values and practices that become symbolic of the in-group. The only difference is that these are maintained exclusively in and through digital communication technologies.

One of the key requirements of CoP membership is that the individual must align with the in-group values and identity. On the internet forum, Mumsnet, for instance, it is reasonable to assume that the majority of users are parents of children and teenagers (most often mums), given that this forum is intended to be a space where users can share tips and discuss issues around parenting and raising children. 'Having children' and 'being a parent' are therefore likely requirements of becoming a member of a CoP on Mumsnet.

In virtual CoPs, it is common for users to explicitly authenticate their membership of the CoP by introducing or affirming their identity. For instance, on Mumsnet, users will often introduce themselves as a parent before offering their own perspective. By referencing their own experiences of being a parent and raising children, they authenticate themselves as a member of the group. An example of this type of authentication is found in Extract (1) below. The message is in response to a post which asked, 'what buggy would you get in my shoes?!'. In the extract, we see that those who respond to the post draw on their own personal experience of being a parent when offering advice. Notice that Poster 2 uses the personal pronouns 'we' and 'our', which presumably refers to themselves and their partner, to introduce their comment. This allows users to authenticate themselves as a parent who has similar experiences of raising children. In this instance, someone who has experience of using a particular brand of buggy/pushchair.

(1) Poster 1: We had a baby jogger city mini double from birth with our twins as could swap in our 2 year old when needed, or use sling (back carry for 2 year old) or front for baby twin. Never needed bassinet as it lies flat so seats can be used from birth.

Poster 2: I second the double OutNAbout, we don't use ours at the moment, but when we do DC love it.

4.4.2 Language in Online Communities

As noted above, members will often develop norms and values (e.g., language, practices, clothing styles) which become associated with a particular CoP. In digital settings, users might start to use distinctive words, spellings, or phrases to signal their in-group identity. If you are not part of this community, it might be hard to know what people mean or are talking about. For instance, in the above example taken from Mumsnet (Extract (1)), we see the use of the term <DC>. Readers who have not been on Mumsnet before are unlikely to know what this acronym means. However, community members are likely familiar with this acronym and its specific reference ('darling child'). Other platforms and communities develop other styles of interaction. This includes Twitch where the following terminology and phrases are common:

- **<F>**: A way of a user paying their respects or offering condolences following some announcement or news.
- **'Jebaited'**: A Twitch emoticon featuring Alex Jebailey, the owner of CEO Gaming, which refers to the act of baiting (i.e., to manipulate or trick) an opponent in a video game (see Figure 4.5).

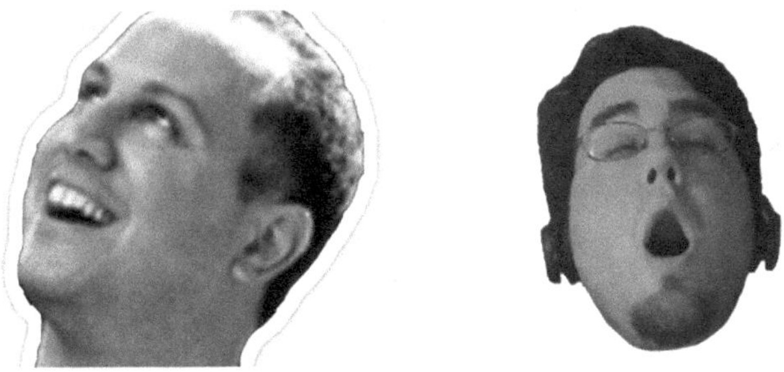

Figure 4.5 Two examples of popular Twitch emotes: 'jebaited' (left) and 'kreygasm' (right)

- **<KEKW>**: An emote for a Twitch extension called FrankerFaceZ. Originally from a video of the Spanish comedian and actor, Juan Joya Borja, this is now used as a way for the user to show they're laughing in the chat.
- **'VODs'**: Referring to 'Video on Demand' – an archive of content previously streamed live on Twitch.
- **'Kreygasm'**: A Twitch emote used to show a sign of happiness, pleasure, and satisfaction. The emote is an image of the streamer, KreyG, with a satisfied facial expression (see Figure 4.6).

Many of these examples are specific to the platform, Twitch. For instance, the term 'jebaited' is a Twitch emoticon which features the founder of CEO gaming, Alex Jebailey. This is unlikely to make much sense on other platforms or to users outside of this community. This means that, potentially, on different platforms, users will develop other language styles, words, and spellings which become typical of that context. As sociolinguists, we might want to study the various linguistic conventions and styles that are used on those sites and what their functions are. Returning to the example of Mumsnet, Mackenzie's (2019: 24–25) work has identified a number of interesting typographical forms and creative spellings which are commonly used on the platform. Many of these are used to achieve particular stylistic or rhetorical effects. This includes:

- **Strikethrough text**, e.g., 'little ~~cow~~ darling'; 'don't fight it ~~or are you shallow~~': Text which is potentially offensive or taboo is struck out
- **Asterisks**, e.g., *voice; explana*tory*: Asterisks are used for a variety of reasons including emphasis and corrections
- **Non-standard punctuation and spelling**, e.g., 'these threads are.... .... boooooooooooring'; 'you clean your loo brush in the dishwasher?!?!?!?!?!': Used to indicate a range of meanings such as timing, emphasis, or surprise
- **Acronyms**, e.g., 'PITA' (Pain In The Arse), 'DC' (Darling Child), 'PFB' (Precious First Born', and 'AIBU' (Am I Being Unreasonable?).

Readers will likely recognise some of these features whilst others may be more obscure. This is because some of these conventions and spellings are used across other platforms (e.g., asterisks for emphasis and corrections). However, the meaning of others might not be as transparent, unless, of course, you are familiar with Mumsnet. For instance, the use of acronyms like PITA and DC are not used widely outside of Mumsnet or the 'mommyblogging' community more generally. An example of these conventions in use is found in Extract (2).

This extract is from a discussion of 'how to balance being firm vs. enjoying your kids. The acronym <DS> 'darling son' is used twice:

(2) Poster 1: Pick your battles so is what he is doing an annoyance if so distract so he doesn't see it as a punishment or a way to push your buttons. Is it dangerous if so be firm but along the lines of **DS** don't do that's we don't want you getting hurt or X breaking.
DS is nearly 10 and other than a bit of attitude that gets the luck he's no bother. I can't remote the last time I actually told him off so it does get better.

What we have seen here is that, quite often, different CoPs will use different styles of digital communication. By using features of the in-group language, individual users can align or index their participation in this community. For instance, if I use <DS> and <PITA> in my messages, I might be signalling my alignment with a particular community of users, such as those who use Mumsnet. Whereas if I use 'jebaited' and <F>, you might conclude that I want to align with the community of users on Twitch.

Points for reflection

- Are you part of any online communities that use distinctive language styles?
- If so, are there any words or phrases that you know or use that you think would be difficult for people outside of those communities to understand?

As discussed above, users will collectively negotiate which linguistic features become adopted by the community. This process is on-going. Those who participate in the community will develop new conventions which have the potential to become adopted by others. Sometimes these conventions will become recognised by other people as markers of that group identity. This is what sociolinguists call **enregisterment** – that is, the process through which language *comes to be* associated with particular identities and social groups (Agha, 2005).

Key Term: Enregisterment

The process by which language varieties, styles, and features become associated with social practices, persons, and communities.

4.5 Participatory Culture

As we have seen in the previous examples, a community is formed through user engagements. As users upload content, interact with one another, and establish in-group norms and activities, they develop and maintain online communities. These types of engagements are facilitated by the affordances of social media which encourage people to create and circulate user-generated content. This is because social media relies on a **participatory culture** where users do not just consume content but they actively produce it too.

Social and digital media encourage a participatory culture through the promotion and circulation of user-generated content such as family photos, personal messages, and streams of gaming sessions. This type of content is not very often professionally produced. Rather, it is often created and distributed by everyday people like me and you (see Figure 4.6).

Key Term: Participatory Culture

A culture in which everyday people (i.e., the public) do not just act as consumers but also participate actively as producers. Social media, which relies on user-generated content such as personal messages, live streaming, and direct messages, are a type of participatory culture.

According to Jenkins and colleagues (2009: xi), a participatory culture refers to "a culture with relatively low barriers to artistic expression and civic engagement, strong support for creating and sharing creations, and some type of informal mentorship whereby experienced

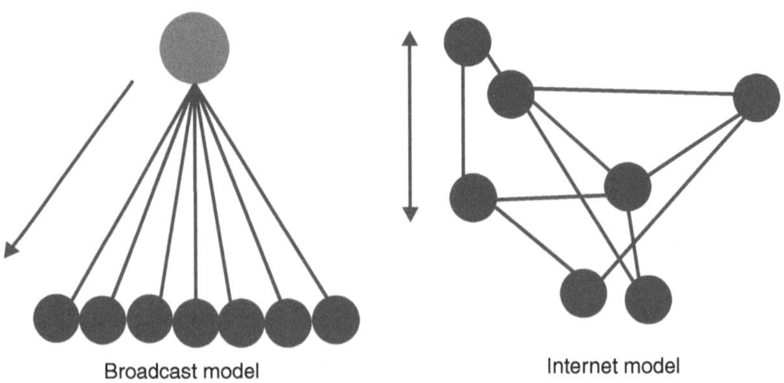

Figure 4.6 Models of producer-consumer relationships in broadcast and digital media

participants pass along knowledge to novices". This type of culture is found on the internet in four main ways:

- **Affiliations:** Digital technologies permit us to forge connections with other members and build online communities. Examples include Facebook groups, entertainment channels on Instagram, and Tumblr communities.
- **Expressions:** Users will engage in new creative practices. This includes digital sampling, video making, fan fiction, and internet memes.
- **Collaborative problem-solving:** People use social and digital media platforms to work as a team to complete certain tasks and activities. For instance, users write and edit articles on Wikipedia – the online encyclopaedia.
- **Circulation:** Users shape the flow and style of information. This includes user generated podcasts and weblogs.

All of these possibilities are enabled by the affordances of the internet and social/digital media where user-generated content is often central to social engagement and interaction. Two obvious examples are the video-sharing platforms YouTube and TikTok. These platforms encourage participation in three main ways: (i) through the creation of content uploaded to the platform, (ii) through the videos that users decide to watch and engage with, and (iii) through the distribution of videos and other content.

This type of consumption is quite different to how we consume traditional forms of media, like television and film. In 'broadcast' media, there is an established hierarchy of producer and consumer. Media is produced by a team of professionals and consumed by the public. Take, for instance, a television programme. Professionals such as script-writers, actors, and videographers produce the programme. It is then distributed via television networks and consumed by an audience, i.e., members of the public who watch it. In this way, the creation and distribution of information is highly controlled – access to broadcast media is restricted to a few select individuals (i.e., professionals). However, in digital and social media, this hierarchy is flipped. Many people who create and share online content are members of the public with no professional training. This, arguably, leads to a more democratic form of information sharing. Bruns (2008) has labelled this type of sharing **produsage** referring to the fact that content can be created and consumed by the same people – the producers are the consumers and vice versa (see Figure 4.6).

Today, the accessibility of camera-enabled smartphones, mobile internet, and other digital devices means that very many people can create and distribute content in ways unlike before. On TikTok, for instance, whilst some videos are professionally produced (e.g., remediated clips of television shows, professional interviews) the vast majority of videos uploaded to the platform are created by those with little to no professional training. Very often platforms which centre on user-generated content will include video editing tools and other affordances which encourage users to create and distribute user-generated content.

One type of information which has been dramatically altered by digital technologies is the news. As noted briefly above, news about current events has traditionally been disseminated through broadcast media such as newspapers, television, and radio. This type of media is often influenced or run by the state. It therefore operates as a constrained source of information: It is distributed by individuals who have a professional responsibility to report the news. A restricted number of individuals, typically newsreaders and/or celebrities, are elevated to these positions. In this model, the news is created and disseminated by a single authority (e.g., a newspaper) and it is consumed by an audience: The general public. The internet has revolutionised how we consume and engage with the news. Services like weblogs and Twitter have given rise to so-called 'citizen journalism' – a type of journalism where non-professionals actively participate in the reporting, 'analysis', and circulation of news and information. Many users who participate in citizen journalism have utilised the affordances of digital technologies to capture videos and images of newsworthy events, circulate stories to large audiences, and analyse unfolding events. Journalism has been dramatically altered by the proliferation of user-generated content and rise of citizen journalism in recent decades. It is now common for broadcast news to integrate user-generated content and information in their own reports. For instance, the BBC will often include amateur videos and photos (typically taken from Twitter) when reporting on a news event. Sometimes, these forms of journalism report events before broadcast media. The death of American singer and actress, Whitney Houston, for example, was reported on Twitter roughly 45 minutes before it was announced in mainstream media.

The participatory affordances of social and digital media and the rise of citizen journalism have played an important role in reporting breaking news events in recent years. This includes coverage of the COVID-19 pandemic, natural disasters such as the Türkiye-Syria earthquakes in 2023, and international political uprisings such as the Arab Spring in 2011. However, sometimes the role of social media has been overstated. In the context of the Arab Spring, for instance, social media was often credited as the *cause* of the uprisings to the extent that they were often dubbed the 'Facebook revolutions' or 'Twitter revolutions'. The 2011 uprisings followed protests in Tunisia in response to government corruption and economic stagnation.

Various anti-government and pro-democracy protests erupted across the Middle East and North Africa, leading to the eventual removal of several leaders, including Muammar Gaddafi of Libya and Hosni Mubarak of Egypt. In the wake of the protests, many social commentators focussed on the role of social media in the uprisings. It was argued that social media and digital technologies allowed users to not only share information and participate in activism, but also to circumvent state-run broadcast media channels. This led some to claim that social media was a causal mechanism in the uprisings. Academic research on the Arab Spring, however, argues that social media played a more indirect role in the protests. Rather than being a *cause* of the protests, social media was used to mobilise people, circulate information about the cause, and raise awareness about the protests, both locally and globally. It is precisely because of the participatory nature of social media that users could organise themselves in this way.

4.6 Memes

A prime example of the types of participatory culture that social and digital media facilitate is the creation, remixing, and circulation of internet memes. Originally coined by the evolutionary biologist, Richard Dawkins, the term meme was used to refer to "a unit of cultural transmission, or a unit of imitation" (1976: 207). Dawkins developed this label to refer to cultural phenomena such as songs, catchphrases, idioms, and other ideas that are passed from one individual to another through imitation and other non-genetic means. Most readers, however, will be more familiar with the modern day use of this term to refer to *internet* memes. These are digital images, GIFs, videos, or textual artefacts that are (intended to be) humorous and which are often adapted, remixed, and edited by others as they are shared from one individual to the next. This includes viral memes such as 'the Harlem Shake' – a video-based meme which saw people dancing to the opening of the song of the same name. At the height of its popularity in 2013, thousands of 'Harlem Shake' YouTube videos were uploaded daily. Figure 4.7 depicts one example.

As users are involved in their creation, remixing, and distribution, internet memes are now a classic example of the participatory nature of social and digital media. When users edit memes and contribute to their circulation, they expand the use and meaning of that meme. What emerges as one meme in one context may take on very different meanings as it is circulated and remixed by different users. A quite dramatic example of this is the Pepe the Frog meme (or 'sad frog meme') which depicts a humanoid cartoon frog (see Figure 4.8). As an internet

Figure 4.7 An example of the Harlem Shake meme - 'Harlem Shake (on a Plane)': www.youtube.com/watch?v=vRuHRsoAOZc

Figure 4.8 Pepe the Frog meme

meme, it gained popularity on Myspace, Gaia Online, and 4chan from around 2008. By 2015, it was one of the most popular memes on Tumblr. Versions of this meme were also popular on Chinese social media, such as Baidu Tieba, where it is known more commonly as 'shangxin qingwa' (傷心青蛙). Although this meme was originally used as a humorous reaction or to convey how the author felt about something, Pepe the Frog became appropriated by white supremacists, especially during the 2016 US presidential election. Following this, and in Autumn 2016, the original creator of the character, Matt Furie, teamed up with the Anti-Defamation League to start a #SavePepe campaign to reclaim the meme.

As in the case of Pepe, an internet meme is only successful if people can recognise the cultural references of the meme and its social meanings (Sobande, 2019; Shifman, 2014; Wiggins, 2019). Often, internet memes reference culturally niche events, jokes, or topics that are familiar only to a subset of users. You may not understand or 'get' the reference if you are not part of the target community. For instance, the image in Figure 4.9 is a popular internet meme in China. The image includes the catchphrase '芭比Q了' (bā bǐ Q le) which when pronounced sounds like the English word, 'barbeque'. The catchphrase appears to have emerged from a video game blogger on the Chinese social media platform, Douyin, but has become used more widely as an internet meme. The meaning of the phrase is something similar to 'I'm finished' and/or 'mentally and physically exhausted'. To readers outside of China, this meme alone is unlikely to make much sense. But at least to the Chinese students in my class, this is a very well-known and popular meme.

Another example is found in Figure 4.10. This meme is only really likely to be meaningful to individuals who are familiar with the

Figure 4.9 芭比Q了 (bā bǐ Q le) – barbie Q meme

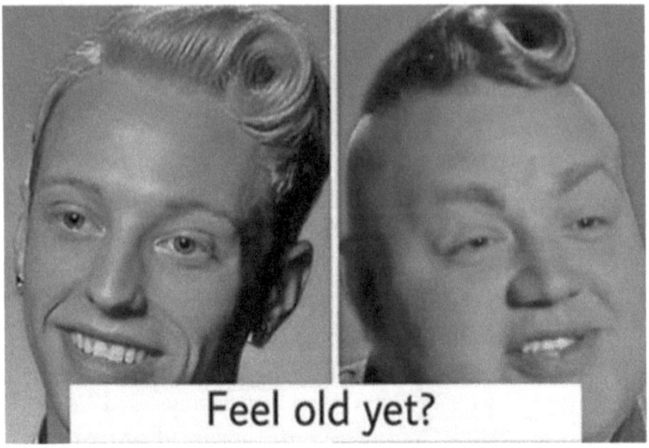

Figure 4.10 'Feel old yet?' Drag Race meme

television programme, RuPaul's Drag Race. This meme depicts two Drag Race competitors: Laganja Estranja and Eureka, side by side. The text references a broader meme genre, 'feel old yet?'. Typically, memes in this genre include a photograph of a celebrity when they are younger and in their prime, alongside a recent image of the same individual. The purpose of the 'feel old yet?' meme genre is to evoke feelings of nostalgia. The meme in Figure 4.10 is a tongue in cheek interpretation of this genre. It suggests that the two images are of the same person at two different timepoints of their life. However, anyone who is familiar with RuPaul's Drag Race will know that these photographs are of two different queens: Laganja Estranja and Eureka. Evidently, to understand that these two images are *not* the same person, and this is a humorous play on the 'feel old yet?' meme genre, we'd need to be familiar with the television series, RuPaul's Drag Race, as well as have some understanding of drag culture.

As in the example of 'feel old yet?' individual memes tend to reference some broader meme genre or subtype. Popular meme subtypes like 'dank', 'emotional damage', 'the Harlem Shake' exhibit commonalities in structure, language, and design. We recognise different Harlem Shake videos as belonging to this broader meme genre because they have very similar characteristics and follow a similar chronology, namely:

- The video starts.
- The song 'Harlem Shake' by American DJ and producer, Baauer, starts. It has a 15-second intro.
- During the intro, one person (typically masked or wearing a helmet) is filmed dancing to the song. Other individuals in the frame do not pay attention.

- After the 15-second intro, there is a bass drop. As the beat hits, all individuals in the video are then filmed dancing.

Although a variety of different users contribute to this meme genre and record the Harlem Shake in various different contexts – such as at a business meeting, on a plane (as the example above), in a lecture theatre, and so on – the basic structure of the video outlined above is consistent across videos and authors. The shared characteristics of the videos enable us to recognise different interpretations as belonging to one meme genre – in this instance, the 'Harlem Shake'.

Because memes encourage engagement and sharing, some platforms have built affordances of participatory culture into their design. For instance, on the short-video platform TikTok, imitation and replication of memes are encouraged through various platform affordances. Zulli and Zulli (2020) identify three main ways that TikTok encourages sharing and imitation:

1. **Through the user sign-up process and default page:** When users sign-up to the platform, they are asked to indicate their interests. Videos presented on the FYP page are algorithmically tailored to the individuals' interests.
2. **Through its icons and video-editing features:** TikTok offers numerous ways to share videos both within the app and across different platforms. Additionally, 'sounds' which include clips from TV programmes, films, and other media, can be added to videos. Users can click on these sounds to find other videos which use the same clip.
3. **Through user and video creation norms:** Most users create TikTok videos to gain visibility and popularity. By using similar concepts and ideas from others, the video puts that author in conversation with others in the meme genre.

It is therefore perhaps unsurprising that meme videos such as lip-syncs, dance routines, and parodies, have become defining features of the app. This includes viral TikTok memes (or trends) such as 'Jungle – 'Back on 74' dance routine', '#Okboomer', 'Although enjoyment' duet, 'Face warp challenge' (see Figure 4.11, for example).

Points for reflection

- What is your favourite meme? Are there any features (e.g., language style, songs, activities) of this meme that you would consider to be characteristic of the meme genre?
- Have you ever participated in a meme trend, such as the choreography for 'Back on 74' by the band Jungle? If so, what were your

Figure 4.11 Two examples of popular TikTok memes. On the left, the dance choreography for ‘Back on 74’ by Jungle, and on the right, the popstar Billie Eilish participating in the #TimeWarpScan or ‘face warp challenge’ trend

motivations for participating in the trend? Did you use hashtags and other affordances to increase the visibility of your post?

4.6.1 Language in Memes

As we have seen above, different aesthetics, trends, music clips, and other semiotic features often become characteristic of meme genres. This includes language. It is common for particular types of words, spellings, and grammar to become enregistered with different meme genres. Two now classic examples are ‘doge’ and ‘LOLcat’ – two meme genres that are associated with two very different linguistic styles. Typically, both memes include an image of an animal (For doge, a dog, more specifically a Shiba Inu; for LOLcat a cat) along with some text. The text is written in a style that contains various orthographic and stylistic choices that many will recognise as the language of ‘doge’ or ‘LOLcat’.

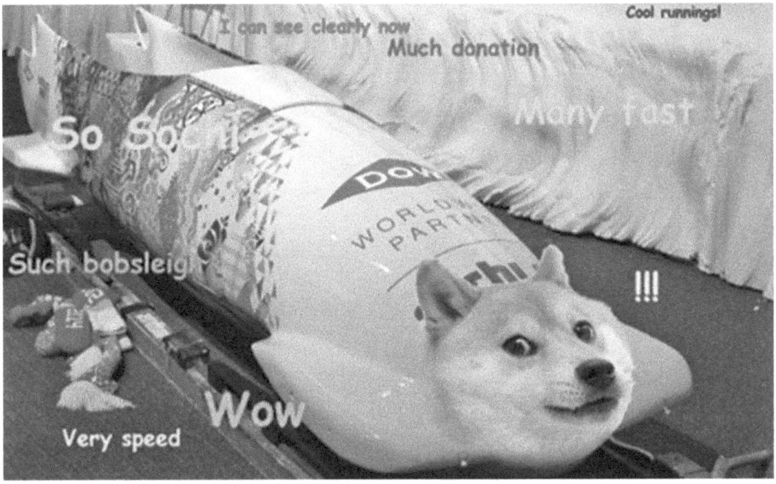

Figure 4.12 An example of a doge meme (Guardian, 2014)

The first example, doge, is an internet meme genre which remixes images of a Shiba Inu. The standard doge format is an image of the dog surrounded by comments in non-standard English written in comic sans font. The comments, which are intended to be interpreted as the dog's internal dialogue, exhibit several distinctive linguistic features (see Figure 4.12). To most readers, these sentences will appear ungrammatical because they contradict the grammatical rules of Standardised English. Features typical of the doge meme include:

- Phrases which typically start with a modifier: 'so', 'many', 'much', 'very', 'such'
- Phrases which are typically two words or less
- Short forms such as 'excite' and 'amaze'.

These features are often considered characteristic of doge memes and of a 'doge style' more generally. As users engage in doge memes, by creating and remixing new images, they develop rules about what does and doesn't constitute the language style of doge. The features outlined above (e.g., short forms such as 'excite' and 'amaze') have now become symbolic elements of a language variety – doge. This means that if we were to create a doge meme using the image of the Shiba but with Standardised English sentences such as 'so many donations' not 'much donation', it is likely that it would be rejected by the community of users as it wouldn't be a *true* doge meme.

Figure 4.13 An example of a LOLCat meme

A similar example is LOLCat. Where the doge style is primarily based on its divergence from Standardised English grammar, LOLCat memes employ a more diverse range of non-standard features. The LOLCat format typically includes an image of a cat accompanied with some text that is written in a style called LOLspeak (Gawne & Vaughan, 2012). Many LOLcat memes feature cats involved in typically human activities, such as using a computer keyboard (see Figure 4.13). The linguistic variety or style of LOLspeak is characterised by:

- **Non-standard spellings,** e.g., <haz> for *have*, <cheezburger> for *cheeseburger*, <teh> for *the*
- **Non-standard grammar,** e.g., the over/under-application of plurals and over regularisation of verb paradigms (*stuffs* for *stuff; eated* for *ate*)
- **Non-standard punctuation,** e.g., the intentional use of <1> in a series of exclamation marks <!!!1>
- **Specific lexis,** e.g., 'Ceiling cat' (God), 'Basement Cat' (Satan), 'Happy cat' (Jesus).

Like doge, these features are considered part of the grammar of the LOLcat meme. Failure to use the LOLcat style appropriately negates the effectiveness of the meme. For instance, in her analysis of LOLspeak, Miltner (2011) finds that because these types of memes adhere to a specific set of rules (or norms), users can distinguish between successful and unsuccessful attempts to master the variety. In her study, one participant suggests that you can spot a newbie by the "wrong font, wrong syntax" (Miltner, 2011: 27). Thus, whilst memes may initially appear to use an idiosyncratic or haphazard language style, in reality, many memes appear to adhere to a set of grammatical rules. As sociolinguists, a common goal is therefore to explain and describe the grammar of a meme genre, such as doge or LOLCat.

Points for reflection

- Do you recognise the Doge and LOLCat examples? Have you seen these memes being used on social media?

4.7 Summary

In this chapter, we have explored the relationship between language and identity. The focus here has been on how users perform their identities in and through social and digital media. We have seen that many platforms offer users a range of different ways to construct their identities online (e.g., profile photos, bios, status updates). This includes offering users a way of connecting with likeminded individuals which may lead to the formation of distinct online communities organised around shared interests and themes. Within the participatory spaces of social media, we have seen that users develop shared norms, values, and forms of creative expression. This includes internet memes which are created, remixed, and circulated by users. The chapter concludes by considering the distinct linguistic varieties that become associated with particular types of meme genres.

4.8 Activities

1. Choose three different platforms (e.g., LinkedIn, Twitter, Instagram). Select a public figure of your choice who has accounts on each of the three platforms. Now collect a sample of 20 posts from each of their profiles of the three platforms. Compare and contrast their identities across the different platforms:
   - Are there differences in the type of content uploaded to the three platforms?
   - Are there differences in the language used by the individual across the three platforms?
   - If the answer is 'yes' to either of the above questions, try to explain why you observe differences (hint: Think about the imagined audience!)
2. Reflect on your own engagement with online communities. Are there any communities that you engage with that use distinctive styles of language? If so, collect 50 posts from that community

and identify the words, spellings, and phrases associated with that community.

3. Doge and LOLCat are now relatively dated examples of internet memes. Are you familiar with any other meme genres that have distinctive language styles associated with them? If so, collect 10 examples of that category of memes. Try to explain the grammar of that meme genre:
   - What features (e.g., image, colour, sound) are typical of the meme genre?
   - What cultural reference(s) does the meme genre make?
   - What are the linguistic features of that meme genre?
   - What makes a meme in this category successful or unsuccessful?

4.9 Further Reading

Brock, André (2020). *Distributed Blackness: African American Cybercultures*. New York: New York University Press.

Jenkins, Henry, Mizuko Ito & danah boyd (2016). *Participatory Culture in a Networked Era*. Cambridge: Polity.

Jenkins, Henry, Sam Ford & Joshua Green (2013). *Spreadable Media: Creating Value and Meaning in a Networked Culture*. New York: New York University Press.

Kannen, Victoria & Aaron Langille (eds.) (2023). *Virtual Identities and Digital Culture*. Abingdon: Routledge.

Milner, Ryan M. (2016). *The World Made Meme: Public Conversations and Participatory Media*. Cambridge, MA: The MIT Press.

Nakamura, Lisa (2002). *Cybertypes: Race, Ethnicity, and Identity on the Internet*. Abingdon: Routledge.

Papacharissi, Zizi (2010). A *Networked Self: Identity, Community, and Culture on Social Network Sites*. Abingdon: Routledge.

Shifman, Limor (2014). *Memes in Digital Culture*. Cambridge, MA: The MIT Press.

Wiggins, Bradley E. (2019). *The Discursive Power of Memes in Digital Culture: Ideology, Semiotics, and Intertextuality*. Abingdon: Routledge.

Yus, Francisco (2019). Multimodality in memes: A cyberpragmatic approach. In Patricia Bou-Franch & Pilar Garcés-Conejos Blitvich (eds.), *Analysing Digital Discourse*, pp. 105–131. Cham: Palgrave Macmillan.

4.10 References

Agha, Asif (2005). Voice, footing, enregisterment. *Journal of Linguistic Anthropology*, 15(1): 38–59.

boyd, danah (2014). *It's Complicated: The Social Lives of Networked Teens*. London: Yale University Press.

boyd, danah & Nicole Ellison (2007). Social network sites: Definition, history, and scholarship. *Journal of Computer-Mediated Communication*, 13(1): 210–230.

Brock, André (2020). *Distributed Blackness: African American Cybercultures*. New York: New York University Press.

Bruns, Axel (2008). *Blogs, Wikipedia, Second Life and Beyond: From Production to Produsage*. New York: Peter Lang.

Castells, Manuel (2002). *The Internet Galaxy: Reflections on the Internet, Business, and Society*. Oxford: Oxford University Press.

Danet, Brenda (1998). Text as mask: Gender, play, and performance on the Internet. In S. G. Jones (ed.), *New Media Cultures, Vol. 2. Cybersociety 2.0: Revisiting Computer-Mediated Communication and Community*, pp. 129–158. Thousand Oaks, CA: Sage Publications.

Dawkins, Richard (1976). *The Selfish Gene*. Oxford: Oxford University Press.

Dubé, Line, Anne Bourhis & Réal Jacob (2005). The impact of structuring characteristics on the launching of virtual communities of practice. *Journal of Organizational Change Management*, 18(2): 145–166.

Ellison, Nicole B., Charles W. Steinfield & Cliff Lampe (2007). The benefits of Facebook 'friends': Social capital and college students' use of online social network sites. *Journal of Computer-Mediated Communication*, 12(4): 1143–1168.

Gawne, Lauren & Jill Vaughan (2012). I can haz language play: The construction of language and identity in LOLspeak. In Maia Ponsonnet, Loan Dao, & Margit Bowler (eds.), *Proceedings of the 42nd Australian Linguistic Society Conference—2011*, pp. 97–122. Canberra: Australian National University.

Herring, Susan C. (2004). Computer-mediated discourse analysis: An approach to researching online behaviour. In Sasha A. Barab, Rob Kling, & James H. Gray (eds.), *Designing for Virtual Communities in the Service of Learning*, pp. 338–376. Cambridge: Cambridge University Press.

Jenkins, Henry, Ravi Purushotma, Margaret Weigel, Katie Clinton, Alice J. Robison (2009). *Confronting the Challenges of Participatory Culture: Media Education for the 21st Century*. Cambridge, MA: The MIT Press.

Jurgenson, Nathan (2012). When atoms meet bits: Social media, the mobile web and augmented revolution. *Future Internet*, 4: 83–91.

Lave, Jean & Etienne Wenger (1991). *Situated Learning: Legitimate Peripheral Participation*. Cambridge: Cambridge University Press.

Miltner, Kate (2011). *Srsly phenomenal: An investigation into the appeal of LOLcats*. Unpublished manuscript, London School of Economics and Political Science.

Rheingold, Howard (1993). *The Virtual Community: Homesteading on the Electronic Frontier*. New York: Harper Collins.

Shifman, Limor (2014). *Memes in Digital Culture*. Cambridge, MA: The MIT Press.

Sobande, Francesca (2019). Memes, digital remix culture and (re)mediating British politics and public life. *Progressive Review*, 26(2): 151–160.

Sobande, Francesca (2020). *The Digital Lives of Black Women in Britain*. Cham: Palgrave Macmillan.

Triggs, Anthony Henry, Kristian Kristian Møller & Christina Neumayer (2021). Context collapse and anonymity among queer Reddit users. *New Media & Society*, 23(1): 5–21.

Turkle, Sherry (1995). *Life on the Screen: Identity in the Age of the Internet.* New York: Simon & Schuster.

Wiggins, Bradley E. (2019). *The Discursive Power of Memes in Digital Culture: Ideology, Semiotics, and Intertextuality*. Abingdon: Routledge.

Zulli, Diana & David James Zulli (2020). Extending the Internet meme: Conceptualizing technological mimesis and imitation publics on the TikTok platform. *New Media & Society*, 24(8): 1872–1890.

5 Methods

5.1 Introduction

In this chapter we cover the following topics:

- Developing a research project
- Research ethics
- Ethics in digital communication research
- Some common sociolinguistic approaches to studying digital communication:
  - Variationist approaches
  - Corpus approaches
  - Digital ethnographic approaches
  - Blended offline-online approaches.

Ok! So, you're now five chapters into this book. And some of you will have some exciting ideas in your head. Maybe you're now at the stage where you're thinking of designing your own project. But how do you even begin? There are so many platforms that you could study, so many practices you've observed, how do you even begin to identify a feasible research project? How do you get started doing a research project on digital communication?

The first stage of designing a research project – and potentially the most challenging – is finding a research topic. For research on digital communication, we often develop a research project in response to some anecdotal observation. For instance, perhaps you've seen that some people use <xoxo> at the end of their WhatsApp messages whilst others opt for <xxx>. Or maybe you've seen that some users on Twitter use alternating caps such as 'HoW LOnG iS ThIS GoNna TaKE?'. You might have even noticed that some people use non-standard spellings on Tumblr, like spelling *you* as <u>. Alternatively, you might want to know whether emoji or stickers are more commonly used in Weibo posts than in Twitter. All of these observations have the potential to be developed into a full-scale sociolinguistic research project. From here, we can formulate a research question such as 'are there age differences

DOI: 10.4324/9781003391838-5

in the use of <xxx> and <xoxo> in WhatsApp messages?'. A research question is central to the project design and helps us focus our project.

Once we identify a project idea and research question, we will need some data. For the above project ('are there age differences in the use of <xxx> and <xoxo> in WhatsApp messages?'), we'd need to collect some data from the WhatsApp conversations of older and younger users. However, we can't simply go extract a load of WhatsApp messages. We have to consider the **ethical** implications of extracting and analysing that data. We might even need ethical clearance from our institution. Then, once we've got past this hurdle, we'll need to use some framework to interpret our data. If we're interested in knowing why some people spell *you* as <u> on Tumblr, for instance, we'll need to use some type of framework to make sense of the data we have.

The purpose of this chapter is to provide readers with an overview of the various stages involved in designing and operationalising a study on DMC. We first focus on identifying a project idea and developing a research question. From here, we delve into the ethics of using digital data before turning to the nuts and bolts of research by considering different analytical approaches that are commonly used in sociolinguistics.

5.2 Developing a Research Project

All research projects start with a seed of an idea. Typically, we can identify a potential research topic because we have noticed someone or some people using a feature in a way that stands out or appears novel. This is how I developed the ideas for nearly all of my published articles. For instance, my paper on variation in <?> in WhatsApp conversations (Ilbury, 2024) was based on my own observations of how my friends used this feature on WhatsApp. In our group chats, I noticed that whilst <?> was often used in its conventionalised sense, that is to signal a question as in '*Why do you think he has left?*', sometimes my friends would use it in the context of a statement such as in the following Extract 0 marked in bold:

(1)
1 Sam I might meet my friend John for a drink, y'all welcome
2 Tilly Whose [sic] John????
3 Sam He's the guy from University? He lives like opposite us?

I then realised this was much more widespread than my group of friends. It was common in emails and was discussed online. This simple observation – that <?> was being used in statements – led me to develop a research project that focussed on the variation in the use of

<?> in WhatsApp chats. In this project, I was interested in examining the extent to which <?> in statements could be considered a textual trace of a feature of spoken language – what sociolinguists have called 'High Rising Terminals' (HRTs). Also called uptalk, HRTs refer to the use of a high rising intonation on a declarative sentence. Although this is a feature of spoken language, the use of <?> in declarative phrases like 'he lives like opposite us?' looked to me to be a textual representation of this feature. To understand this variation, I developed a research question: 'does declarative <?> function in similar ways to HRTs in speech?'.

When developing a project on digital communication, it is often worth spending some time on a platform to simply observe how people communicate. Platforms like Twitter and Reddit which are publicly accessible are great for this type of exploratory research. We can quickly determine whether our initial idea is worth developing into a full-scale project. Good questions to ask are: Is the feature frequent enough to study? Does the feature vary? Does it look like different people are using the feature in different ways?

Points for reflection

- Having got this far in the book, have you thought of any ideas for a potential research project?
- Are there things you've noticed people doing online that you'd be interested in exploring?

Another way to think about developing a research project is by adapting an existing study. For instance, if you've read a paper which finds gendered differences in the use of emoji on Twitter, you might want to see if these gendered differences in emoji use are found in another platform, such as Weibo. Alternatively, if research has found that American teens prefer <haha> to <lol> in WhatsApp conversations, you may want to see if this pattern holds in the WhatsApp messages of Australian teens. Both of these research projects replicate an existing study. In your own work, you may want to simply adapt the research questions, methodology, and background of an existing study to enable comparisons between those findings and your own.

Once we've settled on an idea, we ideally want to develop a **research proposal**. This is a concise and coherent summary of the project. The proposal should do three main things:

1. Establish the research background of the proposed project. What other research has been done on the topic that relates to the project? Why is this project original or interesting?

2. Discuss the aims and objectives of the research project. In research on digital communications, we typically start out with research questions. Though depending on the type of study you're designing, developing some hypotheses may be more appropriate.
3. Detail the methodology and analytical framework(s) that will be used to obtain data and analyse it.

The purpose of the proposal is to help keep the research project focussed. It provides a clear outline of what the project is and how you are going to do it. However, nothing is set in stone. We often adapt and change elements of our research design as the project develops. Perhaps a particular methodology didn't work or data that you thought was available in fact was inaccessible. Adapting the project design is very common when doing digital communications research and shouldn't be seen as a failure!

When we develop the research proposal, we need to make several decisions. These decisions include what literature to include, which methodology to use, what data we're going to get, and how we're going to do the analysis. One of the things we need to think about in some detail is the data. There are lots of interesting questions about language and digital communication but some are difficult to answer because we cannot access the data needed to answer those questions. Dating platforms, for instance, are very difficult to study because the types of conversations people engage in are often filled with emotionally sensitive topics. Getting consent from users to analyse these conversations is quite complex. When writing your proposal, you should have a good idea of what your data will look like, how it will be obtained, and which platforms you intend to get the data from.

Your choice of platform will necessarily have an impact on the types of approaches you use. Projects on Zoom, for instance, will likely need to use recordings of actual conversations between users. We would therefore need to identify the relevant methodological approaches and software that will enable us to capture and analyse audio-visual data. The format of the data will also shape how we analyse it. For some approaches, such as analyses of Twitter data, we might only focus on the text-based content of tweets. However, for other platforms like Zoom which use text, video, and sound, we'll likely need to employ a **multimodal** analysis. These types of approaches allow us to consider the interaction between different semiotic systems (i.e., text, video, and sound; not just one or the other).

5.3 Research Ethics

For all these types of analyses, we will need to first consider the ethical issues involved in collecting, storing, and analysing digital data.

Because our focus in this book is on digital communication, most of the research that we are interested in analyses messages, posts, videos, and other forms of digital content produced by actual people. This data often includes lots of sensitive information like personal names, addresses, and images. Extracting, analysing, and storing this data presents a number of ethical challenges and issues.

Put simply, **research ethics** is a universally agreed set of principles that govern the standards of academic research. The purpose of ethical guidelines and protocols is to ensure that our research does not do any harm or bring people into disrepute. Generally, guidelines are published by institutional or governmental committees who have responsibility to ensure that the research is both legal and ethical.

Key Term: Research Ethics

A set of principles which ensure that research is conducted in an appropriate and responsible manner. Research ethics include things like ensuring you have informed consent from participants, making sure you have stored the data securely, and guaranteeing participant anonymity (if this is agreed).

Although, the exact guidance will vary depending on the institution and the country in which the research project is carried out there are some common principles of research ethics. These include:

- **Respect for autonomy**: People must be free to decide whether they want to participate in the study of not. They are free to withdraw at any time.
- **Minimise risk**: Participants should not be harmed by the research.
- **Benefits outweigh any possible risks**: The research should be worthwhile and should yield some meaningful outcome and be of scientific/scholarly interest.
- **Justice**: The research should treat people equally and participants should not be exploited.
- **Confidentiality**: The participants' personal details and data should be kept safe and confidential. Any data should only be shared with the research team (unless otherwise agreed).
- **Integrity**: All research should be conducted to the highest academic standards. Unacceptable practices include: Falsification of results, plagiarism of ideas, and fabrication of data.
- **Conflict of interests**: Researchers must be upfront as to whether there is personal or economic gain for conducting the research.

As discussed briefly above, research institutions like universities will often have committees which publish specific ethical guidelines. Most universities will have a Research Ethics Committee (REC) or Institutional review board (IRB). These are committees which ensure that research involving human subjects is conducted in an ethical manner and in accordance with national and international law. Alongside issuing ethics guidance, ethics committees will often assess applications and give researchers ethics clearance to conduct their study. Because research projects involving human participants cannot commence until ethical clearance is granted, the ethics application should form part of the overall study design. Researchers will often build ethical protocols (e.g., the right to withdraw) into their research projects from the very beginning. When completing an ethics application, you will often be asked to provide information on various aspects of the research design of the project. This includes questions about how you will (i) get consent from participants; (ii) collect, store, and analyse the data; and (iii) ensure the confidentiality and anonymity of participants.

5.4 Research Ethics and Digital Communication

Given that ethical decisions need to be made in all types of research projects, many of the issues we discuss here are relevant to other types of research projects, not just those on digital communication. However, there are a number of unique ethical issues that arise when doing research on DMC. A main issue is that there are rapid changes in digital technologies; new platforms and services emerge very quickly. Platforms will often be released (and sometimes disappear!) before ethics committees have had the chance to develop guidelines for extracting, analysing, and storing that data. Currently, there is little to no institutional guidance on doing research on newer multimodal apps like TikTok/Douyin. Even when there are ethical guidelines, these can sometimes be contradictory or dated. Unfortunately, and often frustratingly for students and ethics committees alike, there isn't really a one size fits all model for doing ethical research on digital communication. Students and researchers will often want to do research projects where there's no established protocol for extracting or analysing the data that the researcher has in mind. This means that researchers will often have to make decisions based on their own intuitions or follow similar approaches.

In addition to institutional guidelines, there may also be academic communities, groups, and organisations which publish ethical advice which is more tailored to digital communication. For the kinds of projects we are interested in, guidelines published by the Association of Internet Researchers (AoIR; www.aoir.org/ethics/) and the British

Association for Applied Linguistics (BAAL; www.baal.org.uk/who-we-are/resources/) are particularly useful.

One of the big questions in analysing digital data is the issue of consent. Generally speaking, ethics committees will require the researcher to obtain ethical approval for their study and obtain 'informed consent' if the data is collected from 'human subjects'. Informed consent means that we must give participants sufficient information about the study, how the data will be analysed, and so on, as well as the option to participate or not. Usually, participants receive an information sheet which details the study aims and purposes and are then asked to give consent typically by signing a consent form (either in physical or digital format). Sometimes this involves the individual responding to various different requests on how the data will be used.

For most projects that involve human subjects, the question as to whether we need consent or not is relatively straightforward. Say we wanted to do a project on perceptions of climate change, and we wanted to record people discussing this topic in interviews, we would need to get consent from individuals before we interviewed them. Similarly, imagine you are doing a study on the digital practices of a group of five individuals who are known to you. Your study involves you interviewing these individuals and then extracting some of their WhatsApp conversations. Since you are interviewing the participants and obtaining some of their private conversations, you would need to issue them with an information sheet and get their consent to extract and analyse their data.

However, for other types of digital projects, the issue of consent is a much more complex issue. First, it may be not possible to obtain consent from participants. This could be because the user is anonymous and so there is no way of contacting them to ask for consent or because the dataset is very large. In Chapter 6, we introduce a set of approaches that use 'big data' methods and tools to analyse linguistic patterns in datasets made up of thousands if not millions of users. Obtaining consent from all of these individuals is simply not feasible. The question here then is *do we always need consent?*

Whether we need informed consent or not is a decision often based on whether the data is 'public' or 'private'. Generally speaking, ethics committees do not require researchers to obtain ethical clearance or consent when the data is in the 'public domain'. Data in the public domain tends to come from public facing publications like newspapers, magazines, and television programmes. If we wanted to undertake a project on the use of different pronouns in a tabloid newspaper, for instance, we wouldn't need to apply for ethics approval for that project. This is because newspaper articles are in the public domain and they are intended to be read by the public.

This is the argument made for some types of social media data. Take, for instance, Twitter. When a user tweets, their tweet appears in their timeline where it is visible unless it is deleted. By default, profiles are set to public. This means just about anyone can go and read that tweet. If we assume that consent only needs to be obtained for private data, we will conclude that, as Twitter data is in the public domain, it is comparable articles in newspapers or magazines. We therefore do not need ethical approval or consent to collect and analyse public tweets. In reality, however, the public/private debate and the question of consent in digital communications research is much more complex than this.

Points for reflection

- Consider the following platforms – Instagram, WhatsApp, Snapchat, TikTok. Is content on these apps public or private? Do you think we would need consent to analyse the various different posts on these apps? If so, why? If not, why not?
- In the above discussion, we said that researchers do not typically get consent to analyse tweets because they are in the public domain. Do you agree with this approach? In other words, would you be happy if a researcher analysed your tweets or used them in a research project?

5.4.1 Private Content

As briefly noted above, a general rule of thumb is that ethics committees will require the researcher to obtain informed consent if the data is considered private. For instance, if you wanted to do a project on spelling variation (e.g., <bbz> for <babes>, <walkin> for <walking>) in WhatsApp messages sent by a group of young adults, you'd need first need to get ethics clearance from the relevant institutional body. After this, you'd need to get informed consent from all of the contributors to that group. This will likely involve sending everyone an information sheet which outlines the aims of the study and explains how their data will be stored and analysed, and also a consent form. Only once you obtained consent from each and every one of the users in a given group chat could you go ahead and start extracting and analysing their messages. This is because WhatsApp is a private or closed platform. In other words, messages on the app cannot be viewed by individuals who are not members of a conversation or group (unless, of course, those messages are shared elsewhere). Evidently, WhatsApp conversations are very different to public domain sources, like newspapers or magazines, which are intended to be read by anyone.

In an ideal world, if you were conducting this project, every member of the group would happily consent to participating in the study. However, even if you do obtain ethical approval and get consent from all of the users involved, we still need to be mindful of several ethical issues throughout the research process. Ethics committees will often ask us to explain how we will store the data. Sometimes, the country that the researcher is working in will have legal requirements for data storage. For instance, in the UK and the EU, researchers must adhere to the principles set out by the General Data Protection Regulation (GDPR). This dictates things like where the data is stored, who has access to the data, and how the long the data can be retained. We must adhere to these guidelines to ensure that we are storing personal and sensitive data appropriately.

Researchers also have a duty of care to participants to use their data in responsible ways. What this means is that we should not bring people into disrepute or cause harm to them. Participants have often generously donated their data and so we have to be careful not to misrepresent or misconstrue that data. This is a particular concern of research that considers interactional data, such as conversations from DMC. If you use WhatsApp (or any other private messaging service), think about the content of your messages and/or who you send those messages to. Many of our conversations on WhatsApp are very similar to those that we participate in in private contexts like at home or at work. These are conversations that we have with our friends, colleagues, or family – essentially, groups of people that we are close with. Due to this level of intimacy, WhatsApp conversations often include messages about private and personal topics. Users may have sent their friends their address or bank details, conversations might cover taboo topics, and identifiable multimedia content like selfies may be shared in the group. All of these conversations were sent on the assumption that they would remain private and would only ever be viewed by members of the group or message. Even if we do get ethical approval and consent to use this data, we have to be mindful that we now have access to conversations that were never intended to be shared or read by non-members of the group or message. In other words, people sent these messages long before they were ever aware that they could be analysed as part of a study on digital communication.

In some ways, we could think of this as an advantage, not a disadvantage, of digital data. Because we are extracting data from the private conversations of users, we will often get very naturalistic conversations. And, given that participants sent the messages at a time when they weren't part of a study, we're not going to see any observer effects in our data (i.e., the tendency for people to change their behaviours when they become aware that they are being studied). These types of data are often very casual, between friends and family, and on relatively informal topics. In very many ways, this is exactly the kind of data that sociolinguistics aims to collect.

Still, we should be mindful of the assumptions that users had when sending these types of messages. If the dataset contains personal details like phone numbers or addresses, this is identifiable information that must be deleted or anonymised in the dataset. For personal names, we can usually assign someone a pseudonym (i.e., use a fake name) but for other personal information like bank details, we probably want to avoid extracting this entirely or at the very least delete this information from our dataset.

The second issue relates to the topics of conversation. As discussed above, people often engage in very intimate topics in WhatsApp precisely because these are often private conversations between friends and family. When we get consent to analyse and extract those conversations, we need to be mindful of how we present and use this data. For instance, if your corpus of WhatsApp messages contained discussions of substance use or intimate details of someone's love life, it wouldn't be a good idea to use these examples in a paper.

Of course, not every paper on DMC will need to present stretches of the conversation verbatim. One very common approach that is used in sociolinguistic analyses of DMC is to analyse the quantitative (i.e., numerical) distribution of a feature. For instance, we may want to know how many times the different variants of laughter are used in the WhatsApp messages we have extracted. To answer this, we could count how many times the different variants (<lol>, <haha>, and <hehe>) occur. And, if we have different groups of people, we could look at whether one group (e.g., users aged 40 and over) use more or less of one variant over another when compared with another group (e.g., users aged under 40). Since we are simply counting how much a given variant is used, we don't necessarily need to present excerpts of WhatsApp conversations in the paper. Our interest here is solely on the *aggregate* patterns of the variation in the dataset. It may not really matter what people were talking about when they used <lol>, <haha>, or <hehe> since we're not going to use excerpts of the actual conversation.

However, if we *do* want to analyse how <lol>, <haha>, or <hehe> are used in actual conversation, what do we do then? In this type of project, you might want to show that the different laughter variants are used in different conversational contexts, e.g., when joking vs. when being sarcastic. Unlike the quantitative approach above, this study will likely involve close analysis of conversations to explore why and how a given variant is used. We now need to present actual extracts of the conversations – words and sentences – that were produced by actual people. This could potentially be problematic for a number of reasons. First, when we use extracts of conversations, we are almost always presenting data that is decontextualised. We need to be aware that an utterance is often interpreted differently when it is presented alone, separate from the rest of the interaction. Presenting an excerpt in isolation risks misrepresenting what someone really meant when they sent the original message. For instance, calling someone an 'idiot' might be playful or serious depending on the intention of the message. To understand the meaning of this single message, we'd need to know the relationship between the users and the preceding and following conversation. We therefore need to provide enough context so that the example is not misinterpreted. Second, we should be aware that we have a duty to minimise risk to our participants. As noted above, it's possible that taboo or offensive labels or topics will be discussed in DMC. If we are presenting stretches of the discourse in our analysis of <lol>, <haha>, and <hehe>, we would want to avoid presenting excerpts that contain potentially inflammatory or sensitive content. A simple way of doing this would be to use excerpts and examples that are mundane or innocuous. Whilst we anonymise all data, we don't want to run the risk of misrepresenting or harming our participants who have very generously donated their conversations to us!

Points for reflection

- Which 'private' social media platforms do you use? Can you think of any strategies or approaches to reduce the ethical challenges of using this data?

5.4.2 Public Content and Consent

Other types of digital data are in the 'public domain'. Data is considered 'public' if that message, video, or other content is accessible or visible on a platform without registering for an account. Often, the terms and conditions of the platform will determine whether the content is public or private. Most accounts on Twitter, Reddit, Instagram, and TikTok are set to public by default. When users register for an account on these platforms, they would have agreed to some type of condition that specifies that their data will be public. For instance, when a user registers for an account on Twitter, tweets are set to public by default. It is often possible to view a public timeline without personally having an account. If an account owner wishes, they can make their tweets and profiles private by selecting the 'Protect your Tweets' option in the privacy settings. When selected, only users who follow the account can view the users' tweets and profile information. New followers then have to be approved by the user. The terms and conditions (at least in 2024) even state that '[Twitter/]X is a public platform'. Indeed, few users elect to protect their tweets. In a 2021 study of the Twitter practices of over 2,500 adults in the US, only 11% of respondents reported that they had protected their tweets (McClain, Widjaya, Rivero & Smith, 2021).

As discussed above, most of the time researchers do not need ethical clearance to extract and analyse data that is in the public domain. Public social media data – like tweets, Reddit posts, and so on – are often compared to newspapers, magazines, and television programmes. As such, many have argued that since data on these platforms is publicly accessible, it is not necessary to obtain consent from individual users. In most circumstances, this negates the need to apply for ethical clearance.

Because a lot of social media data is in the public domain, it is extremely accessible to researchers. The sheer quantity and style of social media posts is potentially a goldmine for the kinds of research questions and projects we're interested in. Researchers have been able to gather very large datasets comprising conversations from public social and digital media sites. The types of data we can collect from these sites are diverse. Platforms like TikTok and Instagram provide us with access to multimodal (e.g., textual, visual, and oral) content. Now, with the increasing availability of computational tools, we can download and analyse this content far more easily than previously. This means that we can study linguistic phenomena in datasets comprising millions of messages. For instance, in work on lexical variation in Twitter, Grieve and colleagues examine geographical patterns of dialect lexis in a 1.8-billion-word corpus consisting of 180 million tweets posted by 1.9 million unique accounts. This is a huge amount of data! Importantly, collecting a dataset of this size and power is only made possible because the tweets in the dataset are in the public domain.

The increasing use of social media and digital data in sociolinguistics has, in part, been promoted through greater academic access to this data. In fact, some platforms have actively encouraged research on user data. Twitter and Reddit offer a dedicated API for academic research and in 2023, TikTok announced that it would be opening up its API to academic researchers.

Nevertheless, even if this data is in the public domain and the platforms may encourage its use for academic purposes, we still need to be mindful of the implications and ethical issues of using this data. Although ethics committees or institutions may not require us to apply for ethical clearance or obtain consent, we still have a duty of care to those whose data we use. This is particularly true for apps and platforms where data is 'public by default' (e.g., Twitter, Reddit, TikTok, Instagram, and most internet blogs, like Tumblr). Whilst the *majority* of data on these apps is set to be publicly visible, not *all* data is public. It is common, as we saw in Chapter 3, for users to exploit the privacy and security functions of platforms to hide their data. For instance, on Instagram users will often elect to make their profiles private so that only followers who are accepted can view their timelines and, on Tumblr, users can choose the audience of particular posts, making them private if they so wish. Even if posts are publicly accessible, many of these platforms have affordances that are private. This includes the direct messaging functions on TikTok and Instagram.

A related issue that we need to consider here is whether people are truly aware of the status of their data and how that might be used. Although Twitter is often used in academic research because it is publicly accessible, many users appear to be unaware that their tweets are public. In the same 2021 Pew research survey discussed earlier, 53% of the respondents claimed to have set their profile to public. However, after crosschecking these claims, Pew research found that in reality, 89% of the participants' profiles were set to public. This suggests that people aren't truly aware that Twitter is a 'public by default' site and that they may be unintentionally posting content that is seen by an audience much larger than they had imagined.

Points for reflection

- If you use Twitter, would you be happy for a researcher to use your tweets in their paper?
- Would the following factors affect your response?
  - If you were asked permission to use your tweets
  - If your tweets were quoted in full
  - If your tweets were anonymised
  - If your tweets were analysed with millions of other tweets
  - If your tweets were analysed automatically by a computer.
- What concerns do you have about academics using social media data in their research?

The mismatch between users' expectations and how the data might be used is a major issue for researchers. If people aren't aware that their content is public, they probably don't realise that that content could be used in an academic study. This is an issue addressed by Fiesler and Proferes (2018) in a study on 'participant' perceptions of Twitter research ethics. In that work, the authors show that the majority of Twitter users felt that research should not use tweets without express consent. In fact, 48.5% of the 268 participants expressed the view that they were uncomfortable with the idea of their entire Twitter history/timeline being used in research. Only 33.2% of the participants felt comfortable with their tweets being used in this way. 67.4% of users indicated that they would change their view on a tweet of theirs being used in a study if express consent was obtained first. Clearly then, whilst the data might be technically public, people are not always aware that it is accessible and could be used for research purposes.

One very interesting finding of the Fiesler and Proferes (2018) paper is that people responded differently depending on how the data were used. One of the main differences people distinguished between was research which analysed aggregate patterns versus those which explored aspects of their conversations in detail. Fiesler and Proferes (2018) found that participants felt more comfortable with their tweets being analysed along with millions of other tweets from other users (53.2% were comfortable), than in isolation. Only 38.6% of respondents indicated that they would be happy with their tweets being used verbatim in a research paper.

The findings of this type of work can be interpreted with reference to a concept we introduced in Chapter 3: The imagined audience. Recall that we introduced work on Twitter that showed that users generally imagine an audience that comprises their friends, family, or people similar to them. Users often design their tweets with this imagined audience in mind. Fiesler and Proferes' (2018) findings are likely indicative of a mismatch between users' expectations of the imagined audience and the actual potential audience (i.e., academics who may use this data in their research). Very evidently, the users in the study did not anticipate that the audience of their tweets could, one day, be a researcher or even, if the tweet is published in a book or a journal, an entire academic community!

Another related finding was that Fiesler and Proferes (2018) found that users were more comfortable for researchers using their data to examine some topics than others. In fact, for many of the respondents, whether or not their tweets could be used in academic research was heavily dependent on the topic of the study. This leads the authors to conclude that quoting tweets might be less appropriate for research on sensitive topics such as medical conditions or drug use than, for instance, in a study on television habits.

What digital content we quote and how we quote it is a major dilemma for sociolinguistic analyses of DMC. Although we generally think of sociolinguistic questions as fairly innocuous (e.g., *do men and women use <lol> in different ways? Are there generational differences in emoji use?)*, there are some sociolinguistic questions which engage with much more sensitive or risky topics and issues. For instance, there is now quite a lot of work on the so-called 'manopshere' – that is, websites and other digital content that promote toxic masculinity and misogyny. Much of this work analyses social media and digital content in the public domain. This includes work such as Krendel's (2020) analysis of the linguistic construction of gender identities in an anti-feminist forum on the popular discussion website, Reddit. Many of the posts analysed in this work contain highly offensive and discriminatory remarks. Messages are often reproduced in verbatim and so could, potentially, be traced back to the individual user. We will discuss how to balance these issues in Section 5.4.4 when we introduce a 'reflexive approach to research ethics'.

5.4.3 Data from Public Figures

One possible work around for dealing with questions of whether the data is public or private is to use content from celebrities, politicians, and other public facing figures. Many of the issues we've discussed so far apply to everyday users because, as Fiesler & Proferes show, there's little or no expectation that their content will be scrutinised or analysed by anyone but their friends and family. Public figures, on the other hand, cultivate an online presence and profile that is intentionally designed to encourage public engagement.

Nevertheless, whilst using data from public figures might address some of the ethical quandaries we've discussed so far, it equally raises some other issues which may or may not be problematic depending on the scope of the study. Perhaps most obviously, celebrities and other public figures are not representative of a community as a whole nor are they typical of the everyday user. If we are using data from public figures, it is very likely that they are cultivating an online persona that is highly monitored and polished. The topics of posts will also likely be restricted. Many celebrities will only post about topics directly related to their profession and/or role. Consider, for instance, the following tweets from a politician (the current Indian Prime Minister, Narendra Modi) and a music artist (the American singer-song writer, Lady Gaga):

(2) @narendramodi: His Royal Highness Prince Mohammed bin Salman bin Abdulaziz Al Saud and I had very productive talks. We reviewed our trade ties and are confident that the commercial linkages between our nations will grow even further in the times to come. The scope for cooperation in grid connectivity, renewable energy, food security, semiconductors and supply chains is immense.

(3) @ladygaga: Lady Gaga Jazz & Piano returns to Las Vegas for 12 shows between August 31 and October 5 🎷🎼
Sign up now for the Little Monsters pre-sale on http://vegas.ladygaga.com for early ticket access tomorrow!
Tickets go on sale to the public this Friday, August 4 at 10 am PT ✨

This type of data would be suitable for a project that examines the linguistic strategies that public figures use to engage with their audiences.

However, the data would be less useful in projects that examine topics like non-standard spellings or creative typographic strategies, given how standardised these tweets are.

The second issue, and perhaps the more problematic issue for the types of research we're interested in, is that the public figure might not be responsible for creating the content that is posted to their profiles. Often, celebrity accounts are maintained by a third-party, usually a social media manager. If the tweets aren't actually written by the user, we can't argue that the language used in those tweets is representative of that public figure. Especially problematic is we seem to have no way of distinguishing tweets written by the public figure themselves and a marketing assistant. The two examples above seem very unlikely to have been written by the public figures themselves given how formulaic and standardised they are but we really have no way of verifying this.

A third and final issue with using data from these types of accounts is ascertaining whether the individual is actually a public figure. Influencer accounts pose a problem here. Whilst influencers with millions of followers are virtually indistinguishable from actors, television hosts, and other celebrities, it is debatable as to whether so-called 'nano-influencers' (1–10K followers) and 'micro-influencers' (10–100K followers) can really be considered public figures. A counter point to this is that it could be argued that influencers, like other public figures, cultivate an online presence that is intended to be engaging and public facing.

5.4.4 Making Ethical Decisions

In some ways, the previous sections raise more questions than provide answers. At times, working on digital communication feels like an ethical minefield. As discussed above, it's not always clear whether the data is public or private, we may not know if we need to obtain consent, and sometimes there aren't specific institutional guidelines to follow. Given these issues, how do we go about actually designing an ethically responsible project on digital communication?

The first thing to do is check whether there is institutional guidance that is relevant to your project. Given that more and more researchers are working with this type of data, ethics committees will now have more guidance on researching digital platforms and practices. If your institution does not offer any guidance, it is worth having a look at the information produced by BAAL and AoIR (links in Section 5.4).

However, a more radical approach would be to overhaul our thinking of 'research ethics'. So far, we've been discussing ethics as a fairly procedural process that we need to abide by: We read institutional guidance, fill in an application form, get clearance from our institution, and off we go and do the study. But this is a fairly generic process that doesn't account for the fact that research projects often develop in ways we didn't initially foresee. Sometimes, the data we want to collect will be very different to what we first set out to study. Equally, as we build relationships with participants, they might have different expectations about how their data is used or feel more comfortable in disclosing sensitive information to the researcher.

To tackle these issues, Tagg and colleagues (2017) have argued that we should reframe digital research ethics away from a set of obligations that the researcher 'ticks off' and instead we should view ethics as a series of decisions that are made in response to changes in the project design as it evolves. In some studies, this might mean changing aspects of the research project as the dynamics between participants and researchers shift. For instance, in longitudinal studies where participants' digital practices are tracked over time, there is a possibility that participants may reveal more intimate data as they become more familiar with the researcher. It may not always be appropriate for researchers to collect this data even if they have permission from the participants to do so.

The approach that Tagg and colleagues advocate for is a **reflexive** approach to ethics. Reflexivity involves making conscious efforts to reflect on our own thoughts, feelings, and emotions when making decisions in the research process. As a process of continuous self-questioning, reflexivity forces us to consider the *whys* of doing research to ensure that we are making ethically responsible decisions and choices. To many students, reflexivity might seem quite an abstract and academic concept. But in reality, we do this kind of thinking all the time. One of the recommendations I often make to students working on digital communication is to put yourself in the shoes of the community or the user you're studying. Imagine you are the individual who originally uploaded the video, image, or message. Ask yourself, if that were my post, would I be happy for an academic researcher to extract it and analyse it in a paper? If the answer is no, then I'd suggest reconsidering whether the project is feasible or whether different types of data can be analysed.

Points for reflection

- If you are currently working on a research project, take a moment to think about your data. If that were your message, image, or video, would you be happy for a researcher to analyse it? What steps would you want the researcher to take to make sure they using your data in a responsible way?

Key Term: Reflexivity

In research ethics, reflexivity should guide the decision process. Reflexivity means thinking about your own beliefs, judgments and practices as you carry out a research project. Some decisions can be made by thinking about your own practices, e.g., if that were your own post or video, would you be happy with an academic analysing it?

The types of issues around data and consent are heightened when studying the digital practices of minoritised communities. These are individuals who belong to groups that are minorities in the population. This includes people who have minoritised racial, ethnic, sexual, and gender identities. We need to consider this issue carefully because there is a higher likelihood of harm given that research has historically often misrepresented and mischaracterised minoritised communities. When working with minoritised communities or on topics related to these communities, we should pay extra attention to how we gather, store, and analyse the data. It may be appropriate, for instance, to obtain consent from users of minority groups even if that data is publicly available.

We also need to critically reflect on how our world views and assumptions shape our understanding of the data. This is what researchers refer to as **positionality**. Considering our positionality means critically reflecting on how our race, gender, class, and other social identities inform and shape our understanding of and relationship to the data. Very often, researchers working with minoritised communities are part of those communities themselves. The research is therefore heavily shaped by the individual's participation in and membership of the community under study.

Key Term: Positionality

Positionality refers to the fact that the identity of an individual influences their research. How we interpret patterns and social behaviour are all influenced by our own social background and experience of the world.

It's clear then that research ethics aren't just a set of boxes that we must tick off to get clearance for the project. But we should see ethics as an ongoing process of making decisions based on the research objectives. These decisions should be made in relation to participant expectations and the evolving research project, as well as our own experiences and positionality in the field.

5.5 Common DMC Approaches in Sociolinguistics

In the remainder of this chapter, we step away from research ethics to briefly introduce four main approaches that are used in sociolinguistics of DMC. These sections are intended to provide an outline of the approach, with key readings introduced as a way of reading beyond the summaries.

5.5.1 Variationist Approaches

Variationist sociolinguistics explains the social and stylistic factors that constrain language variation and change. To use a common example: You've probably noticed that whilst many people who speak English pronounce the word *butter* as [bʌtə], some people will pronounce this word with a glottal stop [ʔ] in place of /t/ as in [bʌʔə]. What we've identified here is a basic pattern of variation in the English language. Variationist sociolinguists will identify the rate of this variation, and also isolate the linguistic and social factors that influence that variation.

A key argument in variationist sociolinguistics is that variation isn't random. Rather, variationists demonstrate that variation is structured and predictable. This is because these studies have consistently shown that variable patterns of language are influenced by social (or external) and linguistic (or internal) constraints. Social factors include socio-demographic categories like social class, age, gender, and sexuality. Linguistic factors include things like the preceding sound, the word class, or the frequency of the lexical item. In the case of the above example, the variable realisation of /t/ as a glottal stop – what is often called 't-glottalisation' – has been shown to be sensitive to both social and internal factors. Higher rates of t-glottalisation have been observed in the speech of younger and working-class speakers, and in words where /t/ appears in intervocalic position (i.e., between two vowels) such as *better* and *butter*. A central concept in this field is the 'sociolinguistic variable'. Initially conceptualised as 'two or more ways of saying the same thing', a variable like (t) has (at least) two possible alternations: [t] and [ʔ].

Though most research has focussed on variation in spoken language, there is now a growing body of variationist approaches on DMC. A lot of work has demonstrated the application of theories, concepts, and methods that were initially developed to account for spoken language phenomena to digital data. A common approach in variationist analyses of digital communication is to analyse the orthographic representation of some spoken language feature. In these studies, the goal is to identify the social and linguistic factors that constrain the orthographic variable.

A case in point is Iorio's study (2009) on orthographic variation in Massively Multiplayer Online Role-Playing Games (MMORPG). In that paper, Iorio examines the extent to which (ING) variation (i.e., <running> vs. <runnin>) is influenced by the audience. His analysis identifies strong social effects on the realisation of (ING). Notably, Iorio finds that individuals use more of the non-standard (i.e., <runnin>) in private messaging contexts versus public contexts where the standard (i.e., <running>) is more common.

A similar type of approach is found in Tagliamonte and colleagues' (2016) two-year study of the language used in digital interactions by Canadian youth. In that study, the authors analyse variation in a 179,000–word corpus of emails, instant messages, and SMS messages. They focus on the use of three main phenomena associated with digital interaction: (i) acronyms, short forms, and initialisms (e.g., <lol> as a marker of laughter) (ii) intensifiers (e.g., *it was **really** easy* vs. *it was **very** easy*); and (iii) future temporal reference (e.g., *yo **shall** we go to see that on friday?/ wat **will** u be doing in the summer?*). The authors find that there are sizeable differences in the rate of the three features across the different datasets. Notably, in the context of emails, they identify lower rates of the non-standard features, suggesting that users style-shift according to the perceived formality of the interactional context. They propose that this finding could be explained by the fact that users associated email with more formal registers that they engaged in with interlocutors like their professors, teachers, and bosses. The authors observe some gendered effects in the use of <lol>. Males were seen to significantly favour this laughter variant over others (e.g., <haha>, <hehe>).

Typically, a variationist sociolinguistic to DMC asks questions like: *What are the sociolinguistic factors that constrain the use of <lol>, <haha>, <hehe>, and <lmao>? Do men use <lol> more than the other variants as identified by Tagliamonte and colleagues (2016)?* And *are there other social factors that constrain its use*?

To start this type of study, you'll need to get some conversational data from a digital platform. This could be data from 30 friends (10 males, 10 females, 10 non-binary individuals) who have very generously donated their WhatsApp conversations to you. You could then go through the data identifying all the different types of laughter variants and quantifying their rate. Once you've done this, you could see whether males use one variant more than the other groups. If you find that one group use a particular variant more than another, you have evidence that the variation in laughter particles is constrained by the user's gender identity. This type of approach has been used widely in studies of DMC and is useful in identifying broad level patterns in the social distribution of a particular feature.

5.5.2 Corpus Approaches

A corpus is a collection of texts (written, spoken or signed) in a digitally readable format. Researchers build corpora (the plural of corpus) of natural language to examine some linguistic phenomena in that dataset. This includes questions like:

- What differences are there between spoken and written registers of English?
- What types of words co-occur most frequently?
- Do people use more swear-words now than at some other point in time?

In work on social media, researchers have often compiled large corpora of DMC. This includes datasets of WhatsApp conversations and Twitter posts. These types of studies have examined topics such as the quantitative distribution of different spelling variants (e.g., <wot> for *what*), the differences between tweets of 140 and 280 characters, and the most common types of emoji in a Facebook corpus (see Tagg, 2016; Eberl, 2020; Collins, 2020).

Because these datasets are often so large, researchers use computer software (often called concordancers) to analyse and explore patterns in corpora. Well known programmes include AntConc, Sketch Engine, and Wordsmith. Many of these tools are free to download and can be used to analyse patterns in DMC. Often, corpora are tagged or 'annotated' for various different features, including the grammatical category of tokens. Researchers will also add metadata to corpora. This could include social information about the individuals whose data make up the corpus.

In corpus-based approaches, it is common to use computer software to identify 'concordances' – these are words or phrases that are displayed one-example-per-line. This allows researchers to identify the common contexts in which that word or phrase is used. Additionally, researchers will often explore 'keywords'. These are words that appear more frequently in the corpus when compared with others. Finally, 'collocations' may be identified to explore the co-occurrence of words with others.

5.5.3 Digital Ethnographic Approaches

A 'digital ethnography' is a subtype of 'ethnography'. Although ethnographic approaches are used in very many academic fields of research, this method was originally developed in Anthropology. Ethnographers are interested in systematically analysing the distinctive features of cultures and peoples. Researchers will ask questions like *why people do [X]?* or *what does [X] mean for this community of people?* To answer these questions, ethnographers will often spend a lot of time observing and documenting people in their own environments to understand the norms, values, and systems of that culture. The aim of this work is to provide a rich or 'thick' description of a community and their practices. Researchers have done this by becoming a 'participant-observer', engaging with the community beyond the scope of their research questions. The focus here is then to understand what is meaningful to a culture or community. In this way, studies which employ ethnographic principles do not attempt to understand individuals' practices in relation to a set of existing social categories (e.g., age, gender, social class). Rather, they attempt to understand what meaningful systems of distinction people participate in. Ethnographers will often spend quite a lot of time in the 'field' to understand a community. The 'field' here refers to the site or context in which the study is conducted. This could be a school or workplace, for instance.

One of the key methods in ethnography are fieldnotes. To make sense of the context, the researcher will often document what they see, hear, and feel, keeping notes about their experiences in the field site. These notes may include photos or drawings of the field site as well as leaflets, letters, and other information from the community.

With the increasing prevalence of digital technologies, researchers have extended this approach to the online by undertaking digital ethnographies of communities and online subcultures. This approach applies the principles and methodological approaches of traditional ethnography (e.g., participant observation, thick descriptions, field notes) to digital contexts and platforms. Ethnographic approaches have a long history in digital media studies. For instance, Turkle's now seminal work on 'The Second Self' from the 1980s provided an earlier ethnographic account of the digital identities of a group known as 'hackers'. Today, these types of approaches are very common in work on digital interaction. Researchers have used ethnographies to understand a variety of different digital practices including 'micro-celebrity' and influencer branding (e.g., Senft, 2013; Abidin, 2015; Glatt, 2022), meme cultures (e.g., Haynes, 2019; Ilbury, 2022a), and teenagers' digital practices (e.g., boyd, 2014; Stæhr, 2014; Lane, 2019; Ilbury, 2022b).

Digital ethnographies have also been employed to understand patterns of DMC. Students are often excellent ethnographers because they have already observed a practice used by an online culture or community that few academic researchers are aware of. If you wanted to develop an ethnographic study, you would need to engage with a community over some period of time. For instance, let's imagine you're interested in exploring the language used by influencers in developing a relationship with their followers. We could start out by systematically observing the practices of some influencers over say, a three-month period. This might be following ten beauty influencers who regularly upload posts to Instagram. Over the course of this period, we would want to focus on the similarities and differences between the influencers. We could record these observations as digital fieldnotes. Over time, it might be that see the different influences use different language strategies to engage their audience. We might see that some influencers might encourage viewers to sign up to their mailing list whilst others might avoid this recommendation entirely. When we come to explaining these differences, we would want to draw on our ethnographic knowledge that we've built up of the influencers. Perhaps it's that one of the influencers we are studying is sponsored by a commercial brand and so does not need to recommend a mailing list or perhaps they don't use email newsletters. These insights are the kind of insights we'd want to get from a digital ethnography.

As the study progresses, we might even want to engage directly with some of the influencers to get their perspectives on their communication style. We might ask to observe an influencer in the process of creating a video or we might interview a few of the beauty influencers to get their perspectives on the topic. The point of the ethnography is that it helps us contextualise why people do what they do and it explains differences in communication styles not in terms of general factors, but rather things that are meaningful to individual communities, like 'beauty influencers'.

5.5.4 Blended Approaches

So far, we've mainly been discussing approaches which focus squarely on the digital practices of users and their online communicative practices. We have discussed a variety of different studies, including those which study digital topics such as: Variation in the use of <?> in WhatsApp conversations and the alternation of <in> and <ing> in role playing games. These studies can only really say something about how people are communicating online. This is, after all, the focus of the book: Digital communication.

However, as we discussed in Chapter 4, it is very difficult to disentangle digital communication from other contexts and types of social interaction. A very clear example are 'selfies'. When we take a selfie, we create a photograph of some offline context. If we upload this to Instagram or WhatsApp, this offline context – and the selfie – now becomes part of the 'digital'. Similarly, when people interact on platforms like Snapchat, they often move between speaking to someone face-to-face and online. We'd ideally want to use a method that allows us to understand how people's digital communications are *embedded* in their offline practices.

Here's where a blended approach to digital communication may be useful. Instead of trying to distinguish between the offline and online, blended approaches consider how both dimensions influence and affect one another (Androutsopoulos, 2008). In these types of approaches, we might want to look at how people's digital interactions reflect their offline identities or how people use digital technologies in everyday conversation.

Designing a blended approach is difficult because it means looking beyond 'just' the digital. Adopting this approach means that we can't just focus on patterns of digital communication in isolation but rather, we have to start to think about how they reflect practices and identities that aren't in the digital sphere. A blended approach to digital communication, for instance, might collect two types of data: Digital communications and spoken interactions. You could, for instance, follow Sierra's (2021) approach and look at how young people make intertextual references to internet memes in conversation. This would require you to record young people engaged in interactions, as well as studying the types of memes that they engaged with in digital contexts. Alternatively, you could compare the language used by people on a platform like Snapchat, with that used in an 'offline' context like a youth group (see Ilbury, 2022b). All of these studies view digital communication as just one aspect of social interaction.

5.6 Digital Tools

There are now quite a lot of accessible and user-friendly tools that students can use to extract and analyse data from DMC. Some tools require some coding experience whilst others are intended for those with little to no knowledge of programming languages. Some of the recommended resources are paid for, others can be used during a free trial period, and the rest are freely available to use. These tools will be useful for those looking to gather large amounts of data or if manual data collection (e.g., screenshots) is not possible. The following tools and programs are recommended:

- **FireAnt:** Social media and data analysis software that comes with various data visualisation tools (www.laurenceanthony.net/software/fireant/).
- **4CAT:** A Python based tool that allows users to create dataset comprising posts from various platforms including Reddit, Telegram, and 4Chan (https://wiki.digitalmethods.net/Dmi/ToolDatabase).
- **Zeeschuimer:** A browser extension which can be used to scrape data from various platforms including TikTok, Instagram, and LinkedIn

(https://github.com/digitalmethodsinitiative/zeeschuimer). The .ndjson file can be converted to .csv (which can be read in Excel) using 'zeehaven' (https://publicdatalab.github.io/zeehaven/).

- **YouTube data tools:** A range of tools that can be used to extract YouTube comments and channel metadata (https://ytdt.digitalmethods.net/).
- **Apify:** A cloud platform for web scraping and data automation. The website lists a variety of different 'actors' (most are paid for) that can be used to extract social media data. This includes TikTok, Instagram, and YouTube (https://apify.com/store).
- **Chrome Plugins:** Google Chrome has a few scrapers on their web store that can be used to extract social media data. This includes plugins that allow the user to download TikTok videos and comments, as well as scrape data (comments and posts) from Weibo.
- **Python:** If students have some coding experience, there are a variety of Python based packages that can be used to extract social media data. This includes TikTokApi – an unofficial API wrapper for TikTok.com in Python (https://pypi.org/project/TikTokApi/) and Instaloader – a Python wrapper that can be used to download public and private profiles, hashtags, user stories, feeds and saved media (https://github.com/instaloader/instaloader).

All of the above programs were available and accessible at the time of writing. However, restrictions may be imposed by platforms that will affect their use over time. This is the case for FireAnt which can no longer be used to extract Twitter data after the restrictions introduced on the Twitter API in February 2023. It should also be noted that some of these apps collect data in a way that technically contravenes the terms and conditions of some platforms. For instance, platforms like Instagram actively prohibit scraping.

In some projects, we may not even need to use a specialist tool or programme. Some platforms have affordances which can be used to download data:

- **WhatsApp:** Chats can be exported via .txt. To do this, go to the three dots in the right-hand corner of a chat. Go to 'More' and click 'Export chat'. You will be given the option to export with or without media. The .txt file can then be imported into word or transformed into an excel document.
- **TikTok:** Most videos can be downloaded from the app to your local storage. Long press a video and click 'save video' or go to 'share'.
- **Instagram, Snapchat, and others:** Screenshots of content on most can be taken on most contemporary smartphones.
- **Zoom, Teams:** Video conversations can be recorded using in-app/platform functions.

- **Email:** Most email services (e.g., Outlook) allow you to export emails to a text file. This is typically done via the 'print' or 'save as' functions.

5.7 Digital Datasets

There are also a number of datasets that are publicly accessible. I've suggested three relatively large datasets here but I am sure there are very many more elsewhere:

- **Twitter corpora of Brexit related tweets from pro and anti-Brexit accounts, January – March 2022:** Lynch, Gareth (2022). Twitter datasets: Brexit related tweets from pro and anti-Brexit accounts January – March 2022 (Brexit leaning based on their Twitter bios), *Harvard Dataverse*, V1. https://doi.org/10.7910/DVN/FXEFZT
- **WhatsApp corpus of messages from Italian students aged 12–13:** Sprugnoli, Rachele et al. (2018). Creating a WhatsApp dataset to study pre-teen Cyberbullying. In *Proceedings of the 2nd Workshop on Abusive Language Online* (ALW2). https://doi.org/10.18653/v1/W18-5107 (https://github.com/dhfbk/WhatsApp-Dataset)
- **Twitter corpora of COVID-19 related tweets, January 2020–March 2023:** Banda, Juan M. et al. (2021). A large-scale COVID-19 Twitter chatter dataset for open scientific research – an international collaboration. *Epidemiologia,* 2(3), 315–324; https://doi.org/10.3390/epidemiologia2030024 (https://zenodo.org/records/7834392)

5.8 Summary

This chapter has provided an overview of some common research principles and methodologies in studying digital communication. First, we discussed the initial procedure of designing a research project. Then, we considered the ethical challenges and decisions involved in collecting and analysing digital data. Unlike more established areas of academic inquiry, often advice and guidelines on doing this type of project are lacking. Researchers therefore must make conscious and active decisions to ensure that they are undertaking ethical research. Finally, we introduced some popular methodological sociolinguistic approaches to studying DMC.

5.9 Activities

1. If you are developing a project of your own, write up a list of the possible ethical challenges and concerns that you might encounter in your project. Now, write down some strategies for addressing these challenges.

Table 5.1 Twitter 'participant perceptions' based on Fiesler & Proferes (2018)

Question	Very uncomfortable	Somewhat uncomfortable	Neither uncomfortable nor comfortable	Somewhat comfortable	Very comfortable
How do you feel about the idea of tweets being used in research?					
How would you feel if a tweet of yours was used in one of these research studies?					
How would you feel if your entire Twitter history was used in one of these research studies?					

2. Informally replicate the Fiesler and Proferes (2018) study by asking your friends the questions in Table 5.1 (note: Twitter can be substituted for TikTok or another public platform).
3. Choose an approach from those listed in this chapter (e.g., corpus, blended, variationist, etc.). Now do a literature search for socio-linguistic analyses that take this approach. Answer the following questions:
   a. What similarities and differences are there in the methodological design of the papers?
   b. Do any of the papers explicitly discuss the ethical challenges of the approach?
   c. What types of research questions do the papers attempt to answer?
   d. Are there any future directions in the paper?

5.10 Further Reading

Androutsopoulos, Jannis & Andreas Stæhr (2018). Moving methods online: Researching digital language practices. In Angela Creese & Adrian Blackledge (eds.), *The Routledge Handbook of Language and Superdiversity*, pp. 118–132. Abingdon: Routledge.

Rogers, Richard (2024). *Doing Digital Methods*, 2nd edition. London: Sage Publications.

Snee, Helene, Christine Hine, Yvette Morey, Steven Roberts & Hayley Watson (2016). *Digital Methods for Social Science: An Interdisciplinary Guide to Research Innovation*. Basingstoke: Palgrave Macmillan.

Variationist Approaches

Squires, Lauren (2016). *English in Computer-Mediated Communication: Variation, Representation, and Change*. Berlin: De Gruyter Mouton.

Tagliamonte, Sali A. & Derek Denis (2008). Linguistic ruin? LOL! Instant messaging and teen language. *American Speech*, 83(1): 3–34.

Corpus Approaches

Di Cristofaro, Matteo (2024). *Corpus Approaches to Language in Social Media*. Abingdon: Routledge.

Rüdiger, Daria & Daria Dayter (2020). *Corpus Approaches to Social Media*. Amsterdam: John Benjamins.

Digital Ethnographic Approaches

Heyd, Theresa (2023). Complicating the field: World Englishes and digital ethnography. In Guyanne Wilson & Michael Westphal (eds.), *New Englishes, New Methods*, pp. 243–262. Amsterdam: John Benjamins.

Pink, Sarah, Heather Horst, John Postill, Larissa Hjorth, Tania Lewis & Jo Tacchi (2016). *Digital Ethnography: Principles and Practice*. London: Sage Publications.

Varis, Piia (2016). Digital ethnography. In Alexandra Georgakopoulou & Tereza Spilioti. *The Routledge Handbook of Language and Digital Communication*, pp. 55–68. Oxford: Routledge.

Blended Approaches

Blommaert, Jan (2019). From groups to actions and back in online–offline sociolinguistics. *Multilingua*, 38: 485–493.

Dovchin, Sender, Alastair Pennycook & Shaila Sultana (2018). *Popular Culture, Voice and Linguistic Diversity: Young Adults On-and Offline*. Basingstoke: Palgrave Macmillan.

5.11 References

Abidin, Crystal (2015). Micromicrocelebrity: Branding babies on the Internet. *Media and Culture Journal*, 18(5).

Androutsopoulos, Jannis (2008). Potentials and limitations of discourse-centred online ethnography. *Language@Internet*, 5(8).

boyd, danah (2014). *It's Complicated: The Social Lives of Networked Teens*. New Haven: Yale University Press.

Collins, Luke C. (2020). Working with images and emoji in the 🦆 Dukki Facebook Corpus. In Sofia Rüdiger & Daria Dayter (eds.), *Corpus Approaches to Social Media*, pp. 175–196. Amsterdam: John Benjamins.

Eberl, Martin (2020). Are 280–character tweets comparable to 140–character tweets? In Sofia Rüdiger & Daria Dayter (eds.), *Corpus Approaches to Social Media*, pp. 131–146. Amsterdam: John Benjamins.

Fiesler, Casey & Nicholas Proferes (2018). 'Participant' perceptions of Twitter research ethics, *Social Media + Society*, 4(1): 1–14.

Glatt, Zoë (2022). Precarity, discrimination and (in)visibility: An ethnography of 'The Algorithm' in the influencer industry. In Elisabetta Costa, Patricia G. Lange, Nell Haynes, & Jolynna Sinanan (eds.), *The Routledge Companion to Media Anthropology*, pp. 546–559. Abingdon: Routledge.

Haynes, Nell (2019). Writing on the Walls: Discourses on Bolivian immigrants in Chilean meme humour. *International Journal of Communication*, 13: 3122–3142.

Ilbury, Christian (2022a). U Ok Hun?: The digital commodification of white woman style. *Journal of Sociolinguistics*, 26(4): 483–504.

Ilbury, Christian (2022b). Discourses of social media amongst youth: An ethnographic perspective. *Discourse, Context, and Media*, 48: 1–9.

Iorio, Josh (2009). Effects of audience on orthographic variation. *Studies in the Linguistic Sciences: Illinois Working Papers*, 127–140.

Krendel, Alexandra (2020). The men and women, guys and girls of the 'manosphere': A corpus-assisted discourse approach. *Discourse & Society*, 31(6): 607–630.

Lane, Jeffrey (2019). *The Digital Street*. Oxford: Oxford University Press.

McClain, Colleen, Regina Widjaya, Gonzalo Rivero & Aaron Smith (2021). The behaviours' and attitudes of U.S. adults on Twitter. *Pew Research Centre Report*. www.pewresearch.org/wp-content/uploads/sites/20/2021/11/PDL_11.15.21_Twitter_users_final_report.pdf (accessed May 2025).

Senft, Theresa M. (2013). Microcelebrity and the branded self. In John Hartley, Jean Burgess, & Axel Bruns (eds.), *A Companion to New Media Dynamics*, pp. 346–354. Oxford: Wiley-Blackwell.

Sierra, Sylvia A. (2021). *Millennials Talking Media: Creating Intertextual Identities in Everyday Conversation*. Oxford: Oxford University Press.

Stæhr, Andreas (2014). *Social media and everyday language use among Copenhagen youth*. Unpublished PhD thesis, Københavns Universitet.

Tagg, Caroline (2016). Heteroglossia in text-messaging: Performing identity and negotiating relationships in a digital space. *Journal of Sociolinguistics*, 20: 59–85.

Tagg, Caroline, Agnieszka Lyons, Rachel Hu & Frances Rock (2017). The ethics of digital ethnography in a team project. *Applied Linguistics Review*, 8(2–3): 271–292.

Tagliamonte, Sali A., in collaboration with Dylan Uscher, Lawrence Kwok, and students from HUM199Y 2009 and 2010 (2016). So sick or so cool? The language of youth on the Internet. *Language in Society*, 45: 1–32.

6 Big Data Approaches

6.1 Introduction

In this chapter we cover the following topics:

- 'Big data'
- The emergence of Computational Sociolinguistics (CS)
- CS analyses of language variation and change
  - Twitter dialectology
  - Case study of MLE
- Some limitations of these approaches.

Earlier, in Chapter 2, we introduced and discussed some foundational work which attempted to define the language variety that was used on the internet. As we saw in this chapter, a lot of earlier research focussed on analysing and describing variable patterns of language and communication in CMC. One of the main aims of this work was to understand the form, distribution, and function of non-standard spellings (e.g., <bbz> *babes,* <u> *you,* and <fink> *think*) that were often considered characteristic of CMC. However, as discussed, one major limitation of this early work, was that the conclusions made by scholars were often based on introspective observations and/or small datasets. This was most often because, at this time, digital data was quite hard to access and analyse. And even if the data was freely available, researchers did not always have the tools to extract and analyse vast quantities of data.

As the field has developed, so too have the methods and approaches used to collect and analyse digital datasets. Researchers now have access to a variety of computational tools that can be used to automatically extract and analyse digital data. Today, we now face an altogether different dilemma to those working in the early days of CMC – what people have referred to as an "avalanche of big data" (Barnes, 2013: 297).

Our lives are now defined by digital data. From tweets to Instagram posts, blood pressure readings from Fitbit to digitised books, digital data is everywhere. As researchers, we have far greater access to this

DOI: 10.4324/9781003391838-6

data than ever before. We also have the means to analyse it. We no longer need to use specialist tools and computers to download and analyse this data. We can now extract this type of data using software that is often freely available and, importantly, many of these tools require little to no knowledge of coding.

In this chapter, we introduce 'big data' approaches to studying digital communication. The chapter focusses on research that employs computational tools and methods to understand large-scale patterns of language variation in social media texts. From here, I introduce and describe a new area of sociolinguistic research, what has been called 'Computational Sociolinguistics' (CS), before discussing some case studies which have used these methods. Finally, we critically reflect on the potentials of computational tools in shaping and informing our understanding of sociolinguistic phenomena.

6.2 The 'Big Data' Turn

Across the social sciences, there has been a shift toward 'big data' approaches – what some have termed the 'data revolution' (Kitchin, 2014). From sociology to geography, history to media studies, scholars are increasingly using computational methods to explore social phenomena in very large and complex datasets. This includes:

- The prevention and control of infectious diseases such as in the COVID-19 global pandemic
- Predicting and understanding consumer habits
- Understanding population movement and migratory patterns.

As we will see in this chapter, these developments have not bypassed sociolinguistics. Researchers have increasingly used big data approaches to analyse a diverse range of sociolinguistic phenomena including mapping the geographical distribution of different linguistic features across entire nations, tracking the emergence of new lexis (i.e., words), and analysing the representation of spoken dialects in social media texts.

Key Term: Big Data

The use of computational tools to extract and analyse large and complex datasets. These types of datasets have been used to explore human behaviours across multiple communities and users. These approaches are increasingly being used in the social sciences – what some have called the 'big data turn' or 'data revolution'.

The big data turn is indicative of the increasing availability of computational tools and digital data. In research prior to the digital revolution, data was seen as a scarce commodity. Today, however, digital technologies have turned this situation on its head. Data is now widely accessible and is numerous in volume. Think, for instance, how much digital data you've already produced today. Perhaps you've already posted a tweet about your favourite TV show or uploaded a new post of your morning coffee to your Instagram story. Now imagine that every other user of that platform is also doing the same. That is a lot of data! All of these posts and messages could be extracted and analysed by a researcher who is interested in understanding some social issue or trend.

Historically, 'big data' has often been used in the sciences to refer to datasets that could only be read and analysed by supercomputers. However, the software that we need to be able to extract, read, and analyse big data is becoming more accessible. In fact, most big datasets can be analysed using non-specialist software that can be installed on a standard desktop computer.

Before we discuss this development further though, a word of caution is needed in how we interpret the qualifier 'big' in 'big data'. More often than not, people assume that 'big data' = 'massive datasets'. But as many have pointed out, the qualifier 'big' is a somewhat misleading. Big data approaches do not necessarily analyse phenomena in datasets that are 'big' in size. Rather, this approach is more about the complexity of the dataset. As boyd & Crawford conclude, the big data movement is "less about data that is big than it is about a capacity to search, aggregate, and cross-reference large data sets" (2012: 663).

Points for reflection

- Before we introduce this discussion, briefly think about some potential advantages of using a big data approach in sociolinguistics. What benefits do you think a big data approach would have?

6.3 'Big Data' and Sociolinguistics

As noted earlier, these approaches have been used in a variety of different disciplines. This includes sociolinguistics. Researchers using big data approaches have emphasised the value of big data in understanding patterns of social interaction. Nevertheless, the types of methods and datasets that big data focusses on are quite different from those typically used in sociolinguistics. Traditionally speaking, sociolinguists have typically done research on social interaction by going out into different communities and recording people engaged in conversations. Most of these studies analyse language in audio and/or video recordings. This is the approach typical in variationist sociolinguistics, where researchers have often collected data through a well-established methodological strategy: The sociolinguistic interview. This approach has been used in a wide-range of settings and contexts and has been shown to be an effective methodological approach in collecting naturalistic recordings of spoken language interaction.

However, gathering data in this way is extremely resource intensive. Researchers often spend a lot of time recruiting participants and even longer interviewing them. Sometimes, people will change their behaviour during the interview because they become aware they're being studied – what Labov (1972) famously described as the 'observer's paradox'. After they've managed to record people, the researcher then has to spend a great deal of time transcribing and coding the data for various features of interest.

When we consider how laborious and time-consuming collecting and analysing this data is, big data approaches look very attractive. Many of the issues we discussed about collecting, coding, and analysing spoken language corpora are resolved when we use social media data. First, big datasets typically comprise posts and messages from text based social media sites. Because interactions on many digital platforms are text based, we don't have to spend hours on end transcribing the conversations – users do this for us! Second, given that people largely use social media to communicate with their friends and family, most interactions on social media are casual and conversational. This is exactly the type of data that sociolinguists are interested in. We don't have to design some experiment or study to elicit conversations (cf. the sociolinguistic interview), since people are already interacting with each other online. And because they are not participating in an experiment or interview, we don't have to contend with the issue of the observer's paradox. As we have previously discussed, most users imagine an audience of their friends or people like them (Marwick and boyd, 2011); they don't expect their messages or content to ever be analysed for the purposes of research. Finally, given the scale of social media, we can very likely extract a range of conversations from a variety of different people – many of whom we would not have been able to reach through participant recruitment. Overall, then, it seems that big data approaches are potentially very promising in sociolinguistic research because the data generally comprise naturalistic and informal social media conversations. These conversations can be gathered from a diverse population of users and can be downloaded in a text-based format ready for analysis, addressing quite a few issues involved in the collection and processing of spoken language data.

To illustrate the analytical potentials of a big data approach, let's use a hypothetical example of a study which explores the geographical distribution of lexis in the US. For the purposes of this example, we will focus on the lexical alternation of *pop-soda-coke*. One way of analysing this type of variation would be to physically go out to several towns, cities, and neighbourhoods, stop people on the street and ask them: '*What do you call a can of generic carbonated, sweetened beverage?*'. We could then scribble down their answer and, once we got back to the lab, we'd count how many people say each word in each area. From here, we could use these responses to plot where across the country people use 'pop', 'coke' or 'soda'. The quantitative picture that we build would allow us to identify whether there's any regional variation in the use of *pop-soda-coke*.

The kind of approach I'm describing here is one that has been traditionally used in dialectology – a branch of linguistics that explores variation in dialect, such as the lexical alternation of *pop-soda-coke*. The random survey study of *pop-soda-coke* is comparable to work in early dialectology. In this type of research, teams of fieldworkers went out into different communities and asked people similar questions to the one we're asking here. After recording what each speaker said, researchers would quantify how many times a particular feature occurs within a given area. If different areas use *pop-soda-coke* at different rates, the researcher could conclude that there was dialectal variation in this lexical alternation. This is the approach used in the Survey of English Dialects (SED; e.g., Orton & Barry, 1969), for instance.

Points for reflection

- Think of some limitations and issues with the traditional dialectological approach described above.
- Do you think a big data approach to *pop-soda-coke* might account for some of these limitations?
- Are there other issues and/or limitations that we might we encounter if we did this analysis on social media data?

Clearly, there are some major limitations of this method. The main issue is that this approach is it is extremely resource intensive. Collecting this type of data will take a lot of time, energy, and money. In our study of *soda-pop-coke*, even if we surveyed only ten people from ten different areas (a total of 100 participants), we would spend a great deal of time and money travelling between different neighbourhoods and cities. It would only really be feasible if we had a team of researchers who were based in the different areas we wanted to study, as was common in dialectological surveys such as the SED. Even then, it would be extremely time consuming. The SED took over ten years to complete.

Realistically, then, this approach is not suited to the type of research project we're designing. Even if we could dedicate a substantial chunk of time and money to this project, we then couldn't guarantee that the people that we stopped in a given area would be willing to participate in the survey. And even if they did, since we are only collecting data from a limited number of participants per area (N = 10), we would be making inferences based on a small number of responses from a few people who may or may not be representative of their neighbourhood or city.

This is where a 'big data' approach is promising. Imagine if we could collect data on the geographical distribution of *soda-pop-coke* from individuals across the US without travelling all the way to their neighbourhoods and asking them what word they'd use. Imagine if that data already exists. Imagine if we could collect hundreds, thousands, or even millions of tokens of *pop-soda-coke*. Well, this is exactly where big data is revolutionary. For the purposes of this research project, let's consider data from Twitter. Below are a series of real tweets 1.–3. that contain a token of *soda-pop-coke* extracted from the platform through the search function.

1. haha I love cocacola, it's my fav **soda**, FAVOURITE!!!
2. Dear pepsi, Please send me a fountain **pop** machine please and any amount of regular Pepsi to fill it up with. That is all. Thank you for your time 😂😎
3. Clearly you're not Southern cause all fizzy drinks in the south are **Coke**

These three examples demonstrate that the *soda-pop-coke* alternation exists in Twitter as it does in speech. If we think about the sheer number of tweets posted every minute (estimated to be roughly 350,000 tweets!), that's potentially a lot of messages with the *soda-pop-coke* alternation that could be analysed. One of the advantages of this data is, as we discussed in Chapter 5, tweets are generally set to 'public'. This means that we can search and extract these tweets without explicitly obtaining the users' consent (though the issues we discussed in Chapter 5 still apply!).

Now, let's redesign our *pop-soda-coke* study using a big data approach. This time we won't go and collect this data from speakers by asking them to respond to a questionnaire. Instead, we're going to log on to Twitter from and use some computational tools to automatically download millions of tweets containing tokens of *soda-pop-coke*. We can do this by accessing Twitter's API (Application Programme Interface) using a computer programme that is specially designed to enable users to extract and analyse tweets. Prior to 2023, researchers could access the API for free. However, the platform now charges for access to the API. There are other platforms which do not charge access to their API and similar types of data can be extracted.

Key Term: Metadata

Data about the post/message itself. This may include the time, date, geolocation, likes received, and so on.

If we have access to the API, we could extract quite a lot of tweets containing *soda-pop-coke*. Along with these messages, we could also collect the tweet metadata (i.e., data about the tweet itself). Depending on what we're interested in, we could collect information about when the tweet was posted, how many likes it received, or how many times it was retweeted. For the purposes of our *soda-pop-coke* study, we will want to use the geolocation metadata about where the tweet was sent. We can then plot the distribution of *soda-pop-coke* tokens across the USA.

If we don't have access the API ourselves, we can use the app 'Word Mapper' (https://jwgrieve.shinyapps.io/mapper/; see Figure 6.1) to visualise this distribution in a dataset collected by Jack Grieve and colleagues. This app allows users to map the distribution of a word in an 8.9-billion-word corpus of 890 million geocoded Tweets sent from the United States between 11 October 2013 and 22 November 2014 – prior to when Twitter made changes to the API. Using this app in our example study, we see that *soda* is largely concentrated to the West coast and the Northeast of the United States. *Pop,* on the other hand, is much more frequent on the East Coast, whilst *coke* is largely concentrated to the South. Importantly, whilst these maps are based on the geographical distribution of *pop-soda-coke* in Twitter data,

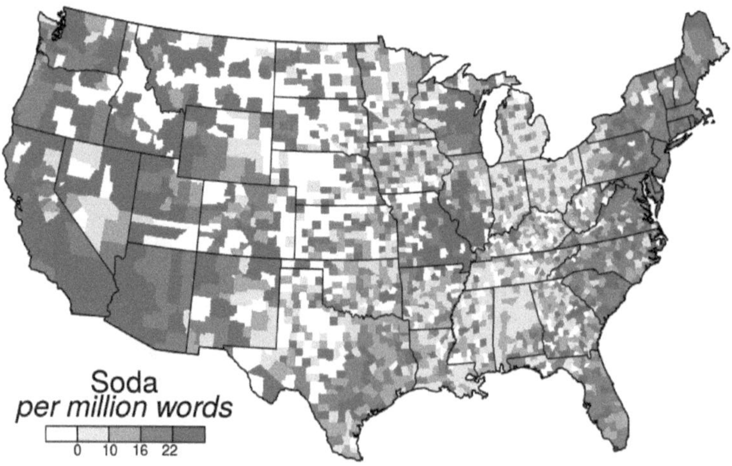

Figure 6.1 The geographical distribution of 'soda' per million words from https://jwgrieve.shinyapps.io/mapper/

these patterns actually mirror the distribution of these words in data collected in traditional dialect surveys.

What we've shown here is that, in a short-space of time with very little effort, we have been able to put together a map that would have been almost impossible to recreate if we were to try and undertake an in-person survey of *soda-pop-coke*. Using a big data approach, we've been able to explore the distribution of *soda* in a massive dataset from a huge number of users across hundreds of different locales. This means that we have a much more coherent picture of the geographical distribution of *soda-pop-coke*. And, perhaps most importantly, we haven't spent any money or even needed to leave the lab!

6.4 Computational Sociolinguistics

The type of approach that I have outlined in the above is now characteristic of those used in a new field of research, what has been termed 'Computational Sociolinguistics' (henceforth CS; Nguyen, 2016). This new area of study – as suggested by its name – combines the methodological approaches of computational linguistics with theories and concepts developed in sociolinguistics. CS researchers use computational tools like web-scrapers and part-of-speech taggers, to extract, analyse, and code digital datasets for sociolinguistic phenomena. The development of CS is part of the big data turn. It is now common for researchers to use computational tools to extract and understand sociolinguistic patterns in very large and complex datasets.

Key Term: Computational Sociolinguistics

A new area of study which uses tools from computational linguistics (e.g., web-scraping, POS tagging, automatic classification) to extract, code, and analyse sociolinguistic phenomena.

Quite a lot of CS research has attempted to understand the socio-demographic factors that influence linguistic variation in social media texts. The example above, the geographical distribution of *soda-pop-coke*, is one such example. Other work has analysed the social and linguistic factors that influence the use of variable spellings. This includes the alternation of <in> and <ing> as in <walkin> vs. <walking>, which will be discussed in more detail below.

The emergence of CS can be seen as a development that is motivated, in part, as a merging of two different research agendas. In computational linguistics, there has been an interest in modelling the social dimensions of language in order to increase the reliability and accuracy of automated classification models. Researchers have long been interested in developing computer models that can automatically predict the authors' social identity (e.g., age, gender) based on differences in text. These classification models have useful applications in fields like advertising and marketing, as they can be used to advertise products to a particular demographic of users. As an example, imagine we have just designed a new perfume aimed at women aged 18–35. It would be very useful if we could advertise *only* to this demographic of user. You may be familiar with the term 'targeted ads' – this is where particular types of adverts are shown to different consumers based on what the advertiser knows about the user. One way of inferring information about the users' social background would be to use a computational model that predicts the gender and age of the user based on linguistic patterns in their posts. This would mean that we could target the marketing campaign only to those who matched our consumer profile, i.e., women aged 18–35. This type of marketing strategy is popular because it increases the response rate to that advertisement and the likelihood that the user will buy the product being advertised.

Although the motivations for identifying social characteristics of users based on variation in text may be different, they share a common goal. Researchers in both computational linguistics and sociolinguistics are interested in the relationship between language and social identities. It is therefore perhaps unsurprising that, in recent years, there has been an increasing move towards embracing computational approaches in sociolinguistics. Those working in this area have been quick to argue for the value of big data in potentially revolutionising our understanding of language and social interaction.

To date, most CS analyses use data from two main platforms: Twitter and Reddit. These platforms are frequently used in CS analyses for three main reasons. First, content on both platforms is – largely – textual (cf. TikTok). This is important because the computational approaches used in CS have mainly been developed to model variation in text. Second, unlike some other social media platforms such as Facebook and Instagram, data is more accessible on Reddit and Twitter. A great deal of CS studies have been done on Twitter because, up until 2023, data on this platform could be easily and freely extracted via the API. Third, and as discussed earlier, platforms like Twitter and Reddit allow researchers to extract not just the post or message, but also its metadata. This information is particularly valuable because it allows us to infer things about the sociodemographic background of the author. As we have already seen, the geolocation of a tweet can be used to plot on a map where the tweet was sent from. Metadata has also been used to infer other social information about the author, such as their age, gender, location, and ethnicity (e.g., Bamman, Eisenstein & Schnoebelen, 2014; Eisenstein, 2015; Grieve et al., 2017; 2018).

Today, CS researchers are working on a variety of different topics related to language and society. Many of these questions are similar to those typically asked in sociolinguistics. This includes the following types of research questions:

- Are there gender differences in the use of emoji?
- Do younger people use internet acronyms (e.g., <lol>) more frequently than older people?
- What is the geographical distribution of a linguistic feature (e.g., lexis, grammar, spelling, etc.)?

The main difference between a typical sociolinguistic approach to digital communication and the CS approach is in the size and type of data collected and how it is analysed. CS research typically investigates the distribution of some linguistic feature in multimillion word corpora of social media posts gathered from millions of users. Given the scale and complexity of these datasets, most of the coding and analysis is done automatically. Researchers will often use computational tools like Part-Of-Speech (POS) taggers, tokenizers, and clustering to code and analyse datasets. These types of approaches are quite different to how sociolinguists have typically analysed patterns of digital communication, such as those discussed in Chapter 2 and later in Chapter 7.

6.5 Twitter Dialectology

One of the most productive areas of CS research has been 'Twitter dialectology' or 'Tweetolectology'. This research has used large datasets of Twitter data to explore regional patterns of language variation. We have actually already discussed one example: Our earlier illustration of the lexical alternation of *soda-pop-coke* in the US. This case study was inspired by a very similar analysis by Jack Grieve and colleagues (2019) on lexical variation in UK Twitter data. In that paper, the authors explore the regional distribution of 139 dialect words in a 1.8–billion-word corpus of geolocated UK Twitter data. To understand whether the regional patterns they observe in this corpus mirror those observed in speech, they compare their social media maps with the dialect maps from the BBC Voices survey. The BBC voices dataset includes 300 recorded conversations from a total of 1,201 people talking about accents and dialects, the words they use, and their attitudes to language. The analysis explores regional patterns of lexical alternation, such as *sofa-couch-settee* across the two datasets. In the BBC Voices survey, *sofa* was the dominant form in the south of England, whilst *settee* is preferred in the north of England, and *couch* more common in Scotland – all refer to the same concept: 'an upholstered seat with a back and arms, for two or more people'. Interestingly, the authors find a broad alignment between the two corpora with the distribution of lexis in Twitter largely comparable to the BBC dataset (see Figure 6.2). This finding is important because it offers some evidence to suggest that the factors that influence language variation in social media might be similar to those in speech. This leads the authors to argue that social media could be used either in place of or alongside traditional dialectological surveys.

Big data approaches in sociolinguistics are not just valuable in confirming existing knowledge about the relationship between language and society, but also have the potential to revolutionise our understanding of sociolinguistic phenomena. We can now analyse datasets much larger in size than previously possible and compare data across various different time and location points. Many of the questions we can now begin to answer would not be possible to address using traditional sociolinguistic fieldwork methods. A case in point is Jones' (2015) analysis of the regional distribution of African American Vernacular English (AAVE) lexis. Jones' paper examines the frequencies of non-standard spellings like <sholl> 'sure' and <eem> 'even' in data from Black Twitter. Some of these features are lexical but others are non-standard spellings which represent AAVE phonology. For instance, the use of <al> in <talmbout> 'talking about' is intended to be an orthographic representation of [aː] or [ɔː] for /ɑː/ - a pronunciation common in some varieties of African American English. To examine the geographical distribution of these words, Jones used the Twitter API to collect tweets containing AAVE words or phrases of interest, along with the tweet ID and the latitude and longitude from where it was sent. He then used the geolocation metadata to map the location of the tweets, in a similar way to Grieve and colleagues' (2019) analysis of *sofa-settee-couch* discussed above. This allowed Jones to explore the geographical distribution of different features, identifying whether there is any regional variation in their use. Interestingly, Jones found that AAVE features are not evenly distributed across the US as a whole. Instead, he identified distinct dialect regions for the AAVE features which do not correspond to those identified for White varieties of American English. For instance, he observed that <yeen> 'you ain't' is largely constrained to the South, with particularly high frequencies in Atlanta, Georgia. These findings not only confirm earlier claims that AAVE exhibits social and regional variation, but his analyses go further to systematically describe and map those differences. Through this analysis, Jones found that the linguistic patterns appeared to mirror large-scale patterns of population movement beginning in the 1910s. Specifically, the dialect regions that Jones identified map on to the movement patterns of the 'Great Migrations' – the movement of six million African Americans of the rural Southern United States into the Northeast, Midwest, and West regions of the US. The computational

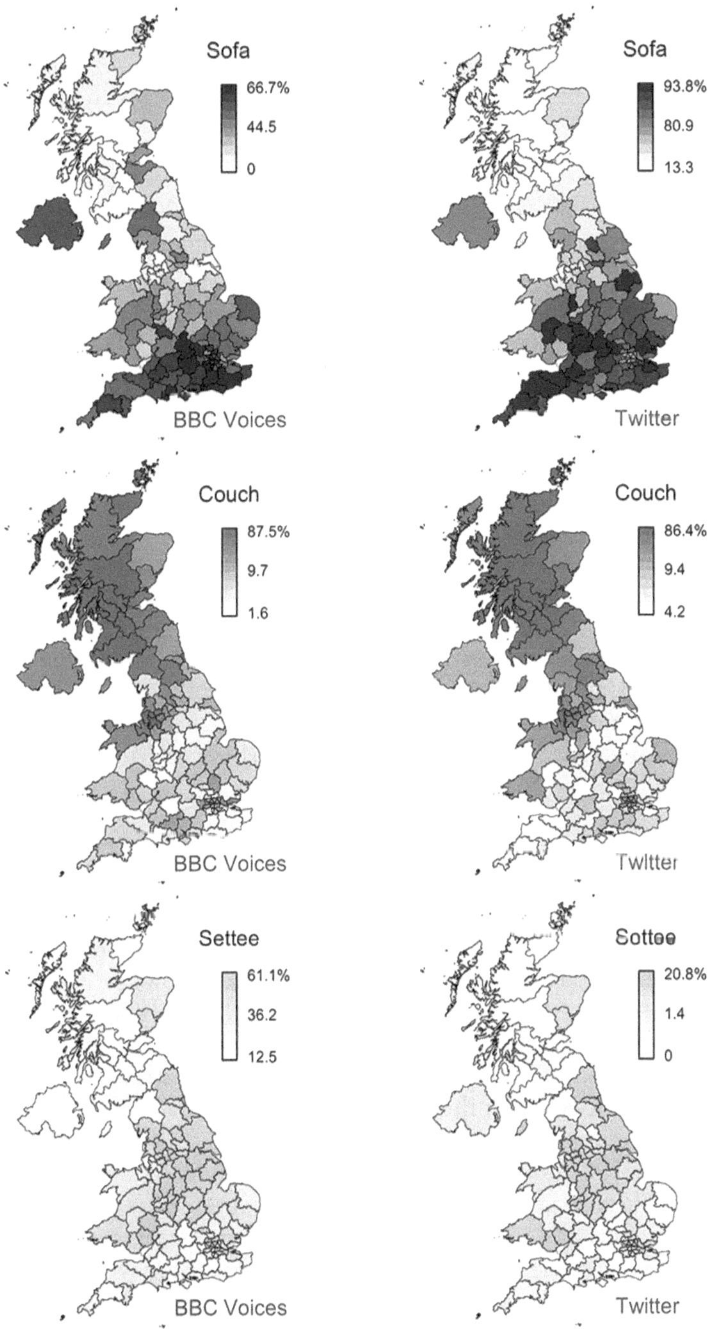

Figure 6.2 Geographical distribution of sofa-couch-settee across the UK in data from BBC Voices and Twitter

approach employed here permitted Jones to describe both the distribution of the variation and, crucially, explain why those patterns exist.

Points for reflection

- Big data approaches often assume that if a linguistic feature is used in a social media text, it is used by someone who habitually uses that feature or the variety from which it is from in speech. For instance, in Jones' (2015) analysis, the use of <eem> and <sholl> are assumed to be produced by speakers of AAVE. Can you think of any limitations of this approach? In other words, can you think of any examples where people use features of varieties that they might not habitually use or speak in everyday life?

It is very difficult to think how we could replicate Jones' analysis without using a big data approach. Theoretically, we could undertake a traditional dialect survey that replicates this type of analysis. But, as with the *soda-pop-coke* example this would be extremely time consuming and resource intensive to the point that the study probably wouldn't be feasible. Thus, as Jones (2015) demonstrates, the value of big data is not just in its size but more so in the ability to explore aggregate patterns and cross-reference these across multiple communities and users. To demonstrate the analytical potentials of this approach further, I now introduce a case study of Multicultural London English.

6.5.1 Case Study: Multicultural London English

In a recent co-authored paper (Ilbury, Grieve & Hall, 2024), we have used a CS approach to understand and track the spread of a relatively new dialect of British English, 'Multicultural London English' (MLE). First documented as a spoken language variety in East London, 'MLE' was defined as a dialect or variety that was used by young, working-class, inner-city Londoners (see Cheshire et al., 2008; 2011). Most of the sociolinguistic work on this variety is based on recordings of MLE speakers. In the first project on MLE, Cheshire and colleagues (2008; 2011) recorded 98 adolescents in two London boroughs (Hackney and Havering). The young people were recorded in naturalistic interviews with their friends and individually. In total, the researchers collected 110 hours of recordings, amassing a corpus of 1.4 million words. This permitted the researchers to define a new variety of English that was characterised by several interesting phonological, lexical, discourse-pragmatic, and syntactic features.

Lots of work has been done on MLE over the past 15 or so years. This includes some work which has documented similarities between MLE spoken in London and a variety used by speakers from other English cities, such as Manchester and Birmingham. Manchester is a city in North-West England, some 163 miles away from London whilst Birmingham, the second largest city in the UK in the West Midlands region of England, is 100 miles away from London. The similarities between MLE and varieties used elsewhere has led some researchers to argue for a more general variety that is largely based on MLE but incorporates features of the local vernacular – what has been labelled 'Multicultural British English' (MBE, Drummond, 2018).

Given that features have been documented outside of London, it appears that MLE has spread beyond the city where it first emerged. Sociolinguists call this **diffusion** – i.e., the process by which linguistic features spread from one social group or speech community to another. Analysing how varieties diffuse and where they spread to has been quite difficult to do. Generally speaking, research on diffusion focusses on the spread of features or varieties in a handful of different speech communities. In work on MLE, researchers have been very interested in understanding where MLE spread to and the social mechanisms that led to its spread. However, it would be very hard, if not impossible, to examine the spread of MLE using traditional sociolinguistic methods. This means that, apart from a few studies which focus on the language used in Manchester and Birmingham and anecdotal accounts of MLE being used elsewhere, we don't really know where MLE is being used in the UK.

This is where a big data approach becomes useful! To answer some questions about its spread, we used a 1.8 billion corpus of geolocated tweets to identify where MLE lexis was used most frequently. By mapping words frequently used in MLE like *paigon* ('enemy'), *leng* ('nice'), and *fam* (an address term), we could determine where MLE was used and by who.

We first started out mapping the frequency of MLE words. Our assumption is that areas where these words are used more frequently are those where the words spread earlier. The map in Figure 6.3 shows the regional distribution of the aggregated list of 47 MLE words. Areas which are striped are those where there are high frequencies of the word. This map shows very consistent pattern of MLE lexis. Perhaps unsurprisingly, given the origins of this dialect, we see that MLE words are used very frequently in the London post code regions. MLE words like *paigon* and *leng* are particularly frequent in the north, east, and south of the city. We also see that the 47 MLE words are quite frequent in areas outside of London where MLE has previously been reported, such as Birmingham.

This map, at first glance, confirms what we already know: MLE is frequently used in London and appears to have spread, being used elsewhere in cities like Birmingham. However, if we look beyond this general pattern, we see some interesting patterns not yet reported. First, the words are not evenly distributed across the UK. In fact, we see very low rates of MLE lexis outside out of England. Notably, MLE lexis is very infrequent in Scotland and Northern Ireland. In fact, we find that the five areas where MLE lexis is used least frequently are all in Scotland. These areas are not only very far from London (e.g., the Outer Hebrides – an island chain off the west coast of mainland Scotland) but they are also much less ethnically diverse than London. In the Outer Hebrides, the majority of the population (98%) identify as 'White British/Scottish/Irish'.

The big data approach we use in this paper also tell us things about *how* MLE spread. If we scrutinise the map in Figure 6.3, it is possible to conclude that the areas that MLE lexis has spread to aren't *just* urban cities that are close to London. There are areas which are urban and close to London, such as cities like Brighton on the south coast and Reading to the west of the city, which show low rates of MLE lexis. We therefore wanted to know: What predicts the spread of MLE? If we look at the areas where we see high rates of MLE lexis and compare this with data from the national census, we can determine two things: (i) These areas are generally close to London, and (ii) they are ethnically diverse. For instance, Luton, which shows the highest rate of MLE lexis outside London, is home to sizeable numbers of people identifying as British Asian (30% of the population) and Black British (9.8% of the population). This finding seems to suggest that MLE lexis has spread upwards from London into areas that are both urban and culturally diverse. It is therefore reasonable to assume that the diffusion was propelled through the social networks of non-White (mainly Black British) speakers.

This type of case study demonstrates the potential of big data approaches in sociolinguistics. In this case, the big data approach that we use allows us to understand the development and subsequent spread of a new dialect of British English across the entire UK. In doing so, we can systematically map the diffusion of this dialect to identify the social mechanisms that propel its spread. An analysis of this type seems impossible if we were to use traditional field methods.

6.5.2 Beyond Lexis

So far, we've focussed primarily on CS research which explores the regional distribution of lexis. This work has demonstrated that patterns of lexical variation in social media data very closely resemble the patterns that have been documented in spoken language datasets. Based on this finding, several researchers have proposed that social media data could be used as a proxy for speech. However, to confirm

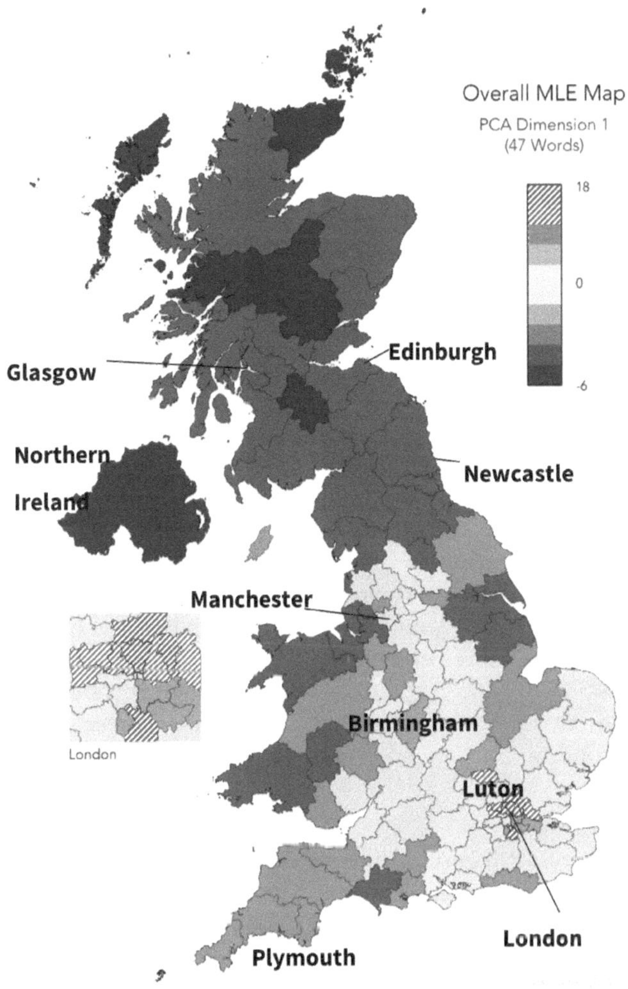

Figure 6.3 Frequency of MLE words across the UK postcode regions (striped sections indicate higher frequencies of MLE words)

this claim, we'd ideally need to study variables beyond lexis, such as syntactic and discourse-pragmatic features.

In other CS research, researchers have examined the orthographic representation of spoken language phenomena. This includes the variable representation of the *-ing* segment in words like <walking>/<walkin>. Many scholars have argued that spelling 'walking' as <walkin> is an orthographic representation of a variable found in speech (ING). This is where people pronounce the *-ing* segment /ɪŋ/ in words like *walking, talking, shooting* as [ɪn], hence [hʌntɪn] *hunting* and [wɔːkɪn] *walking*.

Although (ING) variation is most frequently associated with spoken language, the variation can be represented in text. Sometimes, people write words that contain <ing> with <in>. This leads to spellings like <huntin'> and <walkin> for *hunting* and *walking*. These types of spellings are very common in informal written contexts and can be observed in deregulated spaces like dialect literature, shop signage, and advertisements. The American fast-food restaurant, McDonald's, used this spelling in their now iconic slogan, *'I'm lovin' it'*.

Points for reflection

- Have you seen people spell words with <ing> like *hunting, loving,* and so on as <in> on social media?
- Can you think of some other spoken features that people represent in written messages on social media? Hint: Think about the way some people say the initial sound in the word *think*.

Variation in the representation of (ING) tends to be very common in DMC. Take, for instance, the following excerpt (1) from a WhatsApp group conversation of some young professionals living in London. In the excerpt, there are three contexts (or words) in which contain <ing>, *craving, skipping,* and *coming*. Here, we see that there is variation between the two forms: *Craving* and *coming* are represented as <cravin> and <comin> (lines 1 and 6) and *skipping* is represented as <skipping> (line 4).

(1)	1	Andrea:	I'm cravin a bev soooo bad
	2	Andrea:	Bring it on
	3	Lianne:	Literally can't wait to put beer to my lips
	4	Lianne:	I'm skipping work drinks
	5	Florence:	So am I
	6	Lianne:	Comin straight 2 u all
	7	Florence:	Don't have my ID though so wouldn't get me very far he he

The conversation in Extract (1) is an example of an informal digital communication between friends. It is precisely the type of casual conversation where we'd expect to see non-standard spellings and other types of creative strategies. It is therefore perhaps unsurprising that (ING) is variably represented too.

The question, here, then is whether the variable in social media texts is influenced or constrained by similar social and linguistic factors to the variable in speech. In speech, [ɪn] for /ɪŋ/ doesn't occur in monosyllabic words (i.e., words comprising one syllable) like *thing* or *wrong*. Other factors which influence this variation is word-class. We see higher rates of [ɪn] for /ɪŋ/ in verbs – particularly progressives, such as *walking, running,* and *speaking* – and lower rates in nouns and adjectives. The variation is also influenced by social factors, like the social class and age of the speaker. If the written variable is similar to that in spoken language, we would expect to see similar social and linguistic constraints. It would be reasonable to hypothesise that we would see higher rates of <n> for <ing> in verbs than in nouns and adjectives.

These types of questions have been critically examined by Eisenstein in his (2015) article on this variable in Twitter (he refers to this as 'g-deletion'). The study analyses the orthographic representation of (ING) and other features in a corpus of 114 million geotagged messages from 2.77 million different user accounts. The focus here is whether the orthographic variable patterns in similar ways to the variable in speech. To understand the variation in this very large dataset, Eisenstein first uses part-of-speech tagging to automatically classify *–ing* words as nouns, verbs, or adjectives. This automated procedure distinguishes between words with multiple senses, e.g., *a loving father* (adjective) vs. *I am loving your hair* (verb). He then analyses whether there are quantitative differences between the orthographic representation of (ING) across word classes. Remarkably, he finds that the orthographic representation of (ING) patterns in similar ways to the variable in speech: Verbs show a higher rate of deletion than nouns or adjectives. This means that words like *hitting, getting, messing,* and *rolling* are more frequently represented as <hittin>, <gettin>, <messin>, and <rollin> than say, *wedding* <weddin> (noun) and *boring* <borin> (adjective). In addition to these linguistic factors, he also finds that the orthographic representation of (ING) is influenced by similar social factors to those identified for the spoken variable. Notably, he finds that the variation is influenced by the authors' ethnic background. More specifically, Eisenstein finds that the standard, <ing>, is more frequently used in areas where there are large White populations whilst <in> is more commonly used in areas where there are large numbers of African Americans. Like Grieve's work discussed earlier and the MLE case study I introduced above, Eisenstein's work provides additional evidence to support the idea that social media can be used as a proxy for speech.

Before concluding this section, it is worth acknowledging that I've only really summarised a small area of work in CS. This chapter has focussed only on two types of variation: (i) lexis and (ii) the orthographic representation of phonological variation. And only one language has been discussed: English. However, the field is much more diverse than this. Researchers have explored a wide range of features in a number of different languages. For instance, Wieling and colleagues (2016) used Twitter data to examine variation in hesitation markers (e.g., *um, eh*) across different Germanic languages (English,

Dutch, German, Norwegian, Danish, Faroese) and dialects (American English, British English). They found that *um* was increasing over time relative to the use of *uh* and that this pattern of change was generally led by women and more educated speakers. Similarly, van Halteren and colleagues (2018) used Twitter data to map dialect features (e.g., niet→nie 'not'; dat→da 'that') in the Dutch province of Limburg. Willis (2020) explores Morphosyntactic variation in Welsh tweets, Scheffler (2014) used Twitter data to identify German dialect regions, and Grondalears and Marzo (2023) use a similar approach to that in the MLE case study to understand the social motivations for the diffusion of a new variety of Dutch, Citétaal.

6.6 Limitations

Although we've discussed some advantages of CS and big data in sociolinguistics, these types of approaches are not without their limitations. The first thing to consider is that most CS analyses can only really tell us about 'large-scale' patterns of language variation and change. This is because the available metadata can only be used to infer very general things about the author, identities like 'man', 'woman', 'Black', or 'White'. To explain the variation, authors have examined correlations between a feature and a broad-social category. For instance, Eisenstein's (2015) analysis shows that the non-standard spelling of (ING) is more frequent in areas where there are more people identifying as African American. The use of the spelling <in> is therefore correlated with the broad social identity of 'African American'. As compelling as these approaches are, we must be mindful of the fact that this runs the risk of over generalising identities and linguistic practices. In the case of AAVE, the identity of 'African American' isn't a monolith (as Jones, 2015 study shows) – there are multiple ways of being and sounding African American. The CS approach therefore runs the risk of oversimplifying the variation *within* social categories.

The second issue is that author identities are typically operationalised as binary categories. CS research has examined linguistic differences related to gender, but researchers have generally coded gender as a binary (men vs. women). This approach not only disregards those who identify outside of the gender binary (i.e., non-binary people), but it also neglects the more performative approaches to language and identity that we outlined in Section 4.2. Some CS research does attempt to address these issues, however. A case in point is Bamman and colleagues' (2014) analysis of gender identity and lexical variation in Twitter. In that analysis, the authors use a dataset of 9,212,118 tweets from 14,464 users to explore patterns of gendered variation. First, they take a standard computational approach by identifying broad correlations between linguistic features and the gender identities of users (men vs. women). This approach allows them to determine that pronouns, including non-standard spellings of those pronouns, are generally associated with female authors, e.g., <u>, <ur>, <yr>. In the next stage of their analysis, they employ the computational technique 'clustering' to automatically group language styles (e.g., emoticons, swearwords) and topical interests (e.g., sports, politics). They find that these clusters largely have gendered associations. Nevertheless, there are quite a few users who deviate from these population-level gender patterns. Focussing on users who deviate from population-level gender patterns, they find that these users tend to have social networks that include significantly fewer same-gender social connections. This leads the authors to conclude that the gender-sameness (or homophily) of an individual's social network, explains the use of same-gender language features. It therefore seems possible to use a CS approach to develop a more nuanced account of language and identity beyond generalised binary categories of author identity.

A final limitation of the CS approach relates to how author identities are deduced in this work. Most research in CS has inferred author characteristics from information that is available on user profiles. The author's age, for instance, can be inferred from their birthday (if they have this information available in their profile). Location, on the other hand, can be determined through the geo-location metadata attached to the tweet or post. However inferring author gender is much less straightforward. Researchers have generally inferred the author's gender identity from their username or handle, classifying names into 'male' or 'female' categories on the basis of publicly available name lists, such as baby names. However, this approach assumes that users provide accurate and authentic information. Many users do not provide real or gendered names and some will use intentionally obscure usernames. Bogus or intentionally misleading identities therefore may skew our analyses.

6.7 Summary

In this chapter, we have provided an overview of 'big data' approaches in sociolinguistic research on digital communication. With the emergence of a new field of inquiry – 'computational sociolinguistics' – researchers are increasingly employing big data approaches to understand and explain large-scale patterns of language variation and change in DMC. These types of approaches are very useful in sociolinguistics because we can collect large datasets of naturalistic and casual conversations. One of the most important findings of this research is that variation in social media texts often patterns in similar ways to the corresponding feature in spoken language. This has led some to argue that social media texts can be used as a proxy for spoken language data – a potentially revolutionary finding for fields such as dialectology and variationist sociolinguistics. In this way, big data approaches have potential to not only confirm our existing theories of language and society, but these types of analyses could call into question longstanding concepts and provide new sociolinguistic insights.

6.8 Activities

1. The studies we have discussed in this chapter analyse 'aggregate' patterns of language variation and change. That is to say that linguistic patterns in the tweets are analysed alongside millions of other tweets in the study. Some approaches, however, have reproduced individual tweets (e.g., Tatman, 2015). Considering the findings from the Fiesler and Proferes (2018) study, write down some potential ethical issues and challenges in using this data in this way.
2. Try searching for regional variation in US lexis using 'word mapper' (https://jwgrieve.shinyapps.io/mapper/). As a starting point, have a look at the following words.
   a. *Pop-soda-coke*
   b. *Sneakers*
   c. *Y'all* (enter yall)
   d. *Fleek*
   e. *Bae*
   f. *Slay*
   g. *Squad*
      - What regional patterns can you identify?
      - Are these patterns in line with your expectations?
      - Can you find any sociolinguistic research which explains the patterns you identify in the use of these words?
3. Install the Zeeschuimer plugin (https://github.com/digitalmethodsinitiative/zeeschuimer). Now, navigate to one of the platforms that it supports. Extract some text data and download it in a readable format (e.g., TikTok comments). Manually go through the data you have collected and try to code for any novel or interesting words or spellings. Are there any words you are not familiar with?

6.9 Further Reading

Eisenstein, Jacob (2017). Identifying regional dialects in online social media. In Charles Boberg, John Nerbonne & Dominic Watt (eds.), *Handbook of Dialectology*, pp. 368–383. Chichester: Wiley-Blackwell Press.

Nini, Andrea, George Bailey, Diansheng Guo & Jack Grieve (2020). The graphical representation of phonetic dialect features of the North of England on social media. In Patrick Honeybone & Warren Maguire (eds.), *Dialect*

Writing and the North of England, pp. 266–296, Edinburgh: Edinburgh University Press.
Shoemark, Phillipa, Debnil Sur, Luke Shrimpton, Iain Murray & Sharon Goldwater (2017). Aye or naw, whit dae ye hink? Scottish independence and linguistic identity on social media. In *Proceedings of the 15th Conference of the European Chapter of the Association for Computational Linguistics: Volume 1, Long Papers*, pp. 1239–1248. Available at: https://aclanthology.org/E17-1116.pdf
Tatman, Rachael (2015). #go awn: Sociophonetic variation in variant spellings on Twitter. *Working Papers of the Linguistics Circle of the University of Victoria*, 25: 97–108.

6.10 References

Bamman, David, Jacob Eisenstein & Tyler Schnoebelen (2014). Gender identity and lexical variation in social media. *Journal of Sociolinguistics*, 18: 135–160.
Barnes, Trevor (2013). Big data, little history. *Dialogues in Human Geography*, 3(3): 297–302.
boyd, danah & Kate Crawford (2012). Critical questions for big data. *Information, Communication & Society*, 15(5): 662–679.
Cheshire, Jenny, Paul Kerswill, Sue Fox & Eivind Torgersen (2008). Ethnicity, friendship network and social practices as the motor of dialect change: Linguistic innovation in London. In Ulrich Ammon & Klaus J. Mattheier (eds.), *Sociolinguistica: International Yearbook of European Sociolinguistics*, vol. 22, pp. 1–23. Tübingen: Max Niemeyer Verlag.
Cheshire, Jenny, Paul Kerswill, Sue Fox & Eivind Torgersen (2011). Contact, the feature pool and the speech community: The emergence of Multicultural London English. *Journal of Sociolinguistics*, 15(2): 151–196.
Drummond, Rob (2018). *Researching Urban Youth Language and Identity*. Basingstoke: Palgrave Macmillan
Eisenstein, Jacob (2015). Systematic patterning in phonologically-motivated orthographic variation. *Journal of Sociolinguistics*, 19: 161–188.
Grieve, Jack, Andrea Nini & Diansheng Guo (2017). Analysing lexical emergence in American English online. *English Language & Linguistics*, 21(1): 99–127.
Grieve, Jack, Andrea Nini & Diansheng Guo (2018). Mapping lexical innovation on American social media. *Journal of English Linguistics*, 46: 293–319.
Grieve, Jack, Chris Montgomery, Andrea Nini, Arika Murakami & Diansheng Guo (2019). Mapping lexical dialect variation in British English using Twitter. *Frontiers in Artificial Intelligence*, 2: 1–18.
Grondelaers, Stefan & Stefania Marzo (2023, First View). Why does the shtyle spread? Street prestige boosts the diffusion of urban vernacular features. *Language in Society*, 52(2): 295–320.
Ilbury, Christian, Jack Grieve & David Hall (2024). Using social media to infer the diffusion of an urban contact dialect: A case study of multicultural London English. *Journal of Sociolinguistics*, 28(3): 45–70.

Jones, Taylor (2015). Toward a description of African American vernacular English dialect regions using 'Black Twitter'. *American Speech*, 90: 403–440.

Kitchin, Rob (2014). *The Data Revolution: Big Data, Open Data, Data Infrastructures and Their Consequences*. London: Sage Publications.

Nguyen, Dong, A. Seza Doğruöz, Carolyn P. Rosé & Franicska de Jong (2016). Computational sociolinguistics: A survey. *Computational Linguistics*, 42: 537–593.

Orton, Harold & Michael V. Barry (1969). *The Survey of English Dialects: The Basic Material—vol. II, The West Midland Counties*. Leeds: E. J. Arnold.

van Halteren, Hans, Roeland van Hout & Romy Roumans (2018). Tweet geography. Tweet based mapping of dialect features in Dutch Limburg. *Computational Linguistics in the Netherlands Journal*, 8: 138–162.

Wieling, Martin, Jack Grieve, Gosse Bouma, Joe Fruehwald, John Coleman & Martin Liberman (2016). Variation and change in the use of hesitation markers in Germanic languages. *Language Dynamics and Change*, 6(2): 199–234.

Willis, David (2020). Using social-media data to investigate morphosyntactic variation and dialect syntax in a lesser-used language: Two case studies from Welsh. *Glossa: A Journal of General Linguistics*, 5: 1–33.

7 Small Data Approaches

7.1 Introduction

In this chapter we cover the following topics:

- Language and interaction
- Interactional topics
    - Language alternation: Code-switching and translanguaging
    - Stylisation
    - Politeness
    - Metadiscourse
- Some limitations of these approaches.

If I asked you to think of an iconic feature of DMC, I would imagine that very many of you would say <lol>. Now, if I asked you to define what this feature meant, I bet you would say something like *'well, it originally meant 'laugh out loud', but people don't always use it to mean 'that's funny' or to signal laughter'*. That's because although <lol> originally emerged as an acronym for 'laugh out loud' and was used as a textual representation of laughter, it is now often used in ways which can't straightforwardly be interpreted as the sender signalling that something is funny. Take, for instance, the following examples from the WhatsApp conversations between a group of young Londoners:

(1)	Lisa:	So turns out he's 51 not 32
	Beth:	hahahaha omg **loooooool**
(2)	Isaiah:	Can you send me the council tax money?
	Lisa:	**lol**, yeah, dw I haven't forgot
(3)	Ria:	I've just locked myself out, fml.
	Isaiah:	**lol**, oh no. Is anyone home?
(4)	Kate:	[sends humorous meme]
	Nisha:	**LOOOOOOOL**

The examples above show us that <lol> is used in very different ways. The first function of <lol> is its prototypical function: As a signifier of laughter in a humorous conversation. For instance, in (1), Lisa has just

DOI: 10.4324/9781003391838-7

returned from a date with a man who happened to be almost 20 years older than he initially claimed to be. In the setting of an informal conversation amongst friends, this story is retold as a humorous incident. The use of <lol> in (1) therefore appears to signal laughter. Similarly, in (4), Kate has just sent Nisha a meme. The use of **<LOOOOOOL>** here suggests that Nisha finds this meme to be funny and/or entertaining. The humorous intent of these message is signalled by other linguistic markers which appear to mark the tone of the message: In (1), <lol> co-occurs with the other laughter variant, <haha>, whilst in (4), <lol> is sent in all caps and the vowel <o> is repeated – as a way of signifying intense emotion or expression.

Now contrast (1) and (4) with the use of <lol> in (2) and (3). In these two messages, it is does not appear that the topic of conversation is intended to be perceived as humorous or funny. In (2), which is from a group chat between housemates, Isaiah has sent a direct request asking Lisa to pay her share of the council tax bill. When Lisa responds, she prefaces her comment that she hasn't forgotten to pay with <lol>. Similarly, in (3), with Ria having just locked herself out of her flat, Isaiah responds using <lol> before adding a more sympathetic message. Unlike in (1) and (4), in both of these examples it does not appear that <lol> is being used to straightforwardly represent or signal laughter. Most people would agree that owing someone money or being locked out of the house are not particularly funny situations.

So, what does <lol> mean? And why is it used in contexts that are not really that funny? In order to understand the meaning of <lol> and what discourse function it performs (i.e., laughter vs. non-laughter), we need to explore how this feature is used within specific moments of the conversation. This approach means considering not just the quantitative distribution of <lol>, but crucially analysing the *contexts in which it is used* and *what functions it performs in those contexts*. This includes consideration of the possibility that <lol> might *sometimes* function in more complex ways than simply signalling laughter. It may, as in these examples, signal interactional qualities like sarcasm or fulfil a more mundane role like acknowledging receipt of a message.

The approach we've started to sketch out here is quite different to that discussed in Chapter 6. In the previous chapter, we introduced a set of 'big' data approaches which explain language variation in relation to users' membership of 'macro-level' categories like their age, ethnicity, and regional background. As we saw in Chapter 6, many of these analyses attempt to identify significant correlations between users' social identities (e.g., African American) and linguistic features (e.g., t/d deletion). The present chapter introduces an altogether different set of approaches which can be grouped together under the heading of 'small' data analyses. The focus here is not on correlations between macro-social demographic categories and linguistic features but rather on the interactional or discourse function of linguistic variation.

Before we introduce these approaches, a word of warning is needed regarding the qualifier of 'small' in the chapter heading. As in the case of 'big' data approaches, the 'small' label does not refer (necessarily) to the size of the dataset. Rather, it refers to types of methodological tools and analytical approaches that are employed to understand the 'small' (or 'micro') details of conversation and interaction. Research in this area focusses on describing discourse-level phenomena like the turn-by-turn negotiation of identities, the inferred meaning of messages, and the diverse range of functions that features like <lol> fulfil. In what follows, we introduce this approach in more detail, focussing on four main interactional topics (language alternation, stylisation, politeness, and metadiscourse).

7.2 Language and Interaction

As noted above, the 'small data' label refers to the types of tools and approaches that researchers use to understand *micro-level* (i.e., discourse) phenomena. Researchers working in this area use a variety of tools and concepts from different subfields of linguistics including:

- Discourse analysis
- Conversation analysis
- Interactional (socio-)linguistics
- Linguistic ethnography.

Lots of work has effectively applied concepts, approaches, and theories developed to account for spoken language phenomena to DMC. Researchers working in this area have employed micro-analytical approaches to describe topics such as the use of narratives and 'small stories' in social media (e.g., Georgakopoulou, 2014; Page, 2018), the sequential organisation of conversation in DMC (e.g., Herring, 1999; König, 2019), and the discursive properties of 'hate speech' (e.g., Retta, 2023; Ermida, 2023).

The goal of this type of work is to consider how people negotiate meaning in interaction. This means exploring how people use words, conversational styles, formulaic expressions, and other types of conversational features to express what they mean. Typically, micro-level analyses have focussed on the minute detail of interaction in audio and/or video recordings. Researchers who apply these approaches to DMC have gathered datasets comprising interactions from platforms such as WhatsApp, Tinder, and IM. One particularly productive area of research has been to understand how individuals discursively (i.e., through language) construct and reproduce their identities in and through DMC.

One core concept in analyses of language and interaction is **contextualisation cues**. Essentially, contextualisation cues are signalling mechanisms that are used by people to indicate what they mean by what they say. In spoken interaction, this includes paralinguistic features like pitch, tempo, loudness, as well as facial expressions such as smiling, raising your eyebrows, and so on. In most contexts, when we are interacting with someone in face-to-face communication, we can determine whether they're being honest, sarcastic, or hurtful by making inferences based on the contextualisation cues they use. For instance, imagine you are going clothes shopping with your friends. You enter a store, try on a new outfit, and want a second opinion. You come out of the dressing room and ask your friend whether they like the outfit. In response, your friend says 'I love it'. This simple utterance could mean one of two things:

1. They genuinely like the new outfit
2. They're being sarcastic – they hate the outfit.

To ascertain the meaning of your friend's comment 'I love it', you will likely use contextualisation cues to determine whether they are being serious or not. If they intended this to be a faithful comment – that really do like your outfit – then it's likely they will use contextualisation cues such as a high rising intonation to signal their approval or they might show this through paralinguistic cues, such as smiling whilst saying 'I love it'. Whereas if they are being they sarcastic, they might use falling intonation and a grimacing facial expression. All of these cues – intonation, facial expression, and so on – help us ascertain the intended meaning of an utterance that potentially has a range of different possible interpretations.

Now, contextualisation cues in DMC work a little differently. In most DMC contexts we do not have access to the full range of contextualisation cues that we have in face-to-face or spoken interaction. This is because DMC is often text-based (e.g., WhatsApp, SMS, Email, and so on) so we cannot infer what someone means by what they say based on their facial expressions, intonation, or body language. Without these cues, it is possible that messages will be misinterpreted. How many times have you received an email or DM and thought 'I am not quite sure how to interpret this message' or 'are they being rude or are they just in a rush?'. A couple of years ago, one of my friends mentioned to me that a mutual acquaintance was annoyed with her. When I asked her why, she said it was because all of her texts ended with a 'full stop' <.>. When I explained that using the <.> at the end of messages was her 'style' and that she used this style regardless of her interlocutor, my friend was surprised as thought this was 'rude' or 'abrupt'. In other words, she has misinterpreted the <.> as a contextualisation cue.

Points for reflection

- What strategies or resources do you use in DMC to account for the lack of some contextualisation cues? Hint: Emoji!
- Have you ever received or sent a message which has been misinterpreted? If the answer is yes, what was the cause of the misunderstanding? Could the lack of contextualisation cues have been a factor?

Because our text messages can be interpreted in several different ways, users will often use orthographic and typographic features in creative ways to signal what they mean by what they say. Take, for instance, the following hypothetical SMS messages:

(5) What are you doing
(6) What are you doing?
(7) What are you doing?!
(8) What are you doing?! 😊
(9) What are you doing?!:)

The examples in (5)–(9) are different ways of representing the same text message: 'What are you doing?'. Imagine you have just received these five texts. Now, depending on what stylistic and orthographic features accompany the message, we could interpret this message in four different ways. In (5) and (6), it seems likely that the user wants their message to be interpreted as a straightforward question (it is possible, however, that the omission of <?> in (5) is socially meaningful, but we'll leave this for now!). However, the meaning of <?!> in the other two examples is less clear. In (7), <?!> could signal something like 'what [the hell] are you doing?!' or it could mean 'what are you doing?! [I'm excited to know]'. The addition of the 'Smiling Face with Smiling Eyes (😊) emoji in (8) or the :) emoticon in (9), however, clarifies the meaning of <?!>. It seems at the very least that the message is intended to be friendly. In this way, the emoji in (8) and emoticon in (9) both function as contextualisation cues to help the receiver infer the true meaning of the message, i.e., what the sender meant.

7.3 Emoticons and Emoji

As we saw in the previous examples, emoticons and emoji often function as contextualisation cues in DMC. 'Emoticons' are pictorial representations of facial expressions that are created through punctuation marks, letters, and numbers, as in (9). These features were especially common in older genres of text-based DMC, such as SMS and Emails. Popular emoticons include:

- :) 'smiley'
- :-P 'tongue sticking out'
- :O 'surprise'
- ;) 'winking'
- :('unhappy'.

Interestingly, emotions exhibit a degree of cultural variation. For instance, the happy emoticons :) :-) = :D are most commonly used in the West (e.g., USA, UK, Europe), whilst in East Asia, 'kaomoji' (literally 'face characters') are more frequently used, e.g., (^ u ^)or (^ v ^) 'happy'.

In more recent forms of DMC, emoticons have gradually been displaced by emoji. 'Emoji' is a Japanese word which literally means 'picture letter'. These are digital icons that are used to express ideas, thoughts, emoticons, and activities. Emoji are particularly common in text-based forms of DMC such as WhatsApp, iMessage, and Snapchat. Popular emoji include the 💀 'skull', 😭 'loudly crying face', and 🏊 'person swimming'. Some work on the use of emoji (particularly those that are not related to facial expressions) has suggested that emoji can substitute for words in two ways. The first is 'calquing', referring to those emoji that are literal, word-for-word 'translations' of words. The second is the 'rebus principle', where the emoji is used to refer to its sound rather than its literal meaning to represent a new word (Danesi, 2016). Some examples include:

- Calquing: 💣 🐚 👙 'bomb shell bikini', 🎤🌧 'singing in the rain'
- Rebus: 🐝🍃 'believe', 📖🐦 'book a flight'

As we saw above in example (7), emoji (and by extension, emoticons) often function as contextualisation cues. As we don't have access to facial expressions in text-based forms of DMC, users will often employ emoticons or emoji that reference gestures, faces, and emotions to signal how that message should be interpreted. Consider, for instance, the following examples in (10) and (11).

(10) I hate you 😠
(11) I hate you 😂

The message 'I hate you' has two different meanings in (10) and (11). In (10), the use of 😠 suggests that this message is to be taken at face value – the sender really does dislike the receiver – whilst the use of 😂 in (11) infers that this message is sarcastic or tongue-in-cheek. The fact that emoticons and emoji function as contextualisation cues suggests that both features play a much more complex role in DMC than simply conveying emotion, as is often assumed in popular discourse. Dresner and Herring (2010) argue that emoticons indicate the illocutionary force (i.e., the intention) of the message, as opposed to simply conveying valence or emotion. For instance, they suggest that the use of the emoticon ;-) in a message does not convey some single emotion but rather it signals some joking intent. Similar types of arguments are proposed by Skovholt, Grønning, and Kankaanranta (2014) in their study of emoticons in workplace emails. In that paper, the authors argue that emoticons fulfil three main interactional functions. These are:

1. When following email signatures like 'have a nice day :-)', emoticons signal a positive attitude.
2. When following utterances that should be interpreted as humorous, emoticons signal that the message is a joke/irony, e.g., 'I am 36. I have never had a car. However, I have driven others' cars since I was 18, without making a scratch, but that doesn't count, I guess. :-)'.
3. When following expressive speech acts such as thanks and greetings or directives such as requests and corrections, they function as hedges. They can either strengthen the meaning of the message, e.g., 'great and thanks :-)' or soften the meaning of the message, e.g., 'A little Friday moaning from here :-)'.

Given that emoji appear to function in ways more complex than simply signalling emotion, it is perhaps unsurprising that other research on emoji has found that these features are used by authors to do complex interactional work. For instance, Ge-Stadnyk (2021) analyses the use of emoji across Twitter and Weibo, focussing on the ways in which influencers use emoji sequences when engaging in identity performances. She finds that emoji are not necessarily written expressions of attitudes, gestures, and behaviours but rather they often introduce new meanings to messages. More specifically, Ge-Stadnyk argues that emoji are often used to add emotional appeals (e.g., affection, sympathy, flattery), making their messages more emotionally expressive. This includes messages such as those in (12) and (13):

(12) Happy new year 带着兄弟祝福所有人🙏🙏🙏❤❤❤
'Happy New Year. (I) and my brothers send our best wishes to everyone'
(13) DIY Blotting Paper using @Starbucks tissues & setting powder.
No more oily skin 🙅😉

According to Ge-Stadnyk, all of these emoji modify the 'tone' of the message. That is, they make the message seem less forceful or more friendly. Ge-Stadnyk notes that this practice is especially common amongst influencers. This is perhaps unsurprising given that influencers often attempt to perform a friendly and relatable persona to generate and maintain user engagement.

Points for reflection

- If you use a platform that supports emoji (e.g., WhatsApp, Snapchat), navigate to a recent conversation. Scroll through the chat and take note of the emoji in the conversation. Which emoji do you use most? Are there any emoji that are used for novel or abstract reasons (e.g., the peach emoji 🍑 which is rarely used to refer to the fruit!)?

A similar interactional approach to emoji is found in Gibson's (2024) analysis of Spanish and Danish conversations on the dating platform, Tinder. The focus in that paper is on 'wink emoji' subtypes e.g., 🤪, 😉, and their use in certain 'conversational routines', specifically in 'flirting'. The goal here is to understand *why* people use the wink emoji subtypes and *what* their function is. Example (14) is taken from Gibson's (2024: 13) analysis of the Danish dataset. In this example, we see that the 'wink' emoji 🤪 is used as part of P5's attempt to flirt with EM. The use of 🤪 here, according to Gibson fulfils a nuanced interactional function: It 'downgrades' the flirtation by marking the comment 'I would rather lie under your duvet' as one that has been made in jest.

(14)	1	EM	Vil du låne en bluse af mig?
	2	P5	'Do you want to borrow a shirt from me?' Tror hellere jeg vil ligge under din dyne 🤪
	3	EM	'Think I would rather lie under your duvet 🤪' Nå, men dem har jeg kun en af, og bruger den for ofte til at låne ud
	4	P5	'Oh, but those I only have one of, and I use it too often to borrow/ lend it' Og du deler den heller ikke? 'And you don't share it either?'

Emoji are just one type of resource that users of DMC can employ to signal what they mean. In the remainder of the chapter, we develop our understanding of 'small data' approaches by focussing on four main topics: Language alternation, stylisation, politeness, and metadiscourse. I first start out introducing the general area of study before relating this more specifically to research on DMC.

7.4 Language Alternation

If you are proficient in more than one language, it's highly likely that you will switch or alternate between the different languages you are familiar with. For instance, you might use one language when you're with your family and another with friends. Or you might use one language when you're at work, and another when you are home. These types of practices are very typical of bi- and multi-lingual interaction. Consider, for instance, the following interaction (Extract (15)) between Eleni and her husband, Nikos. Eleni and Nikos are bilingual: They both speak English and Greek:

(15)	1	Eleni	What are we having for dinner tonight?
	2	Nikos	We're having κεφτεδάκια με ρύζι 'We're having meatballs with rice'
	3	Eleni	Καλά, νόστιμο 'good, delicious'
	4	Nikos	It'll be half an hour, εντάξει; 'It'll be half an hour, ok?'
	5	Eleni	Ναί, ok! 'Yes, ok!'

In the above extract, Nikos and Eleni can be seen to alternate between the two languages, English and Greek. Although the conversation opens in English, when the dish (line 2: 'meatballs with rice') is introduced, Nikos switches to Greek. Eleni then responds in Greek with her assessment of the dish (line 3: 'good, delicious'). As the conversation unfolds, we see that Nikos and Eleni continue to alternate between English and Greek. Switching in this way is a very common practice amongst those who are proficient in more than one language.

The above example demonstrates one type of 'language alternation'. In sociolinguistics, a great deal of research has been done on a type of language alternation called **'code-switching'**. This term refers to the common practice where individuals are seen to alternate or 'switch' between two or more languages in a single conversation, such as the example above. Researchers will often distinguish between shifting within a sentence (*intra*sentential or code-mixing) and across sentence boundaries (*inter*sentential or code-switching). Some examples are found below in (16) and (17):

(16)	**Code-mixing:**	We're having κεφτεδάκια με ρύζι 'We're having meatballs and rice'
(17)	**Code-switching:**	Πάω σπίτι. I will sleep well tonight. 'I'm going home. I will sleep well tonight'

A common misconception is that bi- or multi-linguals shift between languages because they simply 'don't know the word in one language or another'. However, sociolinguistic research has found that people code-switch for much more complex social and stylistic reasons. People often switch between different languages to achieve a range of different communicative goals including role-play, establishing their identities, or marking conversational emphasis. Because switching is motivated by certain communicative goals, the output is not a random combination of two or more languages. Language alternation is rule-governed and systematic. Decades of sociolinguistic research has demonstrated that when people code-switch, the syntactic rules of both languages are respected.

Returning to example (15), it is possible to present a hypothesis as to *why* Nikos switches between English and Greek. Note that Nikos initially switches to Greek when he introduces the dish he is cooking. We could therefore propose that the switch occurs in relation to the topic of the conversation: A Greek meal. This type of language alternation based on topic is what sociolinguists call **metaphorical** code-switching. On the other hand, when people alternate between languages on the basis of the situation or speech context, we can refer to this as **situational** switching. An example of situational switching is when speakers use a language like Greek at home with family but English at work with colleagues.

Key Term: Code-Switching

Code-switching is the use of two or more languages in interaction. People will often switch between two or more languages in a single sentence (i.e., **code-mixing**: We're having κεφτεδάκια με ρύζι) or across different sentences (i.e., **code-switching**: Πάω σπίτι. I will sleep well tonight).

So far, we've discussed language alternation between two languages: English and Greek. Our analysis suggests that it is fairly easy to disentangle when one or the other language is being used. One interpretation of this approach to language alternation is that the different languages we switch between are stored as cognitively different systems. However, in some multilingual contexts, it is harder to distinguish between languages, especially if there are multiple languages involved. Where does one language begin and the other end? Take, for instance, the following extract from Wei (2023: 4). The extract is taken from a spoken recording in which the individual can be seen to use features of Chinese, Japanese, and English throughout the dialogue:

(18) **ああそうそうそうそう**(*ah so so so so* 'Oh yeah yeah yeah yeah'), sorry, 我给 (*wo gei* 'I get') confused/的了(*de la* – aspect marker. 'I got them confused/mixed up.'). **あの** (*ano* – discourse marker), 我明天(*wo mingtian* 'I tomorrow') bring you 啦 (la - utterance particle. 'I will bring it to you tomorrow.'), okay 好吗 (*hao ma* 'okay')?
(unmarked font: English, **bold**: Japanese; underlined: Chinese)

In example (18) above, it seems difficult to argue that the speaker is *switching* between English, Japanese, and Chinese. Words, sentences, phrases, and discourse particles from all three languages appear to be entangled. Although this type of utterance may look unusual, in highly multilingual contexts, individuals are often seen to engage in these types of interactions. It is very difficult to isolate where one language starts and another ends.

To account for these multilingual practices, researchers have introduced the concept of **translanguaging**. The main argument here is that multilingual individuals do not switch between language [X] and language [Y]. The languages are not stored as separate systems in the mind. But rather, when people interact, they strategically select features from a single linguistic repertoire for strategic reasons like identity and language creativity.

Key Term: Translanguaging

A theory of language alternation that views languages as part of a single repertoire. According this theory, when individuals interact, they do not 'switch' between separate languages, but rather they draw on a multitude of different linguistic resources.

Importantly then, whilst both concepts capture aspects of language alternation, translanguaging is different from code-switching in that it refers not simply to a shift or an alternation between two or more languages. Rather, it views bi-/multi-linguals as having access to a fluid repertoire of linguistic resources that cannot be easily assigned to a single language or variety. The *trans-* prefix in the term translanguaging refers to the transcending of distinct and, supposedly, artificial boundaries of named languages.

7.4.1 Language Alternation in Digital Communication

When multilingual users interact in DMC, it is inevitable that they will use similar multilingual strategies to those that we described above with reference to spoken interactions. Take, for instance, the following conversations (Extracts (19) and (20)) analysed by Dorleijn & Nortier (2009: 137–139). In the first example, a user is seen to switch between English (in bold) and Dutch when posting to the online forum, www.maroc.nl. In the second example, the user switches between Turkish (in bold) and Dutch in a message posted to www.TurkishTexas.nl:

(19) **Ok, I admit,** maar h0e wil je dan 00it **mr Right** vinden als je t0ch geen relaties mag aangaan . . . behalve het huwelijk?
'OK, I admit, but how will you ever find Mr Right if you're not allowed to have any relations. . . except marriage?'

(20) Is er geen moppen topic of zo, **fikralar topigi falan var, mop guzel ama, her mopa bir topic acilirsa,** is een beetje onnodig.
'Isn't there a topic for jokes, there is a special topic for jokes, joke(s) (are) nice but, if a topic is opened for every joke, it is a bit too much.'

In both examples, we see evidence for language alternation: The use of Dutch and English or Turkish. What language someone chooses to post in is likely to be motivated by interactional concerns like conversational cues, the negotiation of identity, and the relevance of the language to the topic. In the above examples, we see that the use of English in (19) is limited to stock phrases (e.g., 'Ok', 'mr Right'), whilst the use of Turkish in (20) is heavily embedded in Dutch. Dorleijn & Nortier interpret these linguistic practices with reference to the status of the Turkish and Moroccan communities in the Netherlands more generally.

Points for reflection

- If you speak more than one language, reflect on your multilingual practices in DMC.
  - Do you write messages in more than one language?
  - Does it depend on the addressee or audience?
  - Or does the language choice relate to the topic or style of interaction?

Similar themes are explored by Deumert and Vold Lexander's (2013) in their work on 'texting Africa'. In that project, the authors analyse the texting practices of people from five African nations: Côte d'Ivoire, Ghana, Nigeria, Senegal and South Africa. To answer their research questions, Deumert and Vold Lexander draw on a variety of different corpora collected during several research projects:

- **Sengalese corpus** (2005–7): 450 text messages from individuals aged between 20 and 28 years

- **South African corpus** (2008): 2269 text messages from individuals aged between 18 and 22 years
- **Ghanian corpus** (2011): 457 text messages from individuals aged between 16 and 25 years
- **Nigerian corpus** (2011): 199 text messages from individuals aged between 16 and 25 years
- **Côte d'Ivorian corpus** (2011): 35 text messages from individuals aged between 16 and 40 years.

All of these settings are highly multilingual. Typically, speakers from these countries will be proficient in the former colonial language (i.e., English or French) and a local African language (e.g., Wolof in Senegal, Ewe in Ghana). The analysis explores the use of different linguistic resources (e.g., non-standard spellings, different languages) by the texters and the different functions of those features in conversation. Focussing on multilingualism in the corpora, the authors find that the dominant style of texting is in the former colonial languages, i.e., English or French. This is different to spoken interactions which the authors suggest would usually be conducted in the local language. This perhaps unexpected finding leads the authors to explore the social meanings of the different languages in texting. They propose that the use of African languages may be considered marked and so any type of switch or shift would carry some type of socio-symbolic meaning. To explore this possibility in more depth, Deumert and Vold Lexander examine the contexts in which the different languages are used. One such example is found in (21) which is taken from the Senegalese corpus (2013: 538):

(21) Sama téy bunek dina gathiel sama demb rawatina sama euleuk ngir sama thiofél pour yaw. Yay sama xol, yay **qui** tax ma beug téki tuki ted terala **jtm**
'My present will dishonour my past, even more so my future, when it comes to my love for you. You, my heart, you, who make me want to travel, to succeed and make sure that you don't miss anything. I love you'

In the extract, the texter uses features of French (in bold) and Wolof (the national language of Senegal) interchangeably. The authors argue that the choice of language is not random but is rather motivated by the social meanings of the different languages. Based on the patterns they identify, the authors argue that French is often used by the texters to express strong romantic feelings, whilst Wolof is used to communicate a more measured form of love. In this way, writing in the former colonial language (i.e., English or French) allows writers to perform the 'persona of a skilful writer' whilst African languages can be used to create intimacy as they have come to index "sincerity and seriousness as well as respect for the addressee" (2013: 541). Here we see how the choice of language used in the text messages is motivated by the interactional functions that each language can perform or convey.

Another example of multilingual practices in DMC can be found in Seargeant, Tagg, and Ngampramuan's (2012) work on language choice and addressivity strategies in Thai-English interactions. The focus in this study is on the motivations and functions of code-switching in status updates, wall postings and comments to Facebook. The authors find that code-mixing tends to occur when the message is directed at a specific individual, as in the following example (22) between Mint and Aum:

(22) Mint: seng mak loey gae sia dai roob a! kong har mai jer laew **cus lost** nai maddox **anyway thanks** mak mak na jaa **see you soon** na aum:)
'{I'm} very bored! It's a pity that all the photos are gone. I can't find them because I lost them in Maddox. Anyway, thanks a lot. See you soon, Aum'
Aum: **thank u** jaa … . **Love u lots** naaaa:)) xxx

In Extract (22), we see how the users, Mint and Aum, switch between English (in bold) and Thai in their messages. Here, the choice of language is influenced by the social meanings of the language, as well as its discourse function. More specifically, the authors observe that English is used in discourse-organising phrases and closings, whilst Thai discourse particles are used to heighten the intimacy of the conversation, much like the use of African languages in Deumert and Vold Lexander (2013). These choices, the authors argue, are tied to an awareness of the site's affordances and also the users' sensitivity to the addressee.

A related case study is found in Ren and Guo's (2024) analysis of the translanguaging practices used in posts on the Chinese social media platform Weibo (Extract (23)). Their analysis considers 300 self-praise posts from 52 young Chinese Weibo users, focussing on the use of multimodal resources (e.g., emoji, photos, videos), multilingual resources (e.g., different languages), and multi-semiotic resources (e.g., hashtags, punctuation marks) that users employ in self-praise posts. The authors find that Chinese Weibo users displayed a high level of linguistic creativity by mixing Chinese characters with other linguistic features and varieties. This included the combination of Chinese with English, as in the following example (2024: 365):

(23) 洗完澡就觉得自己很beautiful [附作者漂亮的自拍照片]
'Feeling very beautiful after taking a shower'
[The post was followed by a beautiful selfie of the author.]

In this example, Ren and Guo (2024) argue that the combination of the Chinese intensifier '很 (very)' and the English word 'beautiful', rather than using the Chinese word '漂亮 (piao liang)', has the effect of mitigating the intensification of how beautiful she is. Apparently, such mitigation of intensification is a common strategy in the speech of young people from China. In other examples, however, Chinese is combined with English in novel ways. For instance, in the following extract, the user combines Chinese characters with the English progressive suffix *-ing*. Chinese does not indicate the state of the verb through the addition of suffixes, rather the character '在 zai' is used to show the progressive state of a verb (Extract (24)).

(24) 踏青ing [附作者踏青的照片]
'Trekking'
[The post was followed by the author's photos of trekking.]

Ren and Guo (2024) argue that these types of multilingual practices can be interpreted as authors asserting their bilingual identities. By flexibly using elements of English and Chinese, they construct their online identity as 'global citizen'. They observe that such practices often lead to the formation of new scripts, that are created in novel and playful ways (e.g., the use of English suffixes on Chinese characters). In this way, the authors conclude that the use of different linguistic resources cannot be understood as users switching between separate codes, but rather can be interpreted as the translanguaging practices of multilingual users online.

7.5 Stylisation

In the above section, we introduced language alternation to describe when individuals switch between two or more different languages. In this section, we introduce a slightly different type of alternation where individuals can be heard to 'stylise' a variety or language.

To briefly recapitulate a few basic facts, very early on in this book we established that all speakers have an accent. This accent is likely related to the social background of the speaker, such as where they grew up (e.g., Boston, Singapore, etc.) or other aspects of their social background or identity such as their social class, gender identity, or sexuality. In most contexts, people will speak in a way that is expected or 'unmarked'. It is their *habitual* speech style.

But people don't always do this. Sometimes people speak in an accent or style that is different to how they would usually speak. This style is highly marked as it deviates from their habitual speech style. For instance, a young White person from London is likely to habitually speak in a variety of London English. When they speak using a variety of London English, this style is unmarked and unnoticed by most people because it is their habitual speech style. But if they decide to 'put on' a Jamaican English accent, this style is marked because it deviates from how we expect them to sound or speak. This accent may also be markedly different from those who authentically speak the dialect and may sound intentionally performed or hyper-stylised.

What we've been describing above is what sociolinguists have called **stylisation**. In stylised performances, speakers produce "specially marked and often exaggerated representations of languages, dialects, and styles that lie outside their own habitual repertoire" (Rampton, 2009: 149). These types of practices are very common in media, such as in films and TV programmes where actors are often required to emulate the speech style of a character or popular figure.

Key Term: Stylisation

The use of a voice or linguistic variety that is different to how the individual *usually* speaks. Often, stylised performances are exaggerated versions of the variety. For instance, an individual who speaks American English may 'stylise' British English when quoting the speech of their friend who is from the UK.

In addition to media such as TV and film, people can often be heard to stylise dialects in everyday interactions. Stylisation is especially common in retellings of stories and events when speakers perform the voice of a friend, family member, or character. Imagine, if you will, that you are telling your friends about a conversation with a fellow passenger at the bus stop. The passenger happened to be from Australia. When you retell the story, you quote what she said. It is possible that you will perform or 'stylise' the accent of the passenger to make the story more engaging. We do this type of stylisation all the time.

Importantly, when we stylise, we not only emulate the accent or dialect being used but we also perform the identity that is associated with that variety. This could be some recognisable individual (e.g., Queen Elizabeth II, the woman at the bus stop) or some imagined person (e.g., a valley girl, a teacher). Take, for instance, the following Extract (25) in which the Iranian-British comedian Omid Djalili stylises an imagined voice of an individual who has invited him to Dubai:

(25) [British English – habitual voice] When you go there, they always give you some kind of er… there's always a guy who goes [Arabic accented English] "Omid, you come here, you come to Dubai, we are the Las Vegas of the Middle East" (www.youtube.com/watch?v=4yRMNoWeIY0)

In the above example, Djalili switches from his habitual and expected speech style (British English) to a hyper-stylised variety (Arabic accented English) to not only make the story more engaging but also to perform the identity of his interlocutor. As this example is taken from a popular British stand-up comedy programme, we would likely conclude that the stylisation is employed to add humour to the story. As the routine progresses, Djalili voices multiple different characters (an Italian waiter, Godzilla, an Iranian tribute band) that are intended to be perceived as humorous and add 'life' to the story.

Here, we see that the routine is successful in generating humour because there is an intentional disconnect between the individual's expected voice/identity and the voice/identity performed. As in the example of Djalili's stylisation above, the performance is not intended to be taken at face value. In other words, Djalili does not expect the audience to perceive the voice/identity as his own. Nor does he expect the audience to perceive this as a faithful replication of how the individual actually spoke. This paradox is what Coupland (2007) has called **strategic inauthenticity**. It is precisely that the performance is recognised as inauthentic that it is considered humorous and/or entertaining.

Stylisation has often been analysed using concepts borrowed from the works of literary scholar and philosopher Mikhail Bakhtin. Of relevance here is Bakhtin's concepts of **polyphony** and **heteroglossia**. From this perspective, it is argued that language is not original or unique but rather it references the voices of people with whom that language is associated. In other words, when we use certain words, phrases, and accents, we not only speak or interact, but we reference images of the person or people who have used that language before.

Because language is polyphonous, when people stylise, they not only perform a voice, but they also perform the *identity* of the (imagined) person we associate with that voice. In stylisation, we can be seen to voice the stylised identity for our own purposes – what has been termed **double-voicing**. An often-made division is between so-called **uni-** and **vari-directional voicing**. In uni-directional voicing, the individual is seen to align themselves with the voice/identity of the performed style. For instance, this is often the case when people who are not speakers of African American Vernacular English use features of the variety to index their engagement in Hip-Hop. Vari-directional voicing, on the other hand, occurs when individuals attempt to mock or denigrate the voice/identity of the style that they perform. This occurs, for instance, when individuals parody a speakers' voice or way of interacting.

The type of identity that we reference or perform in stylisation is often a type of **characterological figure**. This is a socially recognisable identity or persona that can be performed and enacted by users (Agha, 2007: 177). Often, these figures have recognisable labels that people use and circulate in public discourse. Identities like the 'valley girl' and the 'roadman' have become recognised as distinctive identities that are associated with particular ways of speaking and being.

> **Key Term: Characterological Figures**
>
> Socially recognisable identities that are associated with certain activities, beliefs and language varieties, and can be performed by users. These personae are often labelled as in the case of the 'valley girl', 'Karen', the 'roadman', or the 'bro'.

A particular type of stylisation which has attracted a lot of attention in sociolinguistics is **crossing**. First introduced by Ben Rampton, language crossing refers to moments of stylisation that appear to move across ethnic and/or social boundaries. In his seminal work, Rampton (1995) analyses crossing in the speech of young people at a secondary school, called Ashmead. In that work, he analyses the use of an English-based Creole amongst young people of Anglo and Asian descent, the use of Punjabi by Anglo and Caribbean speakers, and the stylisation of Asian English by all three groups. Unlike in the example of Djalili above, the young people at Ashmead used crossing for a variety of different functions, not just humour. Rampton argues that these practices are important in the construction of a 'youth identity'. In specific contexts of use, crossing can help establish social solidarity across different ethnic groups, helping build friendships amongst the young people.

> **Key Term: Crossing**
>
> A subtype of stylisation that refers to when people transgress ethnic and/or social boundaries. This occurs, for instance, when a White speaker is heard to 'put on' (or stylise) an ethnic speech variety, such as Indian English or Jamaican English that they do not habitually speak.

7.5.1 Stylisation in Digital Communication

In the above section, we introduced and discussed stylisation as a feature of spoken language. Although a lot of sociolinguistic research has focussed on stylisation in face-to-face interaction, more recent work has analysed stylisation in DMC. This includes work which has explored how users stylise non-standard spellings, typographic features, and memes to perform recognisable characterological figures and to perform interactional routines. Consider, for instance, the following WhatsApp exchange (Extract 26) taken from a conversation between a group of young Londoners:

(26)	1	Mark	Ok! I'll meet yaaa
	2	Abi	Yeah George
	3		I'm walking up the road
	4	Stef	We're in the garden bbz
	5	Abi	Cooooool
	6	Abi	C u in a min
	7	Mark	You guys still there?
	8	Abi	Yeeeeee

In the above example, Mark has just agreed to meet his friends at the pub ('the George'). This extract is interesting because we see that Mark, Stef, and Abi alternate between a more standard style of English ('I'm walking up the road) and a more stereotypically DMC style, what some have labelled 'txtspeak' ('C u in a min'; see Chapter 2). If we examine the rest of their messages in detail, we see that all three individuals who use 'txtspeak' primarily use Standardised English spellings in the vast majority of their messages. It seems possible then that the use of non-standard spellings (e.g., 'C u in a min', 'bbz', 'yaaa') represent a type of language stylisation. However, beyond simply identifying stylisation, a goal in small-data approaches to DMC would be to explain *why* the users stylise in this way. In other words, we are interested in understanding the motivations of spelling 'see' as <C> and 'you' as <u>.

In the above example, which I have analysed elsewhere, I suggest that the users stylise elements of 'txtspeak' because of the long-standing association of these spellings with the 'informal' nature of DMC. In other words, the non-standard spellings (e.g., <C> and <u>) function as contextualisation cues to help the interlocutor interpret the tone of the conversation. If we consider the context of this interaction – a group of friends who are organising a friendly drink – it seems reasonable to assume that users are likely to employ strategies to signal to each other that this is a casual, informal, conversation. It is possible, then, that certain words, spellings, and other typographical features are used to 'key' or signal the exchange as a casual conversation. In this extract, we see that the use of <C> and <u> occur alongside representations of lengthened vowels in words like <Coooooool> and <yaaa>, as well as expressive features like the exclamation mark, which appear to be combined as cues to contextualise or 'key' this as a casual conversation.

Points for reflection

- Do you stylise any language varieties in your own DMC? If so, why?
- Does it depend on the audience or addressee?

A similar type of analysis and approach is found in work by Tagg (2016) where she explores the texting practices of a young English woman called Laura. In that paper, Tagg focusses on the creative orthographic strategies that Laura utilises in her texts to perform aspects of her identity, as well as achieve certain interactional goals. The types of features that Tagg analyses includes:

'Non-speech-related respellings'

- Vowel deletion (e.g., <spk>, <gd>)
- Standard clippings (e.g., <thurs>, <mins>)
- Missing apostrophes (e.g., <im>, <dont>).

'Typographic features'

- Missing capitals (e.g., <monday>, <i>)
- All capitals (e.g., 'GO ON, Jonny!')
- Emoticons (:-xx).

'Speech-related respellings'

- TH-fronting (<wiv>, <bruvver>)
- Schwa-representation (<ya>, <ye>, <fella>)
- Letter repetition (<sooo>, <ahhh>, <woo>, <whyyye>).

'Intimate/conversational register'

- Discourse markers (e.g., 'so', 'oh')
- Informal/slang words (e.g., 'grub', 'quid')
- Response tokens (e.g., 'okay', 'nah').

'Language creativity'

- Word play (e.g., 'chish and fips')
- Self-repetition (e.g., 'I think this is your number. This is my number. I think.')
- Metacommentary (e.g., 'Cor, had to teach my phone lots of new words there!').

Tagg's paper combines ethnographic interviews with quantitative and interactional analyses to explore the language choices that Laura makes in her text messages. The first part of the analysis identifies features that are particularly common in Laura's messages by comparing her usage with a larger corpus (CorTxt) collected by Tagg. The analysis reveals that respellings such as <u>, <wot> and omitted apostrophes are significantly more frequent in Laura's text-messages than in CorTxt. For instance, in Laura's messages, <wot> is used in place of <what> in 85% of cases, whilst <u> is used in place of <you> in 55.9% of the time. The high frequency of non-standard spellings in Laura's messages suggests that she attributes some symbolic value to these features.

In the second part of her analysis, Tagg explores the discourse function of features such as <wot> and <u> in Laura's texts. Tagg argues that they are often used by Laura to fulfil some interactional function, such as parodying the voices of others (i.e., stylisation), signalling shifts in footing (i.e., conversational alignment), or to indicate the 'key' (or intent) of the message. Consider, for instance, the following example (27):

(27) Ok that would b lovely, if u r sure. Think about wot u want to do, drinkin, dancin, eatin, cinema, in, out, about... Up to u! Wot about Sammy? X
(Tagg, 2016: 73)

In this extract, we see that non-standard spellings such as the representation of (ING) <drinkin>, <dancin>, <eatin> and abbreviations <b>, <u>, <r> for *be, you, are,* often occur in combination in Laura's texts. Tagg argues that Laura uses these features in this way to create 'conversational informality'. In other words, she stylises features of what we might consider to be 'txtspeak' to draw on their association with informality and casualness to indicate how the intent of the message, in a very similar way to Extract (25). Thus, these non-standard spellings act as contextualisation cues to help the audience or interlocutor understand the intention of a message.

In my own work, I have argued that this type of stylisation is particularly common in social media. And, more recently, with the emergence of multimodal and video-based social media, stylised performances are increasingly commonplace. A nice example of stylisation on TikTok is the #AccentChallenge trend which went viral on the platform in 2023. The challenge involved users uploading videos where they attempted to mimic (or stylise) social and regional speech styles. This viral trend led to videos such as that in Figure 7.1. In the video, the user who elsewhere speaks in a General American accent, can be seen to stylise a variety of different speech styles. This includes national accents ('Indian', 'French', 'Malaysian') and also some accents that are linked to character-types/types of people ('valley girl', 'roadman'). If we focus on the segment in which the user stylises the 'valley girl' (the transcription is provided), we see that this accent – and relatedly the identity – is performed through a number of different linguistic features that become highly associated with this identity label:

Figure 7.1 An example of the #AccentChallenge on TikTok

- High Rising Terminals (HRTs): The use of a rising intonation on a declarative statement
- Discourse marker *like* as in '*like I'm literally like annoying myself*'
- Creaky voice
- Nasal voice.

(28) Ok, but like, which American one? Cos American's are literally gonna come for you. Right, valley girl. Ok, yeah. Umm... that's literally what I was doing ummm I just feel like this is the most obnoxious accent. But you know sometimes when I'm just feeling like a Jessica like I'm just gonna like talk like this cos like. Ok, I'm actually gonna stop right now cos like I'm literally like annoying myself just like talking like this, so...

Although this is part of a series of videos framed as the 'accent challenge' trend, we see that the user combines accent features typically associated with this persona with other semiotic resources, such as bodily features: pursed lips, relaxed jaw setting, hair flick, and hand flick. This stylised performance therefore directly references an imagined character (or characterological figure) of the valley girl.

Points for reflection

- Are there other types of 'characterological figures' that people stylise in DMC which you are familiar with? What are the linguistic characteristics of that identity?

In my own work, I have been interested in this type of stylisation, focussing on parodies of Multicultural London English (MLE) on TikTok. In a recent paper (Ilbury, 2023), I analyse a corpus of TikTok videos that reference a characterological figure, called the 'roadman'. In that paper, I analyse the stylisation of this persona performed through a subset of MLE features and non-linguistic tropes and references (e.g., costumes, participation in certain activities, particular discourse topics). For instance, in one video, the user performs the roadman persona in a hypothetical babysitting scenario. In the video, we see a user (who does not habitually speak MLE) stylise various features of the variety including:

- The use of MLE lexis including *flex* 'dance'
- The discourse marker *still* – which is commonly used in MLE to signal emphasis
- Several accent features including a very front GOOSE vowel, e.g., *do* [dʏː], the monophthongal pronunciation of the vowels PRICE, e.g., *nice* [naːʔ] and FACE, e.g., *ok* [ɔ'ke], the use of [d] for /ð/ in words like *that* [daʔ].

In addition to the hyper-stylised form of MLE, the roadman is performed through various other semiotic resources that reference this persona. This includes his dress (a tracksuit), the background music (a grime track), and his disposition (he is disinterested throughout). All of these qualities are ideologically associated in some way with the identity that the user performs: The roadman. Importantly, as with most types of stylisation, the performance is not to be taken at face-value. The creator is not trying to be truly interpreted as a roadman. Rather, the videos are parodic – they are, strategically inauthentic.

In other videos, I show how these stylised performances link the roadman persona (and relatedly MLE) to a much more contentious set of issues, such as his perceived involvement in crime, drugs, and violence. In very many settings he is positioned as someone who is aggressive or 'angry' (see Figure 7.2, for example). These types of parodies, I argue, are relevant to sociolinguistic analyses of MLE because

Figure 7.2 An example of roadman parody TikTok videos

they have the potential to shape how MLE is perceived. I return to this discussion in more detail in Section 9.3.1.

7.6 Metadiscourse

Metadiscourse is a term that refers to 'language about language' (or 'talk about talk'). This label includes folk beliefs about language, language attitudes and language awareness. Metadiscursive comments can be observed when an individual characterises or makes a remark about some regularity or pattern of language use. For instance, it is common to hear people associate linguistic features or ways of speaking with particular types of users, such as the valley girl or roadman above. It is common to hear people say things like 'that's what [valley girls/ roadmen] say' or 'why are you speaking like a [valley girl/roadman]?' or comment on the appropriacy or social meaning of forms, such as 'I wouldn't usually say [X], because I think it sounds so uneducated' or 'I'm not cool enough to say [Y]'. When people make these types of comments, they are engaging in metadiscourse.

Key Term: Metadiscourse

Language about language. When people say things like '[X people] would use this word' or 'I don't like how [X people] say this', they are engaging in metadiscourse.

Metadiscourse is often prevalent in everyday conversation. For instance, in their research on family dinner table conversations, Blum-Kulka (1997) studies metadiscourse in the context of socialisation. The focus in this work is on the ways in which parents design their utterances to socialise children directly or indirectly into culturally appropriate behaviours and expectations. This includes utterances that function as conversational routine management (e.g., 'wait until your brother finishes talking') as well as politeness strategies (e.g., 'say please').

Metadiscourse is closely related to the concept of **linguistic ideologies**. A language ideology is a set of beliefs or ideas about language users and/or languages. Sociolinguistics has long critiqued the existence and circulation of 'Standard Language ideology' – the idea that there are 'superior' varieties of language. This ideology has led society to conclude that there are 'correct' or 'incorrect' ways of speaking or interacting. Metadiscourse is relevant here because often comments about language enter public consciousness and become 'common sense'. This is the case for 'Standard English' which is often cited by people as the true form of English but rarely (if ever!) defined.

7.6.1 Metadiscourse in Digital Communication

Social and digital media are prime sites in which we can observe metadiscursive actions. Because of its participatory nature, users often comment on or make content which explicitly references types of language use and their assumed users. A cursory glance at TikTok returns the following types of metadiscursive comments (29)–(31):

(29) Why is bro speaking like that? Is he acoustic?
(30) speaking like a roadman lol
(31) What accent is this? 💀.

All of the above comments were posted to different videos on the platform. In (29), the commenter responds to the creators' unusual way of speaking, asking if he is 'acoustic' (an intentional and pejorative misspelling of *autistic* which is problematically used in response to actions deemed stupid or ignorant). In (30), the user associates the creators' style of speaking with the 'roadman' identity – an identity that is often associated with involvement in crime and violence. And in (31), the commenter uses the 'skull' emoji 💀 – suggesting that they find the creator's accent humorous or unusual. All of these comments are examples of metadiscourse because they all comment on some aspect of language use.

Points for reflection

- Next time you watch a TikTok or YouTube video or even a Twitch stream, navigate to the comment section. Do you see any metadiscursive comments? (Often people will comment on the accent or speech style of the user, particularly if their accent is regionally or socially marked.)

An academic analysis of metadiscursive comments is found in Androutsopoulos' (2013) paper on the stylisation of German dialects on the video platform, YouTube. His paper focusses on the ways in which audience comments and participatory videos engage in a type of dialect discourse. This includes an analysis of the content of videos, such as where German dialects are stylised, as well as the comments on those videos. The participatory videos include hypothetical scenes where individuals are seen to use a typical version of a Berliner dialect. For instance, the video *'Rinjehaun—Berlinerisch für Anfänger'* (See ya—Berlinerisch for beginners), depicts an interaction between two girls, a local and a newcomer, in the bathroom of a Berlin nightclub. The scene focusses on the posh and preppy newcomer girl's misunderstanding of local Berliner 'slang'. The following interaction has been reproduced from Androutsopoulos (2013: 59–60, Extract (32)):

(32)	1	A	Ey, Puppe! Wat jeht'n, Alter? 'Hey doll! 'What's up, mate?'
	2	B	Hallo! 'Hello!'
	3	A	Ey, hast mal fünf Minuten Zeit, ick muss dir mal wat erzählen. 'Hey, have you got five minutes? I've got to tell you something'.
	4	B	Ja? 'Yeah?'
	5	A	Cool. Naja, jedenfalls war ick ja am Wochenende
	6		mit meen Atzen aus der Hood erstmal im Freibad.

		'Cool. Well, over the weekend I went with my Atzen (mates) from the hood to the open-air pool'.
7	B	Du warst mit deinen Eltern im Freibad? 'You went with your parents to the pool?'
8	A	Oh man, man, doch nicht mit meinen Eltern. Mit meinen Atzen. Wo
9		kommst du denn her dass du det nicht kennst? 'Oh, man. Not with my parents, with my Atzen. Where do you come from if you don't know that?'
10	B	Also ich komm aus der Lünebürger Heide, falls es dich interessiert.
11		Sonst noch Fragen? Well, I come from Luneburg Heath if that is of any interest to you. Any further questions?
12	A	Nee. Na det merkt man, wer Atze nicht kennt, kann nicht aus Berlin
13		sein. Nope. You can tell that if people don't know Atze, they can't be from Berlin.
14	B	Naja, kann ich ja nicht wissen. gibt ja genügend Zugezogene in
15		Berlin. Well, how should I know that? There are a lot of newcomers in Berlin.
16	A	Zujezogen bin ick höchstens. A newcomer. Maybe that's me

The above conversation emerges as a metadiscursive commentary on the word '*Atzen*'. When the word is introduced in line 6, B misunderstands the referent as 'pool'. What follows is a discussion of this term and its association with the Berliner dialect. As the conversation progresses, we see that A associates the knowledge and use of this word as an indication that the speaker is from Berlin. In the extract, the word is used alongside other Berliner dialect features including word-final /s/ is realised as [t] in words such as *wat* for *was* ('what') and *dat* or *det* for *das* ('the, this') and *ick* or *icke* for *ich* (the personal pronoun, 'I').

The content of the video demonstrates one type of metadiscursive activity: The association of words with particular dialects and people. But Androutsopoulos also finds metalinguistic discussions in the comment section of the videos. This includes users' evaluation of the dialect and questions around the meaning of the words used in the videos (33)–(35):

(33) Berlinerisch klingt doof!
'Berlinerisch sounds stupid!'

(34) I just love that Berlinerisch. Very cool. Weiter machen!
'I just love that Berlinerisch. Very cool. Keep it up!'

(35) Also Atze ist definitiv Bruder, Freunde sind Kumpels. // Atze ist eigentlich sogar der kleinere Bruder, Keule hingegen der große Bruder, und die Schwelle ist die Schwester, also bei uns iss dett so, wa!
'Well, Atze definitely means brother; friends are called mates. // Atze is actually the younger brother, and Keule the older brother, and the sister is called Schwelle. Well, that's the way we do it, right!'

These commentaries, Androutsopoulos argues, are important to study because the ideologies that shape them are not separate from language use. If people think of a word or dialect as 'cool' or 'stupid', this could shape how they use that feature or whether they avoid it entirely.

Similar types of comments are examined in Lee's (2013) analysis of metalinguistic discourses of English proficiency on the photo-sharing site, Flickr. In that paper, Lee analyses users' explicit self-evaluations of their English proficiency-level in their captions, comments, and posts. This includes comments such as *'My English is poor'* and *'I'm sorry I don't speak English well"*. In that context, Lee argues that acknowledging one's proficiency level is not simply a form of self-abasement. Rather, on Flickr, acknowledging a limited knowledge of English encourages social networking, widens engagement, and supports informal learning. For instance, in the following Extract (36) taken from Lee (2013: 81), we see how the photo caption posted by CB 'Sorry, I know my English is so so so bad!!', leads commenters to respond to these comments, offering support and evaluating the users' English as 'good':

(36) Commenter A:		Pretty bento. And I think your English is good!
	Commenter B:	Trust me, your English is a lot better than the English of many native speakers. ^_
	CB:	thank you so much, [commenter A]. . . . I learned english for 5 years at school, but I think it isn't good enough for that >

Many of these metadiscourses relate to language practices and varieties typically associated with offline environments. However, it is interesting to note that internet or digital language practices themselves can also become the subject of metadiscourse. This includes a feature which we discussed earlier, <lol>. For instance, in one popular

TikTok video, a user provides an analysis of the different types of <lol> in British DMC. The video describes the following subtypes of <lol>:

- *lol*
  Can be very passive aggressive in sentence final position, can occur in non-humorous environments like 'did you bring my clothes though, lol'
- *lol???*
  Do you think I am an idiot?
- *LOOOOOOL*
  When you're actually laughing. An appropriate response to a joke.
- *LOOOOOOL+*
  When the laughter carries over two lines. This refers to actual laughter. An intensifier version of the above.
- *loooooool*
  Meant to press caps lock. The topic is still funny.
- lool
  Really wasn't that funny or intended to soften the blow of a statement.

In this way, a common feature of digital interactions <lol> has itself become the topic of metadiscourse. Exploring metadiscourses of <lol> might help us explain why this feature is often used in ways that don't straightforwardly look like laughter. This is because metadiscursive insights often latch onto some imagined or real pattern of language use.

More recently, my colleague, Rianna Walcott, and I, have been analysing metadiscursive commentaries of 'Gen Z' language in TikTok. Lots of these commentaries relate to the use of words like 'slay', 'yaas', and 'kween', and phrases such as 'ate it up', 'left no crumbs', and 'serving [x]'. Many of these features originated in AAVE and were taken up in queer circles but have since been reinterpreted as features of 'Gen Z slang' or 'TikTok language'. Our focus in that work has been to understand how different creators respond to this framing. We find that, on the whole, Black creators reject this framing by arguing that the labelling of AAVE as 'TikTok language' represents a type of linguistic appropriation. White creators, on the other hand, tend to argue that this is a natural process of linguistic diffusion, and embrace the 'Gen Z' framing of this trend.

7.7 Politeness

The final area of micro-analytical approaches we consider here are studies of linguistic politeness. When students encounter the concept of 'politeness', they tend to assume that how we use this term in sociolinguistics is synonymous with its popular definition: Politeness is about using 'please' and 'thank you' and respecting someone's title, 'it's Mrs, not Miss'. However, whilst the sociolinguistic concept includes things like 'please' and deference, the academic use of this term is more related to the types of interactional moves and choices that we make to avoid offense. What we are interested in here is how people use conversational strategies like hedging, overly-polite forms, and indirect questions to perform politeness. Often, utterances which use polite forms (e.g., 'sorry to trouble you but would you mind opening the door for me, please?') are, at least in British English, perceived to be more socially acceptable than those which do not use these forms, such as direct imperatives like 'open the door'.

The focus in sociolinguistic research on politeness has been on how people negotiate both the addressee's wants and desires as well as the speaker's wants and desires. This theory of politeness developed by Brown and Levinson (1987), relates politeness to Goffman's (1967) concept of **face**, that is the public self-image that people claim for themselves. Face comprises two main elements:

- **Positive face**: The desire for community; to be liked
- **Negative face**: The desire for independence; to be respected.

The idea is that politeness is an attempt to maintain each other's face. When we communicate, we try to avoid imposing on others (i.e., negative face). Our wish is for our interlocutor to perceive us favourably (i.e., positive face). However, often we have to impose on someone – we might have to ask them to take the bins out – or we might provide some assessment that may not be perceived positively – you might not like their outfit. In these contexts, Brown and Levinson (1987) contend that the request or assessment functions as a **Face-Threatening Act** (FTA). When individuals are posed with the problem of performing an FTA, they can use a politeness strategy to mitigate the FTA. If the request or assessment is 'bald' or 'on-record' then it is performed without a politeness strategy. Most of the time, however, individuals will use a politeness or negative politeness strategy to mitigate the FTA. For instance, imagine you are at your friend's house. The window is open but it is freezing cold. There are a number of different ways you could shut the window (37)–(40):

(37) Brr
(38) Shut that window!
(39) I'm so sorry, would you mind shutting the window?
(40) Are you cold? I'll shut the window for you.

In the examples above, we see different linguistic strategies used to close the window. The example in (37) is what we would call 'off-record with no politeness strategy'. The use of 'brr' which people often say when they are cold implies that the speaker is cold, but they do not explicitly ask for the window to be closed. Contrast this with (38), the speaker uses a direct imperative and so is on-record with no politeness strategy. In (39), however, we see the use of an apology 'sorry', and hedging 'would you mind' that have the overall effect of mitigating the FTA towards the interlocutors' negative face. A similar type of utterance is seen in (40), where the speaker attempts to mitigate the FTA by appealing to the interlocutors' positive face. A final strategy is not to do the FTA at all and simply stay cold!

Key Term: Politeness

Linguistic behaviours that are used to reduce the potential to cause offense or upset. In Brown and Levinson's framework, it is associated with **face**, i.e., the self-image that we project in public. Politeness is linked to **positive** and **negative** face. The former refers to the desire to be liked, whilst the latter refers to the desire to be free.

7.7.1 Politeness in Digital Communication

Studies of DMC have often focussed on identifying the similarities and differences between the politeness strategies used online and those used in face-to-face interaction. Early on it was suggested that since text-based DMC was often characterised by a short and concise style, users were more likely to use direct forms (e.g., *what did you say?*) with little to no hedging than in face-to-face interaction (e.g., Park, 2008). However, research has identified some similarities between the politeness strategies in both modalities of interaction. For example, researchers found that individuals employ similar types of positive and negative politeness strategies in DMC. This includes positive strategies such as seeking common ground by expressing shared background knowledge, interests, or experiences, in an attempt to foster social relationships with others as well as negative strategies in the form of apologies and giving deference (Luo Carlo & Yoo, 2007; Park, 2008).

More recent research has considered the interactional negotiation of politeness in DMC. A case in point is Darics' (2010) analysis of politeness in conversations between members of a virtual team. A virtual team or a 'remote team' are a group of people (often based in different locations) who use digital technologies to work together. This is an interesting case study because, as members do not share the same physical environment, they will use digital technologies to perform a variety of work activities such as team building, norm negotiation, co-operation, and task completion. To understand these practices, Darics collected a corpus of Instant Messaging (IM) conversations from 18 members of a global management and consultancy company based in London. Although the workers were dispersed geographically across the world and spoke a variety of different languages, English was the official language of the company. Analysing the IMs, Darics finds that there are several different politeness strategies used by the workers. This includes what she calls 'strategies to represent auditory information'. This strategy involves the use of non-standard spellings which emulate paralinguistic cues like pitch or intonation. For instance, in the following extract, Darics analyses Liz's use of the unconventional spelling of 'no' as a representation of spoken language (Extract (41)).

(41)	1	Sarah	its so great you are back
	2	Liz	it is good to be back
	3	Sarah	I am so sorry i have been crap at keeping in touch!
	4	Liz	and thanks for the text messages you sent me
	5	Liz	noooooooooo
	6	Liz	no worries at all
	7	Sarah	no i should have sent more!
	8	Sarah	how are you doing really?
	9	Sarah	100% better???Strategies to represent visual information

Darics argues that the use of <noooooooooo> in line 5 functions to reduce the potential FTA to Sarah's own face when she apologies that she has been 'crap at keeping in touch' (line 3). The exaggeration of the vowel in 'no' which appears to emulate spoken language, intensifies the meaning of the word signalling that Liz did not find it problematic that Sarah had not kept in touch. The strategy therefore maintains conversational harmony and reduces any possibility that Sarah's face is threatened.

Another type of politeness strategy Darics identifies is 'strategies to represent visual information'. This includes the use of emoticons or 'smiley faces' that provide additional contextualising information that help the interlocutor interpret the meaning of the message. In many cases, these are used to signal things like 'friendliness' or 'sarcasm'. For instance, in the following excerpt the emoticons :) and 8-) are used by Mercedes and Tanya to signal the intent of the message (Extract (42)):

(42)	1	Mercedes	hi dear
	2	Mercedes	Can I ask you a quick question?
	3	Tanya	Hi
	4	Tanya	Sure
	5	Mercedes	by chance, have you received the (*abbreviation*) report? No rush ... just checking:)

6	Tanya	Not yet dear
7	Mercedes	ok, thanks!
8	Tanya	I will fwd as soon as get it
9	Tanya	:)
10	Mercedes	got it! thanks!:)
11	Tanya	8-) Monitoring it

Before we interpret this extract, we will need some context: Tanya is Mercedes' boss. However, in this excerpt, the power dynamic is flipped as Mercedes needs to request a report from Tanya. In line 8, following the comment that Tanya will forward the report as soon as she receives it, she finishes the message with a smiley face :). Darics argues that emoticon signals the friendly intent of the message. The informal address term 'dear' (line 1), the use of hedging 'by chance' (line 5), all seem to suggest that this is intended to be a friendly interaction. Finally, in line 8, Mercedes uses the emoticon 8-) which Darics interprets as a graphical representation of the following statement 'monitoring it'. This emoticon, she argues, introduces a level of humour to the conversation. All of these strategies, Darcis argues, help Mercedes negotiate the power imbalance and mitigates the potential FTA of making a request to her boss, Tanya.

Points for reflection

- Next time you send an email, pay attention to the politeness strategies you use in that email. Make a mental note of the types of politeness strategies you use and think about why you use them.

In my own corpus of WhatsApp messages sent by young adults living in London, I have found similar types of politeness strategies to those identified by Darics (2010). Most notably, the users often use stylisation as a politeness strategy. Consider, for instance, the following example (Extract (43). Rachel has just got herself a new job as a marketing analyst that she wasn't keen to start. On her first day, Abi messages to ask how it's all going. Rachel replies saying she had nothing really to do but was familiarising herself with the back end of the website (e.g., checking visitor counts, making edits to the website).

(43)	1	Abi	How was the first morning?
	2	Rachel	Nothing to do really just familiarising myself with the back end of the website
	3	Abi	Haha at least it's a job bbz!!
	4	Rachel	Not complaining

In response to this, Abi attempts to lighten the mood by suggesting that 'at least it's a job'. Abi's response is interesting because she tags this message with <Haha> and <bbz>. In an analysis of this conversation, I have argued that Abi uses these features to mitigate the FTA of her response, 'at least it's a job'. If this message did not contain <Haha> and <bbz>, it would be a 'bald' FTA in that it would directly challenge Rachel's assessment of the job. Including these two features, however, appears to 'dial down' the intensity of the challenge by first keying this as a casual response (<Haha>), before using the address term, <bbz>, to signal their friendly relationship, and ending with a double exclamation mark <!!> to signal excitement or support. This seems to be effective as Rachel's response in line 4 explicitly affirms the intention of her original message.

7.8 Limitations

The limitations of small data approaches are, ironically, opposite to those we discussed related to big data approaches. In the analyses that we have sketched out in this chapter, language practices are analysed at the level of conversation. The types of variation we have discussed here have been understood in relation to discourse phenomena like what is being said in the conversation or who the recipient is. This is a very different approach to that discussed in Chapter 6 where the variation was explained in relation to some broad level social factor, like the demographics of a given geographical area or the gender of the author.

As interactional approaches try to understand how language is used within specific moments of interaction, it is sometimes unclear to what extent the patterns identified in a given dataset apply elsewhere. How do we know that the function of <lol> in one group conversation is comparable to how other people use this feature? The common retort of such approaches is that the analyses are not attempting to make general claims about the *nature* of language variation/change. Rather, they are attempting to understand language in use. That is, in context.

Nevertheless, there are still some limitations that we should be mindful of. One of the main limitations of this type of work is that interactional approaches, such as those outlined here, tend to focus on phenomena in smaller datasets. Tagg's (2016) research, for instance, on Laura's texting practices discussed in Section 7.5, focusses on a relatively modest dataset comprising 1539 text-messages. Similarly, Androutsopoulos' (2013) study of YouTube videos and comments, analyses 310 dialect-tagged videos. Evidently, these are much smaller datasets than the very large corpora of social media posts often analysed in 'big data' approaches.

A further limitation of interactional approaches is that they often neglect the relevance of big data. As we saw in Chapter 6, big data approaches have been able to identify consistent and compelling patterns of language use that can be explained in terms of macro-level factors. For instance, in Eisenstein's (2013) analysis of t/d deletion on Twitter, he finds higher rates of the non-standard spelling (e.g., <tes> for <test) in areas with higher numbers of people who are African American. Here, we see that there is a significant correlation between the use of a particular type of spelling (i.e., the orthographic representation of t/d deletion) and a socio-demographic identity (i.e., African Americans). Nevertheless, little interactional work has considered the relevance or application of these findings in their analyses of the small details of interaction. It seems possible and worthwhile to consider a synergy of the two approaches – an issue we will take up in Chapter 8.

7.9 Summary

This chapter has introduced small-data approaches to studying DMC. The 'small' qualifier here refers not necessarily to the size of the datasets examined in these types of studies but rather the tools that are employed to understand the granular, micro level detail of interaction. Small data approaches to DMC have employed concepts, theories, and methods from Interactional Sociolinguistics, Discourse Analysis, and Conversation Analysis to understand topics such as the turn-by-turn negotiation of identities, the conversational organisation of messages, and the use of contextualisation cues in signalling meaning in interaction. To explore these topics in more depth, the chapter has focussed on four different areas of sociolinguistic inquiry that examine interactional phenomena: Language alternation, stylisation, metadiscourse, and politeness.

7.10 Activities

1. Navigate to TikTok and search for the #AccentChallenge. Now choose five videos of your choice. Do any of the videos reference identities or ways of being associated with those accents and speech styles (e.g., roadman, valley girl, 撒娇 sājiāo)?
2. The account @islandlarder on TikTok is run by a user from Shetland – an island chain some 100 miles from the north Scottish mainland. The user speaks Shetland dialect. This variety is one very many people will have not encountered before interacting with this page. Choose five videos from this account and collect some comments from those videos. Try to analyse the metadiscourses of Shetland dialect that emerge in the videos. Do people like this

dialect? Do they consider it to be a variety of English? Or something else?

3. Go to your recently sent emails and select ten emails at random. Now identify the politeness strategies used in those emails. What are the most frequent politeness strategies that you use? Consider, for instance, your use of devices such as emoji, address terms (e.g., sir, mate), openings (e.g., dear, to), and closing (e.g., best wishes, yours faithfully). Does your use of politeness strategies vary across audiences, platforms, and topics? Finally, compare your emails with another text-based platform, e.g., WhatsApp.

7.11 Further Reading

Georgakopoulou, Alexandra, Stefan Iversen & Carsten Sage (2020). *Quantified Storytelling: A Narrative Analysis of Metrics on Social Media.* Cham: Palgrave Macmillan.

Giaxoglou, Korina (2020). *A Narrative Approach to Social Media Mourning: Small Stories and Affective Positioning.* Abingdon: Routledge.

Jones, Rodney, Alice Chik & Christoph Hafner (2015). *Discourse and Digital Practices: Doing Discourse Analysis in the Digital Age.* Abingdon: Routledge.

Page, Ruth (2013). *Stories and Social Media: Identities and Interaction.* Abingdon: Routledge.

Wilson, Guyanne (2024). *Language Ideologies and Identities on Facebook and TikTok: A Southern Caribbean Perspective.* Cambridge: Cambridge University Press.

7.12 References

Agha, Asif (2007). *Language and Social Relations.* Cambridge: Cambridge University Press.

Androutsopoulos, Jannis (2013). Participatory culture and metalinguistic discourse: Performing and negotiating German dialects on YouTube. In Deborah Tannen and Anna Marie Trester (eds.), *Discourse 2.0: Language and New Media,* pp. 47–72. Washington, DC: Georgetown University Press.

Blum-Kulka, Shoshana (1997). *Dinner Talk: Cultural Patterns of Sociability and Socialization in Family Discourse.* Abingdon: Routledge.

Brown, Penelope & Stephen C. Levinson (1987). *Politeness: Some Universals in Language Usage.* Cambridge: Cambridge University Press.

Coupland, Nikolas (2007). *Style: Language Variation and Identity.* Cambridge: Cambridge University Press.

Danesi, Marcel (2016). *The Semiotics of Emoji: The Rise of Visual Language in the Age of the Internet.* London: Bloomsbury.

Darics, Erika (2010). Politeness in computer-mediated discourse of a virtual team. *Journal of Politeness Research,* 6(1): 129–150.

Deumert, Ana & Kristin V. Lexander (2013). Texting Africa: Writing as performance. *Journal of Sociolinguistics,* 17(4): 522–546.

Dorleijn, Margreet & Jacomine Nortier (2009). Code-switching and the internet. In Barbara E. Bullock & Almeida Jacqueline Toribio (eds.), *Linguistic Code-Switching*. Cambridge: Cambridge University Press.
Dresner, Eli & Susan C. Herring (2010). Functions of the non-verbal in CMC: Emoticons and illocutionary force. *Communication Theory*, 20: 249–268.
Ermida, Isabel (2023). *Hate Speech in Social Media*. Cham: Palgrave Macmillan.
Georgakopoulou, Alexandra (2014). Small stories transposition and social media: A micro-perspective on the 'Greek crisis'. *Discourse & Society*, 25(4): 519–539.
Ge-Stadnyk, Jing (2021). Communicative functions of emoji sequences in the context of self-presentation: A comparative study of Weibo and Twitter users. *Discourse and Communication*, 15(4): 369–387.
Gibson, Will (2024, Online First). Flirting and winking in Tinder chats: Emoji, ambiguity, and sequential actions. *Journal of Internet Pragmatics*. https://benjamins.com/catalog/ip.00107.gib.
Goffman, Erving (1967). *Interaction Ritual: Essays on Face-to-Face Interaction*. London: Aldine.
Herring, Susan C (1999). Interactional coherence in CMC. *Journal of Computer-Mediated Communication*, 4(4): 444.
Ilbury, Christian (2023, First View). The recontextualisation of Multicultural London English: Stylising the 'roadman'. *Language in Society*, 53(3): 1–25.
König, Katharina (2019). Stance taking with 'laugh' particles and emojis—Sequential and functional patterns of 'laughter' in a corpus of German WhatsApp chats. *Journal of Pragmatics*, 142: 156–170.
Lee, Carmen (2013). 'My English is so poor . . . So I take photos': Metalinguistic discourses about English on FlickR. In Deborah Tannen and Anna Marie Trester (eds.), *Discourse 2.0: Language and New Media*, pp. 73–83. Washington, DC: Georgetown University Press.
Luo Carlo, Jessica & Youngjin Yoo (2007). 'How may I help you?' Politeness in computer-mediated and face-to-face library reference transactions. *Information and Organization*, 17(4): 193–231.
Page, Ruth (2018). *Narratives Online: Shared Stories in Social Media*. Cambridge: Cambridge University Press.
Park, Jung-ran (2008). Linguistic politeness and face-work in computer mediated communication, part 2: An application of the theoretical framework. *Journal of the American Society for Information Science and Technology*, 59(14): 2199–2209.
Rampton, Ben (1995). *Crossing: Language and Ethnicity Among Adolescents*. London: Longman.
Rampton, Ben (2009). Interaction ritual and not just artful performance in crossing and stylization. *Language in Society*, 38(2): 149–176.
Ren, Wei & Yaping Guo (2024). Translanguaging in self-praise on Chinese social media. *Applied Linguistics Review*, 15(1): 355–376.
Retta, Mattia (2023). A pragmatic and discourse analysis of hate words on social media. In Anton Granvik, Mélanie Buchart, & Hartmut Lenk (eds.), *Hate Speech in Online Media*, pp. 197–218. Amsterdam: John Benjamins.

Seargeant, Phillip, Caroline Tagg & Wipapan Ngampramuan (2012). Language choice and addressivity strategies in Thai-English social network interactions. *Journal of Sociolinguistics*, 16(4): 510–531.

Skovholt, Karianne, Anette Grønning & Anne Kankaanranta (2014). The communicative functions of emoticons in workplace e-mails::-). *Journal of Computer-Mediated Communication*, 19(4): 780–797.

Tagg, Caroline (2016). Heteroglossia in text-messaging: Performing identity and negotiating relationships in a digital space. *Journal of Sociolinguistics*, 20: 59–85.

Wei, Li (2023). Transformative pedagogy for inclusion and social justice through translanguaging, co-learning, and transpositioning. *Language Teaching*, 57(2): 203–214.

8 Mixed Approaches

8.1 Introduction

In this chapter we cover the following topics:

- Mixed-method approaches
- Three case studies of mixed-approaches to DMC:
  - Androutsopoulos (2023)
  - Ilbury (2019)
  - Lopez & Kübler (forthcoming).

The two preceding chapters on 'big data' and 'small data' sketched out two different approaches to analysing DMC. In Chapter 6, we provided an overview of work which uses computational tools to understand complex datasets, typically comprising millions (or even hundreds of millions!) of messages. In this field, linguistic patterns are quantified and interpretations are made on the basis of the distribution of some feature. This approach was contrasted with that introduced in Chapter 7. This work is focussed more on understanding the 'small' details on interaction, examining how features are used within specific moments of interaction. Qualitative approaches like Discourse Analysis and Interactional Sociolinguistics are employed to examine discourse level phenomena.

That I've decided to present these approaches in two different chapters suggests that researchers take an either-or approach. They either do 'big data' work *or* they study the 'small' phenomena of interaction. The analyses that people employ are *either* quantitative *or* qualitative. To some degree, this is true in research on DMC. For the most part, researchers have tended to assume that a single methodological approach is sufficient in capturing and explaining different aspects of DMC. However, single-method approaches have their limitations. Quantitative approaches have often been criticised for neglecting the relevance of interactional and discourse phenomena whilst qualitative approaches have often disregarded the relevance of population-level trends.

DOI: 10.4324/9781003391838-8

As a response, there has been a push in recent years for the field to move towards so-called mixed method approaches. The argument is that a combination of quantitative *and* qualitative methods can be useful in understanding the sociolinguistic functions and motivations for patterns of DMC. Quantitative analyses can help us understand the more general distribution of a feature, whilst qualitative approaches can explain why they are used in this way. Following this turn, this chapter provides an in-depth survey of three different case studies which combine large-scale methodologies and approaches, with micro-level insights.

8.2 Case Study 1: Androutsopoulos (2023)

Androutsopoulos, Jannis (2023). Punctuating the other: Graphic cues, voice, and positioning in digital discourse. *Language & Communication*, 88: 141–152.

- **Summary:** This paper investigates the function and social meaning of the so-called 'indignation mark', or <!!1!>, in the context of German-language threads on the platform, Reddit. The main argument is that <!!1!> is used intentionally to parody the voice of an imagined political character who is associated with conservative and right-wing beliefs. This includes "nationalists, supporters of xenophobic and Islamophobic sentiment, conspiracy-theorists, climate change deniers, COVID deniers, and car-crazy Germans" (2023: 147).
- **Background:** To understand the use of <!!1!>, Androutsopoulos draws on sociolinguistic research that explores how group relations are constructed in (digital) interaction. The background refers to several concepts that we have already introduced and discussed, notably double-voicing and stylisation. The focus is on how people use elements of digital discourse (in this instance, creative typographical features) to parody non-local voices and to distance themselves from contentious social identities. The work also seeks to add to a limited body of work on variation in punctuation. As is perhaps clear in this book, although non-standard spellings have been examined in detail, punctuation and typographic features of digital communication have been examined to a lesser extent.
- **Methods:** The paper employs a combination of 'computational, sequential, and microlinguistic analysis' (2023: 141). First, a large-dataset of Reddit threads and comments was obtained using Python through the pushshift API. The programme, R, was used for further statistical and computational analysis. The extraction process focussed on one thread 'r/de' – established in 2006, it is the largest German language sub thread on Reddit. The sampling strategy was

to obtain 1000 threads per half year, from 2009 to 2021 (excluding 2013 for technical reasons). This results in a corpus of 23,000 discussion threads with 386,659 comments. Metadata, including the time stamp of the message, the user ID, the flair, and comment depth was also obtained. This allows Androutsopoulos to (i) quantify the number of times <!!1!> occurs, and (ii) obtain a large dataset of Reddit threads and comments, as well as related metadata.

Since the focus here is on the *interactional* function of <!!1!>, Androutsopoulos then moves to a scaled-down analysis of the contexts in which this feature is used. To do this, he uses the flair metadata of the post. On Reddit, a flair is a tag which shows others what the post is about. It could be things like 'video' or 'humour' meaning that the post contains a video or is meant to be funny. This allows Androutsopoulos to identify three main flairs where <!!1!> is used: Politics (74 tokens), Humour (72 tokens), and Query/Discussion (90 tokens) – a total of 236 messages. He then codes this data for a variety of different linguistic and interactional features. This includes:

1. The position of the indignation mark in the message
2. Whether this message is part of a longer comment or if it is the entire comment
3. The stylised voice evoked in the message
4. Whether the people that the voice evokes are referenced in the comment
5. Any groups named in the stylised message
6. Any graphic cues that co-occur with the indignation mark.

Androutsopoulos notes that, since the metadata includes links to the original posts, he also continually inspected the context of the indignation mark as it is used in the specific Reddit post.

- **Analysis:** The analysis identifies some common themes in the flair sample of 236 tokens. It does this first by identifying the *types* of people who are referenced in messages which contain the indignation mark. It is at this point that Androutsopoulos observes that it is often used in messages that are associated with conservative and right-wing political views. He observes that this feature often occurs alongside overt political references, including 'phrases such as irgendein AfD-Jockel 'some AfD dumbass' (2019–08) and FDP Type (2021–08, FDP is a Liberal party)' (p. 147). He also finds that the indignation mark often occurs alongside other typographic features and non-standard spellings which sets the voice apart from their own. This includes strategies such as writing the message in all caps or using quotation marks.
- **Conclusions:** The main argument in this paper is that the typographic feature, <!!1!>, which may have once been an authentic

error, has since become reinterpreted as a symbol of a particular political identity. It is stylistically used by people who orient away from these values, by parodying the voices of those with conservative and right-wing beliefs. In making these arguments, Androutsopoulos argues for a greater focus on how typographical features become socially meaningful for digital communities of practices.

8.3 Case Study 2: Ilbury (2019)

Ilbury, Christian (2019). 'Sassy Queens': Stylistic orthographic variation in Twitter and the enregisterment of AAVE. *Journal of Sociolinguistics*, 24: 245–264.

- **Summary:** This paper explores the stylisation of African American Vernacular English (AAVE) in tweets posted by White British gay men. The paper argues that a subset of AAVE features have been appropriated by the men and are stylistically used to perform a 'sassy' gay persona. This analysis argues that stylisation is not only commonplace in social media, but it poses an issue for computational approaches (outlined in Chapter 6) which have not considered the potential that users may use features of language varieties other than their own.
- **Background:** The background of this paper first introduces work in the emerging field of Computational Sociolinguistics such as work by Eisenstein (2015) which found that patterns of orthographic variation in Twitter broadly correspond to those observed in speech (see Section 6.5.2 for a discussion of this paper). It then goes on to explore research on 'stylisation' – that is when individuals use language that is markedly different from their habitual style. In Section 7.5 we introduced stylisation when we saw that people often use features of non-local dialects (e.g., Jamaican English) to align with identities or meanings associated with individuals who use that dialect. Although CS research has examined language variation in social media, no research had considered language stylisation. This paper suggests that stylisation may be a problem for CS approaches which assume that 'individuals write how they speak'.
- **Methods:** This paper uses a large dataset of Tweets from ten British gay men. The rationale for choosing this demographic was because, as a member of this community myself, I was aware that gay men often stylise aspects of AAVE in speech. For instance, lots of the language which people describe as 'gay slang' like 'hunty', 'slay', and 'kween', are actually words that originated in AAVE and have been borrowed into gay culture. Based on these observations, I wanted

to see if people used features of AAVE in Twitter. This 'insider' perspective is what is called an 'emic perspective'. In other words, my analysis is informed by my own positionality – as a queer British man – who participates in this culture and has an insider understanding of the community under study.

I chose a small number of individuals to study (ten men) because I wanted to make some more detailed claims about the men's language practices. Generally speaking, CS work like Eisenstein's (2015) analysis explores variation in datasets comprising billions of tweets from millions of users. The social identities of users are typically inferred indirectly through things like the users' name and/or their location metadata. This study, however, intentionally restricts the dataset, focussing on the profiles of just ten men. This enabled me to manually inspect the timelines of each of the users to confirm that (i) they identify as male, (ii) they are from the UK and likely speak a variety of British English, (iii) they are young adults, and iv) they identify as gay.

Once I had identified ten users, I extracted all of their tweets through the Twitter API using twitteR (this is a package used in the R language programming software). In total, I extracted 15,804 tweets. I then manually inspected the tweets and coded them for a variety of AAVE features. Many of these are orthographic representations of spoken language processes and phenomena. This includes features such as completive *done* (e.g., 'I *done* bought up all the good ones) and the monophthongisation of /aɪ/ which is orthographically represented as <a> in place of <y>, <ye>, <ie>, <uy>, and so on (e.g., Story of *ma'* fuckin life). I then counted how many times each of these features occurred. From this point, I then used interactional analyses to examine how the features were used in conversation.

- **Analysis:** The analysis finds that, of the 15,804 tweets extracted from the ten users, 307 (1.9%) tweets contain AAVE features. Although this number might seem very low, remember these men are not AAVE speakers. That they are using AAVE features *at all* is potentially interesting. And, importantly, they don't appear to be using just one feature. They use a range of syntactic, orthographic, and lexical features. This includes syntactic features like copula absence – i.e., the absence of *is/are* (e.g., @User @User oh you nasty), phonological features such as the realisation of /ɛː/ as [ɚ] orthographically represented as <ur> (e.g., My huur done gone CRAY!), and AAVE lexis including *bae, hunty, ratchet, thirsty,* and so on.

One of the main findings of my paper is the AAVE features are more common in directed messages, that is when users direct a tweet to another individual by tagging their username. In fact,

60.9% (n=187) of the 307 tweets containing AAVE features are directed. When we break this down even further, we see that they tend to be used in interactions between gay men. 90.9% (n=170) of the 187 directed tweets are to other gay male users. This suggests that using AAVE has a particular symbolic value as a 'gay male' in-group style.

After exploring the quantitative distribution of the different features, interactional analyses are then employed to understand where and how features of AAVE are used. By focussing on the use of AAVE in the tweets, I argue that users are stylistically using features of this variety to perform a strategically inauthentic style. In other words, the use of AAVE in these tweets is not to be taken at face value: The men were not attempting to be perceived as AAVE users. Rather, they selectively and strategically used a subset of features for some more abstract purpose.

To understand this abstract function, I decided to consider how AAVE and AAVE-speaking individuals are represented in broader digital culture. If we look at popular memes of Black women – many of whom speak AAVE – we see that there is a general tendency to characterise or represent Black women as 'sassy', 'fierce' and 'aggressive'. This, I argue, is linked to a long-standing media trope of the 'sassy Black woman'. Memes like the 'strong independent Black woman who don't need no man', for instance, recycle these tropes in the context of DMC.

At this point, I argue that these mediatised representations of Black women might help us to explain why the gay men in my study use features of AAVE. I argue that we should not interpret the use of AAVE by the gay men as an attempt to actually be read as Black women (as a CS analysis might predict). This is a too simplistic reading of the variation. Rather, I contend that the men use features of AAVE to perform social meanings *associated* with African American women. More specifically I suggest that, by using features of AAVE, the men draw on a trope of Black women as 'sassy' – a value which is often valued in certain subcultures of the gay community. In this way, the gay men create and circulate a linguistic style which is associated with a particular gay identity – what I call the 'Sassy Queen' ('queen' is a label used to describe an effeminate gay man).

- **Conclusions:** The paper argues for a greater focus on stylisation and appropriation in digital communication. It argues that stylisation may be problematic for CS approaches which have assumed that people write how they habitually speak. Finally, it calls for more work which combines quantitative and qualitative methods in explaining patterns of DMC.

8.4 Case Study 3: Lopez and Kübler (f.c.)

Lopez, Holly & Sandra Kübler (forthcoming). Contextualization in abusive language annotation and corpora development. *Discourse, Context, and Media.*

- **Summary:** Research on hate speech has typically taken one of two approaches. Interactional work has described the discursive features of hate speech, focusing on issues such as impoliteness and ambiguity. Computational approaches, on the other hand, have focussed on developing models which can automatically identify and classify abusive language. This paper brings the two approaches together arguing that Interactional Sociolinguistic approaches could explain discrepancies in the manual annotation of hate speech.
- **Background:** The paper first surveys computational research on hate speech. In this field, hate speech is generally identified via automated means, such as sentiment analysis (i.e., how positive or negative a text is). These approaches require large corpora which are used to develop models of hate speech. Human annotators must first make decisions about which messages are considered harmful or abusive before these decisions are used to train machine learners. As the authors acknowledge, this is not an objective process: The annotators' biases and beliefs are likely to influence what they find harmful and/or abusive. These biases in turn are fed into the automated systems that identify hate speech. One potential issue is that the annotators do not have access to the context of a message; they must determine whether the message is harmful based solely on the content of an isolated message. The background goes on then to juxtapose this approach with that used in Interactional Sociolinguistics where context is key to understanding the intended meaning of a message.
- **Method:** The authors use a large corpus of messages which is often used for abusive language detection: Jigsaw's Unintended Bias in Toxicity Classification corpus. This corpus was created using content from the Civil Comments platform. A now defunct news sharing platform, Civil Comments, asked other users to review and vet content before it could be posted. When the platform ceased operations in 2017, they made ~2 million messages publicly accessible. The corpus which this paper uses was created as part of a shared competition to develop the best machine learning approaches to identifying harmful speech in social media. Crowdsourced annotators were asked to label the toxicity of messages on a scale of 'very toxic', 'toxic', 'non-toxic', or 'hard to say'.

  The authors of the paper first reclassified a sample of the messages in the corpus to help the classifiers make more nuanced identifications about what the intention of the message. The annotation criteria included three abusive categories (e.g., implicit, explicit, and self-abuse) and five non-abusive categories (non-abusive, argumentative, meta, casual profanity, and irony). The first step was to ask a group of minimally trained people to annotate 325 messages from the original corpus. The annotators were initially introduced to literature on profanity and hateful language in a classroom setting. They then practised their annotations on 20 examples before discussing their coding in groups. After they had completed these tasks, they were given 50 messages to annotate. The authors then compared the coding by the minimally trained annotators with the original annotation from the corpus and also annotations by an expert. Any disagreements were identified and computer mediated discourse analysis (CMDA; Herring, 2004) was employed to understand why those disagreements arose. More specifically, the authors employ concepts from Interactional Sociolinguistics to understand how contextualisation cues, ambiguity, and other discourse phenomena, might have influenced the annotators' decisions.

- **Analysis:** The first part of the analysis explores annotator (dis)agreements. This section compares annotations made by untrained crowdsourced workers, minimally trained annotators, and an expert. High degrees of agreement were found only for the category of irony. Other categories, such as 'argumentative' messages, showed low levels of inter-annotator agreement. The authors suggest that this finding is indicative of the fine line between content that is contentious and that which is harmful, hateful, or inappropriate.

  The second part of the analysis tries to understand the causes of the disagreements. They suggest that contextualisation cues and other interactional phenomena might help explain why there are low levels of agreement between the annotators. For instance, they analyse one instance which includes the message 'toxic feminism is the real problem'. This message was originally labelled abusive by the crowd-sourced annotators but it was labelled 'non-abusive' by the expert. Without an awareness of the context, it is very hard to understand what this message means. In other words, 'toxic feminism' could reference any number of political ideas or perspectives. It is therefore very difficult for annotators to infer whether this type of message is intended to be abusive if they do not have access to the broader conversation in which this message appears.

  A second issue the authors discuss is the fact that annotators often don't have access to or knowledge of popular culture and current events referenced in the message. For instance, one of the messages references the Denver Broncos, an American football team. The message itself, as replicated below, was initially labelled as 'abusive' by the crowdsourced annotator but as 'non-abusive' by the expert (Extract (1)):

(1) 'Actually many Bronco fans do have issues with it. So glad you just lump yourself in as a 'true Bronco fan' because you agree with some of the players (note some of the players, not all). And I am sure the fact that since last year, the ratings continue to go down for NFL games. And the fact that Alejandro Villanueva's jersey overnight became the #6 bestselling jersey at NFL.com. You sure do miss a lot of facts. Did you miss that Denver sunk it up yesterday? Gee, they sure did. A true fan would be more bothered by how they played and the game plan and the coaching decisions rather than this garbage'.

It is unclear from the message alone why the annotator had labelled this as 'abusive'. There doesn't appear to be any explicit hateful sentiment in the message. However, if the reader has some awareness of the cultural references the message makes, it is possible to understand why this message was originally labelled as 'abusive'. The message makes references to Alejandro Villanueva – an American footballer who was involved in a political controversy in 2017. His team, the Steelers, had decided not to take to the field for the national Anthem to avoid controversies surrounding the protest of taking the knee in response to racial inequality in the US. However, Villanueva was unaware of this decision and so walked onto the pitch and stood for the national anthem. Although this was unintentional, his actions were interpreted as an attempt to undermine his teammates and the efforts of those fighting racial inequality. On social media, he was hailed by right-wing pundits for apparently taking a stand against the growing tide of protests. By referencing this event, the author of the above message appears to align with this misreading of the events, using Villanueva's actions to diminish the experiences of African Americans. This interpretation, however, relies entirely on the audience having quite considerable knowledge of American football and racial politics in the US.

- **Conclusions:** The paper shows that annotator agreement on abusive language is difficult to attain given that annotators rarely have access to the context of the message. The researchers suggest that giving access to the entire conversation in which the message is located might help annotators make more informed decisions as to whether the message is abusive or not. In other words, interactional approaches (such as contextualising messages) might help improve the accuracy and efficiency of computational models in detecting hate speech.

8.5 Summary

This chapter introduced and summarised three contemporary approaches which combine 'big' (i.e., computational) and 'small' (i.e., interactional) methods. Androutsopoulos (2022) argues that users deploy typographic features to parody voices of imagined people with a particular world view. Computational tools are used to extract a large corpus of Reddit posts and their related metadata before discourse analysis is employed to understand how <!!1!> is used in conversation. Similarly, in my own work (Ilbury, 2019) I automatically extracted a large corpus of Twitter posts before examining stylised performances of AAVE in the tweets. I argued that the stylisation of AAVE referenced a particular racialised imagining of Black women as 'sassy'. Finally, in Lopez and Kübler (forthcoming), the authors argue that discrepancies in hate speech annotation are due to differences in awareness of the message context. An understanding of the message context might help improve agreement in manual classification. In turn, this would benefit the automatic detection of hate speech as models are trained on manually coded datasets. All three papers demonstrate the analytical potential of combining 'big' and 'small' data approaches and perspectives. A synergistic approach which benefits from quantitative and qualitative insights will enable us to provide a more complete account of language and DMC.

8.6 Further Reading

Androutsopoulos, Jannis (2021). Polymedia in interaction. *Pragmatics and Society*, 12: 707–724.

Androutsopoulos, Jannis (f.c.). Methodological synergies in the study of digital discourse [special issue]. *Discourse, Context, & Media.*

Bamman, David, Jacob Eisenstein & Tyler Schnoebelen (2014). Gender identity and lexical variation in social media. *Journal of Sociolinguistics*, 18: 135–160.

DILCO Lecture Series (2022, 2023, 2024). www.dilco.uni-hamburg.de/activities.html. University of Hamburg.

Nguyen, Dong (2017). *Text as social and cultural data: A computational perspective on variation in text.* Unpublished PhD thesis, University of Twente. www.dongnguyen.nl/thesis/thesis_dong_nguyen_2017.pdf

9 Beyond the Online

9.1 Introduction

In this chapter we cover the following topics:

- Earlier perspectives on media influence
- The concept of 'mediatisation'
- From language change to sociolinguistic change
- The 'post-digital' turn.

Throughout this book, we have introduced and described some innovative and creative ways that people are using digital technologies to communicate. It is now perhaps uncontroversial to conclude that a substantial chunk of our daily interactions take place in and through digital technologies. This new reality often leads people to conclude that digital technologies are radically altering society and social interaction. As a sociolinguist, I often encounter a commonly held belief that digital technologies and social media are fundamentally changing the way that we speak and interact. So *does* social media lead to language change?

If you do a quick survey with members of the general public or your friends and family and ask people the question 'does the media influence the way we speak?', most people will quickly and confidently assert that 'yes, without a doubt, social media, TV, film, and so on, all influence the way we speak'. People will then very likely go on to cite specific examples of how different types of media have led to language change. Common examples include claims that 'we're all now speaking 'txtspeak'', references to an American child who has apparently picked up a British accent from watching the children's TV show Peppa Pig, and the assertion that there is now a 'TikTok accent'. Similar to these claims, newspapers are awash with articles that decry the loss of 'proper grammar and punctuation' apparently thanks to Twitter's character limit, whilst others warn of the serious and detrimental effects of social media on Standardised English. What we see in all these claims is an extremely common and often undisputed belief that media, especially social media, has led to dramatic changes in language and social interaction.

DOI: 10.4324/9781003391838-9

However, if you ask a sociolinguist a similar question – 'do media lead to language change?' – you may be surprised to hear that our answer isn't a straightforward 'yes'. This is because the role of media in language change is heavily contested in sociolinguistics. Although many people will claim that people pick up accents from their favourite films, TV shows, and other forms of media (see the Peppa Pig and TikTok accent examples above), as Tagliamonte (2014: 229) concedes, 'the impact on language of media is surprisingly difficult to substantiate' in sociolinguistics.

You may be even more surprised to hear that quite a few sociolinguists have gone further to dismiss the influence of media on language change. The prominent sociolinguist, Peter Trudgill (2014), claims the influence of media is 'irrelevant' to language change, whilst the founding father of variationist sociolinguistics, William Labov (2010) contends that media do not generate change, but rather reflect it. For many sociolinguists, the only conceivable media influence on language change is at the level of lexis. Trudgill and Labov concede that it is uncontroversial to claim that people borrow words from their favourite programmes they watch or from social media communities they engage in. But beyond lexis, very many scholars have questioned the idea that media has any significant role in language change. In recent years, however, this view has been challenged as sociolinguistics has reassessed the relationship between society, (digital) media, and language.

In this chapter, we survey sociolinguistic approaches and theories of media influence in language change. We will see that the approach to studying media and language has heavily evolved in recent years. The field has gradually moved away from viewing media influence as something that can be measured directly and which has an *influence* on *language change* towards a more holistic approach which considers the role of higher-level media processes (e.g., mediatisation) in *sociolinguistic change.*

9.2 Media and Language Change

Language change is a natural and inevitable fact of life. Evidently, the English that we use today, such as that used in this book, is not the same variety that would have been spoken or written in the 17th century. Some of this language change has occurred above the level of consciousness (what linguists call 'change from above'). Although lots of language change occurs below the level of consciousness ('change from below'). Some examples of language change include:

- **Semantic (meaning) change:** Today, the adjective *gay* is used to refer to 'someone who is attracted to someone of the same sex'. The term can be traced back to the 12th century where it meant 'full of joy or mirth'. In the 1980s, *gay* acquired a pejorative meaning: It is sometimes used to mean 'dumb' or 'stupid' (e.g., *that song is so gay*).

- **Phonological (sound) change:** In Received Pronunciation, a sociolect spoken by the social elite in the UK, the vowel /æ/ was traditionally pronounced [ɛ], such that words like *happy* to be pronounced like 'heppy'. Over time, the pronunciation of this vowel in RP has moved more towards the Standard Southern British pronunciation, [æ].
- **Grammatical change:** The second person singular pronouns *thee* and *thou,* common in the work of Shakespeare for instance, went into decline in Early Modern English. Today, these pronouns are absent from most varieties of Modern English.
- **Lexical change:** In contemporary forms of British English, the term 'cinema' is generally used to refer to the 'place where films are shown for general entertainment'. Some of the older generation, however, use the term the 'pictures'. This term comes from 'motion picture' but is now considered outdated by younger generations.

Language change is often propelled by social change. As people move around and settle in new areas, they bring with them new ways of speaking and interacting. These language innovations **diffuse** through speech communities. Diffusion refers to the process by which features from one dialect or variety spread to another. Trudgill (1986; 2014) argues that linguistic diffusion is primarily propelled through accommodation in face-to-face interaction. Accommodation here can be defined as the tendency for speakers to adapt their linguistic behaviour to that of the person they're interacting with. In simple terms, this means to talk like others do. As speakers interact with one another, they make small adjustments to how they speak (i.e., they accommodate). Over time, these adjustments lead to more general changes in the linguistic norms of a speech community.

Because language change has typically been viewed as a product of synchronous face-to-face interaction, media – especially asynchronous media like television and films which are often defined as 'passive'– have not been typically thought of as possible influences on language change. Trudgill (1986: 40) concludes, the 'point about the TV set is that people, however much they watch and listen to it, do not talk to it (and even if they do, it cannot hear them!), with the result that no accommodation takes place'.

Subsequently, and as mentioned in the introduction to this chapter, for many sociolinguists, the only conceivable form of language change that could be reasonably attributed to media influence is lexis. This type of perspective is evident in Chamber's chapter in the book *Language Myths,* in which he attempts to dispel to belief that 'TV Makes People Sound the Same' by arguing that media are limited to the diffusion of vocabulary and catchphrases. For Chambers, it is perfectly conceivable to assume that we might watch a TV show or film and think, 'hey, that's a cool or catchphrase word, I'll use it'. The term *catfish* 'to deceive someone, typically by using an anonymous or fake persona on a social media site' apparently entered British English in this way, having been first used on the 2010 American documentary of the same name. Other examples include the catchphrase 'ya-ba da-ba doo' from the cartoon, The Flintstones, and the use of '- NOT!' onto the end of positive declarative statements, originally from the American sketch comedy program *Saturday Night Live* (Chambers 1998: 125). Trudgill likewise acknowledges that people may adopt words and phrases from print media having himself acquired "American words like *campus* and *freshman* in the 1960s, without ever having visited the U.S.A., from reading American novels" (2014: 215). But beyond lexis, for these researchers, media is unlikely to play a role in 'higher-level' (i.e., syntactic and phonological) language change. This perspective is perhaps best summarised by Trudgill who dismisses media influence entirely, concluding that "the question of what role the electronic media may play in linguistic change [...] is therefore of no great interest in solving the big challenges of linguistics" (2014: 221).

Points for reflection

- The above debate on media influence on language change focusses mainly on 'old' media like television, books, and radio. Do you think Trudgill's claims regarding the lack of relevance of media to language change apply to 'new' media genres like digital and social media?

Other researchers, however, have not been so dismissive of the potential for media to influence language change. This includes work which has suggested that television – along with other sociolinguistic factors – could be a factor in sound change. For instance, in their work on the speech of young people in the Scottish city of Glasgow, Stuart-Smith and colleagues (2013) find that, in addition to other more conventional factors, television is an important factor in ongoing linguistic changes in the community. They find that the use of two features which had diffused from London (TH-fronting: the use of [f] for /θ/ and L-vocalisation: The vocalisation of coda /l/ in words such as *milk* and *feel*), was accelerated by a strong engagement with the London-based TV soap, EastEnders. Crucially, however, in this study, TV is not attributed to be the cause or sole factor of language change. It is one of many factors. This finding demonstrates why it is difficult to isolate the role of media in language change: Media is highly imbricated in the social fabric of everyday life.

As perhaps evident in the discussion so far, the debate regarding media influence and language change has overwhelmingly focussed on one type of media: Television. Arguably, television is a very different type of media when compared to the highly interactive and participatory spaces of social and digital media that we have introduced in this book. Trudgill (2014), for instance, appears to dismiss the influence of media on language change because his definition of media is based primarily on television – a form of mass media which does not facilitate face-to-face interaction. But the introduction of DMC and video platforms like Zoom, Microsoft Teams, and Skype have complicated this understanding of media engagement. Many of these services enable users to communicate via digitally mediated synchronous, face-to-face interaction. If diffusion takes place via face-to-face interaction, it seems conceivable that platforms like Zoom and Skype could facilitate this. Any theory of media and language change would need to take into account both types of media engagements.

In response, others have suggested that sociolinguistics had been working with a narrow view of media influence. One main critique is that researchers had only really considered the possible effects of media on *language* change. Research had concentrated heavily on the question of whether engaging with types of media could lead to changes in an individual's language variety, such as their accent or grammar. This is quite a narrow view of the role of media in social interaction. As we have seen throughout this book, digital and social media appear to be prime forums in which representations of speakers and varieties are circulated, debated, and consumed. It seems entirely plausible that performances of dialects, metadiscursive commentaries, and other sociolinguistic phenomena will have some impact on how language is used.

The exclusive focus on 'media and language change' in earlier work was, however, not shared in all subdisciplines and traditions of sociolinguistics. Androutsopoulos (2014: 13) observes that German sociolinguists had engaged with this question for some time. He cites work by Holly and Püschel (1993: 148–152) who suggest that television had an impact on contemporary forms of German in four main ways:

1. Promotion of the standard variety
2. Awareness of other (non-standard) varieties
3. Circulation of norms of interaction
4. Intensification of linguistic innovations.

Notably, in this framework, television is not simply 'a platform through which linguistic innovations diffuse'. Rather, the influence of television on language is related to standardisation and dialect levelling

(1), language attitudes and functions (2, 3), and promoting the spread of neologisms (4). The focus here then, is less on language change, and more on how media promote and circulate ideologies, beliefs, and values which have sociolinguistic implications.

9.3 Media and Sociolinguistic Change

In current work on digital communication, researchers have moved beyond a focus on *language* change towards a theory of media and *sociolinguistic* change. Although this might initially seem a minor terminological difference, this reconceptualisation forces us to reconsider how media may be implicated in sociolinguistic processes beyond structural language change, such as the types of standardisation and representation outlined by Holly and Püschel (1993). This approach is summarised by Androutsopoulos (2014: 6–7) who argues that a focus on sociolinguistic change enables us to:

1. Analyse changing relations between language and society beyond focussing on specific linguistic features that are defined as belonging to a 'single' language.
2. Analyse individuals' linguistic practices in interaction, as opposed to examining linguistic features.
3. Analyse the relevance of language ideology in the interaction between use and change.
4. Analyse language use beyond spoken interaction. It considers how language is used across media and institutional contexts.
5. Analyse the relevance of individuals' agencies in sociolinguistic change.

This type of perspective is much more in line with contemporary post-structuralist approaches to language (e.g., Bucholtz & Hall, 2005) that consider how language ideologies and broader processes of socio-cultural change may be implicated in how people use language. In this way, 'the media' can no longer be considered some monolithic entity that has a quantifiable *influence* or *effect* on language and society. Rather, this approach considers how "specific contexts, representations, and actors of media discourse draw on linguistic resources in ways that may be relevant for change in language/society" (Androutsopoulos, 2017: 240).

9.3.1 Mediatisation

A key concept in the move towards understanding the role of media in processes of sociolinguistic change is *mediatisation*. The term has been defined in various ways by different researchers but for the purposes of this book, we use the term mediatisation to refer to "societal changes in contemporary high modern societies and the role of media and mediated communication in these transformations" (Lundby, 2009: 1). In other words, mediatisation allows us to explore both the interrelation of change in media and communication, and social and cultural change. Importantly, whilst this approach acknowledges the fact that our social lives are increasingly configured in and through digital technologies, it rejects the 'external influence' or 'effect' conceptualisations of media that were typical in earlier sociolinguistic research (cf. Labov, 2001; Trudgill, 2014). Instead, it emphasises the relevance of mediatised engagements in shaping sociolinguistic practice. In this way, mediatisation cannot be confirmed or disproved by any single research project but operates at some 'higher level' of social structure, comparable to other socio-cultural forces like globalisation, commercialisation, and commodification.

Key Term: Mediatisation

Mediatisation refers to changes which media bring about in everyday life. This includes the role of media in processes of communication, cultural practices, and social organisations.

This is a much more complex and abstract way of considering the role of media in sociolinguistic change. But what does it actually mean in practice? What types of sociolinguistic projects engage with mediatisation? How is a research project which examines media influence different to one which engages with processes of mediatisation?

A good example of the type of research that emerges from this approach is that which considers how people use media resources in their everyday interactions. Sierra (2021), for instance, shows how American youth make references to popular internet memes in everyday conversation. In her work, Sierra argues that these intertextual media references serve important functions in discourse and in the construction of social identity. Here, we see that, memes – which we typically think of as elements of digital communication – take on new meanings and functions as they are imported into everyday, face-to-face, conversation.

Points for reflection

- Do you or your friends reference internet memes in conversation? Why do you do this? What effect (e.g., relationship building, identity) do those memetic references achieve?

Similarly, in my own work, I have examined the implications of the mediatisation of language varieties. In work which was first introduced in Chapter 7 (Ilbury, 2023), I have argued that the creation and sharing of parodic TikTok videos that reference language varieties and imagined users have the potential to shape how people use those language varieties. My analysis focusses on a persona, 'the roadman', that is closely associated with the dialect, Multicultural London English (MLE). I argue that, as users create and share these parody videos, they contribute to the reinterpretation (or 'recontextualisation') of this variety from a dialect spoken by young working-class people in East London, to a style associated with 'road' culture and, more specifically, an identity: 'the roadman'. This identity is often depicted as hyper-masculine, and is associated with violence and criminal activities and, importantly, it is racialised as Black. TikTok performances of the roadman, I argue, have important consequences for sociolinguistic change because they reconfigure our understanding of what MLE is. In the videos, we see the outcome of the recontextualisation as some TikTok videos inaccurately – and problematically – describe features of MLE as 'roadman English' (see Figure 9.1). Though I focus on digital data here in the form of TikTok videos, my argument is that these performances are likely to influence and shape our understanding of the speech variety more generally.

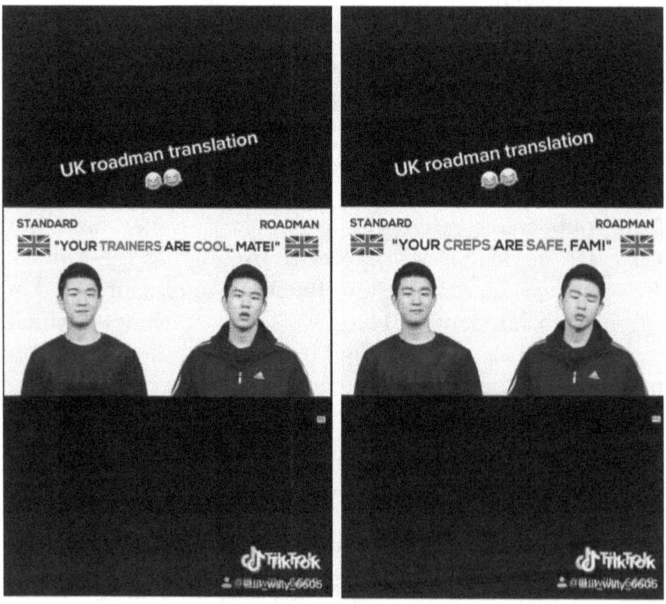

Figure 9.1 Roadman 'translation' TikTok video

As these examples illustrate, in this work 'media' is not considered some external 'factor' that can be operationalised as having a direct effect on language change. Rather, we see how mediatisation – of speech styles, of speakers, of varieties – may have sociolinguistic consequences that go beyond the remit of digital communication. In these examples, we see how references to internet memes are recruited to fulfil interpersonal functions in everyday conversation and, through TikTok parodies, users circulate ideologies of speakers and their speech styles. Clearly, then, media and digital communication can no longer be considered as distinct, locateable platforms that can be easily disentangled from everyday life, each with their own sociolinguistic conditions. Rather, they are now part of our everyday communicative practices and so are likely to have major consequences for social interaction more generally.

9.4 The Post-Digital Turn

Over the nine chapters of this textbook, we have tracked the development of digital communication research from a field squarely focussed on identifying and documenting a unique online variety bounded to 'cyberspace' (i.e., 'internet linguistics'), towards an approach which considers how digital communication is deeply embedded within the infrastructures of everyday social interaction. The contemporary approach we have outlined concludes that individuals' digital practices need to be considered alongside their other sociolinguistic practices, and that media engagements, representations, and ideologies are likely to inform and shape social interaction.

The development of this approach is, perhaps, indicative of just how far we've come in embracing the internet and digital technology. Over the course of 30 or so years, the internet has gone from something that was once novel, used by few, and restricted in use, to a social commodity that is now mundane, highly pervasive, and easily accessible (for most!). Today, very many of us use digital devices and platforms in ways that are not particularly spectacular or even worth deliberating. When I woke up this morning, turned off my alarm, and immediately checked WhatsApp – as I do most mornings – I can't say this event was a standout moment of my day. Digital and social media are so embedded in our lives – in news, in school, in politics – that these interactions and practices are rarely, if ever, remarked upon.

Given that digital technologies are now relatively unremarkable, some researchers have suggested that we are living in a **post-digital** era. This frame acknowledges that although digital technologies are clearly very important in contemporary society, they are no longer considered extraordinary or disruptive in any meaningful way (Tagg & Lyons, 2022; Bhatt, 2023). This term isn't meant to refer to a period *after* digital technologies. Evidently, most people continue to use mobiles, computers, and other digital devices in their work and social lives. But it is intended to describe a shift in our relationship and engagements with digital technologies.

With the *post-digital* turn, we are forced to redirect our attention: Away from studying patterns of communication in specific digital sites and platforms, towards considering how users' digital practices are embedded within broader systems of social differentiation and how these practices are interrelated with offline activities, roles, and contexts. Work which takes a post-digital approach considers not only how users' digital practices take place within everyday contexts of interaction, like the park or at school, but also how those interactions may shape sociolinguistic contexts and relationships that have typically thought of as 'offline'.

Key Term: Post-Digital

Post-digital refers to the fact that digital technologies have ceased to be disruptive. The current period can be defined as 'post-digital' in so far that digital technologies are now considered by most to be relatively unremarkable and have largely become embedded into our everyday social practices in relatively unspectacular ways.

In work that employs a post-digital framework, a common approach has been to undertake blended ethnographic studies of communities to understand how individuals use networked technologies in their everyday communicative practice. Much of this work illustrates that, for very many people, digital technologies have ceased to be spectacular or novel (cf. Chapter 1; Turkle, 1995). Rather, for most people, these platforms, services, and networks are highly mundane and unspectacular. This is evidenced by the fact that people are seen to continually switch between digital and physical contexts of interaction without any real deliberation or effort.

I have found these practices to be especially common in how young people use social and digital media. In what could now be described as a 'post-digital' ethnography of a youth group in East London (Ilbury, 2022a), I found that, although the young people were frequent and avid users of social and digital media, these platforms were so embedded in their everyday communicative practices that they rarely discussed platforms or services in conversation. When I tried to engage them in discussions of 'Snapchat' or 'who uses Facebook', I found that many of the young people found these to be trivial topics that were not particularly interesting. The lack of interest in these topics, I argue, can be understood in relation to the 'post-digital' status – or

Figure 9.2 Snapchat stories depicting everyday life in East London

'domestication' – of social and digital media. For many of the young people (most were between the ages of 12 and 16) at the youth group, social media had always been a fact of life. It was just another way of communicating. Social media platforms and technologies were not particularly remarkable or noteworthy for the young people – they were just another way of interacting with their friends. For instance, in the following excerpt (1), 12-year-old Harinder's response to my question 'do you use social media' suggests that it is a moot point since "everyone uses social media" (Ilbury, 2022a: 4):

(1)	Christian	do you use social media?
	Harinder	yeah everyone uses social media it's just like innit. Contact your friends and stuff, you can call people for free

These comments went hand in hand with the ways in which the young people used social media. Their Snapchat posts did not present some alternate reality or highly edited version of themselves. Far from it. They uploaded stories that documented their everyday lives: From journeys on the bus through Hackney central (an area of East London) to playing basketball in the local park (see Figure 9.2). What we see here then is that digital media – and social media practices – have ceased to be novel. They are now everyday contexts in a post-digital era of social interaction.

9.5 Where Next?

The field we've surveyed in this chapter looks very different to that we introduced and discussed way back in Chapter 1. We've moved quite quickly from a field squarely positioned on studying the 'language used on the internet' to one which attempts to understand how digital communication practices and technologies are embedded in everyday contexts and dynamics. What people do online and how they communicate there now looks less novel or unusual than it once did. We now know much more about the language used in digital communication and the processes which shape the content of those messages. So where does that leave a researcher interested in studying the sociolinguistics of digital communication? What questions are worth pursuing? What are some open issues in the field? What are our research priorities?

In his overview paper of the field, Androutsopoulos (2021: 719) proposes a future research agenda that orients to five main issues:

1. **Digitally mediated interaction:** Research has moved from focussing squarely on the analysis of language variation and change in CMC towards an approach which considers the '[a]ccomplishment of communicative goals, sequential procedures, [and] contextualisation practices' in digital interaction.
2. **The offline/online dichotomy:** The focus should be on how practices transcend the offline/online. How those practices overlap, complement, or contradict one another, as opposed to viewing digital communication as a separate sphere of interaction
3. **Holistic datasets:** Research should examine how user's digital practices entwine with other modes of interaction. To do this, we will need to employ blended ethnographic methods, as opposed to simply focussing on publicly available posts.
4. **Polymedia:** Acknowledges that users will move between platforms and channels for a variety of social and interactional reasons. Analyses of digital communication should take stock of these polymedia practices, as opposed to focussing on a single platform or channel.
5. **Repertoires:** Analyses will consider the multimodal and multilingual practices of users, as opposed to focussing solely on monomodal/monolingual approaches.

Androutsopoulos' agenda quite nicely summarises the theoretical story that we have developed in this book. But I think we could go further to add a few other research concerns:

- **Critically consider the relevance of users' social and personal identities in DMC:** Media research has increasingly demonstrated the central role of digital technologies in the formation of digital cultures related to race, sexuality, and gender. What linguistic practices emerge from the digital publics that platforms enable minoritised users to form? What role do identities like 'Black British' and 'gay' play in the formation and maintenance of digital cultures and, relatedly, DMC?

- **Focus on appropriation and commodification in DMC:** Research such as that discussed in this chapter has argued that people regularly recycle and reuse resources from DMC in everyday interactions (e.g., Sierra, 2021). Some of these features appear to be from varieties that they do not habitually use and potentially reference ideologies of those who typically use those varieties (e.g., Ilbury, 2019; 2022b). A critical approach needs to consider *how* these features are appropriated and for *what* reasons and what the consequences of those appropriations are.
- **Consider users' beliefs in relation to their practices:** In our discussion of metadiscourses, we argued that ideologies and beliefs that people hold shape their linguistic and digital practices. Future work on DMC should therefore engage more seriously with 'lay perceptions' of digital communication. What can user perceptions and metadiscourses tell us about language practices in DMC?
- **Synergistic relationships between fields:** Sociolinguistic analyses of DMC will benefit greatly from a closer synergy between related fields such as digital culture studies, media studies, computational linguistics, anthropology, and communication studies. The increasing availability of tools and approaches from other fields allows us to scale up, scale down, zoom in, and zoom out to provide a more holistic picture of DMC practices.

9.6 Summary

This chapter has introduced and explored a long-standing debate in sociolinguistics: The potential for (digital) media to promote language change. We have seen how the field has gradually moved away from focussing squarely on media 'influence' and 'effect'. By considering this development, we have seen how scholars have started to understand the relationship between media and everyday language more holistically by considering mediatisation and sociolinguistic change. Within this development, there has been a tendency to focus less on digital communication and social media as isolated contexts of interaction and more on how these platforms and services are embedded in offline contexts and interactions. This has led us to introduce the 'post-digital' turn in sociolinguistics which acknowledges that digital technologies and social media are now relatively unremarkable aspects of social life. Finally, we have sketched out a future agenda for the field.

9.7 Activities

1. Informally ask your friends and family what they use social media for. Are their profiles similar to or different from the identities that they perform in everyday life? Consider your findings in reference to the work on the post-digital discussed in this chapter.
2. Check your recent uploads on Snapchat and/or Instagram. What do you post on your stories? Are these mundane posts or are they highly cultivated? Who are you posting for? Why do you upload these types of posts?

9.8 Further Reading

Androutsopoulos, Jannis (2014). *Mediatization and Sociolinguistic Change.* Berlin: De Gruyter.
Cramer, Florian (2014). What is 'post-digital'? *APRJA*, 3(1): 10–24.
Lane, Jeffrey (2019). *The Digital Street.* Oxford: Oxford University Press.
Lyons, Agnieszka & Caroline Tagg (2024). Post-digital connectivities: Framing offline encounters in a digital prospection space. *Applied Linguistics*, 1–20, advance.
Miller, Daniel (2016). *Social Media in an English Village.* London: UCL Press.
Mortensen, Janus, Nikolas Coupland & Jacob Thorgersen (2017). *Style, Mediation, and Change: Sociolinguistic Perspectives on Talking Media.* Oxford: Oxford University Press.

9.9 References

Androutsopoulos, Jannis (2014). Mediatization and sociolinguistic change. Key concepts, research traditions, open issues. In Jannis Androutsopoulos (ed.), *Mediatization and Sociolinguistic Change*, pp. 3–48. Berlin: De Gruyter.
Androutsopoulos, Jannis (2016). Theorizing media, mediation and mediatization. In Nikolas Coupland (ed.), *Sociolinguistics: Theoretical Debates*, pp. 282–302. Cambridge: Cambridge University Press.
Androutsopoulos, Jannis (2021). Polymedia in interaction. *Pragmatics and Society*, 12: 707–724.
Bhatt, Ibrar (2023). Postdigital possibilities in applied linguistics. *Postdigital Science and Education.*
Bucholtz, Mary & Kira Hall (2005). Identity and interaction: A sociocultural linguistic approach. *Discourse Studies*, 7(4–5): 585–614.
Chambers, Jack K. (1998). TV makes people sound the same. In Laurie Bauer & Peter Trudgill (eds.), *Language Myths*, pp. 123–131. London: Penguin.
Coupland, Nikolas (2009). The mediated performance of vernaculars. *Journal of English Linguistics*, 37(3): 284–300.
Holly, Werner & Ulrich Püschel (1993). Sprache und Fernsehen in der Bundesrepublik Deutschland. In Bernd U. Biere & Helmut Henne (eds.), *Sprache in Den Medien Nach 1945*, pp. 128–157. Tübingen: Niemeyer.

Ilbury, Christian (2019). 'Sassy queens': Stylistic orthographic variation in twitter and the enregisterment of AAVE. *Journal of Sociolinguistics*, 24: 245–264.
Ilbury, Christian (2022a). Discourses of social media amongst youth: An ethnographic perspective. *Discourse, Context, and Media*, 48: 100625.
Ilbury, Christian (2022b). U Ok Hun?: The digital commodification of white woman style. *Journal of Sociolinguistics*, 26(4): 483–504.
Ilbury, Christian (2023, First View). The recontextualisation of Multicultural London English: Stylising the 'roadman'. *Language in Society*, 53 (3): 1–25.
Labov, William (2001). *Principles of Linguistic Change, Vol. 2, External Factors*. Oxford: Blackwell.
Lundby, Knut (2009) Introduction: 'Mediatization' as key. In Knut Lundby (ed.), *Mediatization: Concept, Changes, Consequences*, pp. 1–18. New York: Peter Lang.
Sierra, Sylvia (2021). *Millennials Talking Media: Creating Intertextual Identities in Everyday Conversation*. Oxford: Oxford University Press.
Stuart-Smith, Jane, Claire Timmins, Gwilym Pryce & Barry Gunter (2013). Television is also a factor in language change: Evidence from an urban dialect. *Language*, 89: 1–36.
Tagg, Caroline & Agnieszka Lyons (2022). *Mobile Messaging and Resourcefulness: A Post-Digital Ethnography*. Oxon: Routledge.
Tagliamonte, Sali A. (2014). Situating media influence in sociolinguistic context. *Journal of Sociolinguistics*, 18(2): 223–232.
Trudgill, Peter (1986). *Dialects in Contact*. Oxford: Blackwell.
Trudgill, Peter (2014). Diffusion, drift, and the irrelevance of media influence. *Journal of Sociolinguistics*, 18(2): 213–222.
Turkle, Sherry (1995). *Life on the Screen*. London: Simon & Schuster.

Index

FSC
www.fsc.org
MIX
Papier | Fördert
gute Waldnutzung
FSC® C083411

Kolibri 360 GmbH
Ferdinand-Jühlke-Straße 7
99095 Erfurt, Deutschland
produktsicherheit@kolibri360.de